AT POWER'S ELBOW

AT POWER'S ELBOW

Aides to the Prime Minister from Robert Walpole to David Cameron

ANDREW BLICK & GEORGE JONES

Biteback Publishing

First published in Great Britain in 2013 by
Biteback Publishing Ltd
Westminster Tower
3 Albert Embankment
London SE1 7SP
Copyright © Andrew Blick and George Jones 2013

ISBN 978-1-84954-572-3

10 9 8 7 6 5 4 3 2 1

A CIP catalogue record for this book is available from the British Library.

Set in Sabon and Flenja

Printed and bound in Great Britain by
CPI Group (UK) Ltd, Croydon CR0 4YY

For Frederick, George and Nicola
and for Diana

CONTENTS

ACKNOWLEDGEMENTS

Many have helped us with this book over the years, including the serving and former aides who gave us their time to discuss their experiences, and Lords Armstrong and Butler who enabled us to interview them.

We owe further thanks in particular to Lord Donoughue, Lord Hennessy, Professor Dennis Kavanagh, Dr Paul Langford, Sir John Sainty, Dr Anthony Seldon and Professor Kevin Theakston.

Special thanks are owed to Dr June Burnham who helped bring coherence to the transcriptions of the interviews and contributed insightful comments from her social-scientific perspective.

We are grateful to Sean Magee and the Biteback team, including Sam Carter and Hollie Teague.

CHAPTER ONE

INTRODUCTION

The office of Prime Minister is a group enterprise. It is both a position a single politician fills and an institution with staff. Individual holders of the title are famous at home and on the world stage as leaders of the British government. Some of their aides may at times achieve a degree of public awareness – or notoriety – but never on the scale of the person they serve. Most aides are largely unknown but British prime ministers could not function without them. The people who work for the premiership are an important subject of study in their own right, and as a way of understanding the institution to which they are attached.

Aides help premiers decide what to do and try to ensure it is done. They help manage relations with ministers, the civil service machine, the media, Parliament, political parties, and various other individuals and groups. They might be impartial permanent officials, required to serve successive prime ministers regardless of political complexion. They might be attached to particular premiers who have appointed them to support their personal objectives. Some are MPs or peers holding ministerial offices. Aides might have an official role or work in a more informal capacity. They may work within government attached specifi-cally to the Prime Minister or provide support while performing other duties. Often they are based at the famous 10 Downing Street building but they may work out of offices elsewhere. The common thread is they are part of the team upon which the premier depends. They work close to the leading figure within government, deriving importance from being at power's elbow.

David Cameron

All the work that aides do, the problems they encounter, the successes they achieve, the teams they operate within, have a past – that which has gone before shapes their present environment. A consideration of present arrangements at No. 10 helps illustrate the point. During his period as Leader of the Opposition between 2005 and 2010, Cameron and his Conservative team thought much about what they wanted to do if and when they formed a government, but they gave less consideration to the support Cameron would receive as Prime Minister in order to achieve their goals. Cameron had first-hand experience of how Whitehall worked from his time as a special adviser to Norman Lamont as Chancellor of the Exchequer and Michael Howard as Home Secretary during the John Major governments of the 1990s. He could have drawn on this experience to help him put schemes in hand. He did not.

Not all those seeking to become prime ministers have been as reluctant as Cameron to think in advance about administrative structures and processes. Harold Wilson, who first became premier in 1964, provides a contrast. Like Cameron, Wilson had previous experience as a temporary civil servant – his came during the Second World War (and subsequently Wilson served as a Cabinet minister under Clement Attlee). Also, like Cameron, he led his party into power after it had endured three successive general election defeats and thirteen years of opposition. To achieve the changes he wanted, Wilson entered office with firm ideas about how to restructure the prime-ministerial team, and the positions his existing team members would fill. He set out to rebalance power at No. 10, away from the permanent civil servants who predominated within it and towards his party-political appointments. This move ensured he obtained the policy advice he wanted. Similarly Edward Heath, who ousted Wilson from power in 1970, had commissioned a wide-ranging review which included in it a reshaping of the institutions that would support him.

Cameron made no such plans. Why? First he is not greatly interested in the details of administration. Prime ministers may become closely engaged in how their offices function and their day-to-day work, indeed, William Gladstone was obsessive about such processes. But Cameron prefers to choose people he wants and let them work things out between them. This hands-off approach is a characteristic Cameron shares with Gladstone's great rival Benjamin Disraeli, who delegated much work to his private secretary Montagu Corry. A second reason Cameron did not make extensive preparations for a prime-ministerial support team was he wanted to distinguish his premiership from those of his immediate predecessors. During the Labour period of office from 1997, a narrative developed that No. 10 aides, often drawn from outside the career civil service, were playing too prominent a role in government, to the detriment of the Cabinet's influence. Had Cameron come to power and immediately implemented a clearly defined set of new arrangements, he might have looked to be exercising the same 'presidential' approach. A stigma similar to that associated with No. 10 under New Labour had attached itself to David Lloyd George during his 1916–22 tenure of Downing Street, and the two Conservative prime ministers who followed him, Andrew Bonar Law and Stanley Baldwin, made a point of being seen not to replicate his structures or methods.

A third reason Cameron did not give forethought to the organisation of his prime-ministerial team was a simple reluctance to assume the Conservatives were going to win the coming general election. He did not want anyone 'measuring up the curtains' at No. 10, even though Conservative poll ratings were often favourable during his period as opposition leader. If Cameron's staff started talking about possible arrangements in power, he told them to stop. In the event his apprehension about whether the Conservatives could win turned out to be justified. In May 2010 the Conservatives became the largest party in the House of Commons but did not secure a majority of seats. The resulting coalition government with Nick Clegg, leader of the Liberal Democrats and now Deputy Prime Minister, had substantial implications for the Prime Minister's deployment of his staff.

From the outset, Cameron and Clegg were determined to work closely to ensure their government overcame any divisions between the two parties comprising it and that it lasted a five-year term. Out of this desire emerged the concept that No. 10 was, to some extent, a shared resource. The building had been a base for premiers (although with various interruptions) since 1735 when Robert Walpole, commonly regarded as the first Prime Minister, moved in. Now, in the interests of coalition unity, it was to house support structures for both the premier and a deputy of another party. Some staff served both of them, others Cameron and others Clegg, who had by late 2012 appointed five special advisers classed as his 'No. 10 Advisers' (Cameron had twenty).

A combination of Cameron's unreadiness and the advent of a coalition became problematic in one area. Initially he had few policy advisers available. If he had deployed a larger team of aides covering the whole field of government, he might have been better placed to deal sooner with early problems such as the privatisation of forests and a major overhaul of the National Health Service. Margaret Thatcher had been in a similar position when she became Prime Minister in 1979. Seeking to distance herself from her Labour predecessors, she substantially reduced the size of the Policy Unit that Wilson had established in 1974 and James Callaghan had retained. Over time, however, she found this personal source of advice useful in efforts to impose her will upon government. In the 1980s it grew to a size similar to that of the 1970s.

Cameron soon realised he needed more policy support, but he had a problem. How would such an expansion be reconciled with the principle of collaboration with Clegg? Options discussed included having two different policy units, one of Conservatives, the other of Liberal Democrats. Another possibility was to include these two groups together in a single body. Both scenarios could prove divisive. Ultimately Cameron and Clegg agreed on establishing one team answering to the Prime Minister and Deputy Prime Minister simultaneously, which would be composed wholly of impartial career civil servants. In March 2011, Paul Kirby became head of Policy Development and joint head with Kristina Murrin of a newly formed Policy and Implementation Unit, with about eight staff.

This arrangement was a break with recent practice in two ways. Since it was established in 1974 the Policy Unit had directly supported only the Prime Minister and no other member of the government, and it had always been composed mainly or wholly of special advisers who had been appointed on the Prime Minister's personal patronage. Consequently, special advisers had a direct connection with the Prime Minister of the day. They were often supporters of the party of government and subject to rules allowing them to pursue certain partisan objectives. A policy body that excluded such appointments promised to be of a different character. This change, on the surface at least, represented an extension (or revival) of the role of the career civil service, the permanent machine that continues regardless of election outcomes or changes in ministerial offices. Since the 1960s an expansion of special advisers and other outsiders in the premier's support staff had challenged the position of these impartial officials. Developments in the Cameron period represented a significant reversal of that trend. It should be noted, however, that individuals employed as permanent officials in No. 10 were not all from regular civil service backgrounds. Kirby, for instance, was from the accountancy firm KPMG (for whom he had co-authored a paper on extending payment by results for Whitehall staff). Nonetheless, they were employed as impartial staff.

Did the existence of a coalition really dictate that the Prime Minister had to arrive at these particular arrangements for policy support? As war leaders, David Lloyd George and Winston Churchill established prime-ministerial support staffs which were precursors of the Policy Unit and the Policy and Implementation Unit of today. Lloyd George had a Prime Minister's secretariat, or 'Garden Suburb'; Churchill a Statistical Section. Both of these prime ministers led coalition governments. But the new bodies of staff they formed supported them alone and they recruited aides from outside the administrative machine, similar to the special advisers of contemporary government. In eschewing the Lloyd George and Churchill approaches, Cameron seems to have created some problems. It is not easy for policy aides to support two different chiefs, whose parties are often visibly in conflict. Furthermore, party political staff who openly share the orientation of the Prime Minister are useful.

By 2013, Cameron was seeking to obtain a more clearly partisan dimension to his team. Kirby left and Cameron made two ministerial appointments in the Cabinet Office, the first of whom was John Hayes, who became Minister without Portfolio at the end of March. His role was to act as a link with backbench Conservative MPs who were proving troublesome. The second recruit to the Cabinet Office, a month later, was Jo Johnson, younger brother of the London Mayor, Boris. He held the post of unpaid Parliamentary Secretary (in addition to his existing post as an assistant whip). The press release announcing this news stated that he would 'head the Downing Street Policy Unit'. Like a number of Cameron aides, Johnson was an Old Etonian; this trend provoked criticisms that Cameron was drawing on too narrow a social base.

Who have been the key players in the Cameron set-up? Prime ministers often like to have friendly faces around them when they come to the post and some joined him when in opposition. After becoming premier for the first time in 1783, William Pitt the Younger recruited as his private secretary his former Cambridge tutor, George Pretyman. Churchill placed a premium on familiarity and went to great lengths to secure it. As Leader of the Opposition the two most important Cameron aides were Steve Hilton and Andy Coulson. Both accompanied their chief into No. 10.

Steve Hilton

Hilton had worked with Cameron at Conservative Party Central Office on the successful general election campaign of 1992. He worked at the Saatchi & Saatchi advertising agency and then set up his own agency, helping corporations detoxify their images. After Cameron became Conservative leader, Hilton helped him in the attempt to perform a similar decontamination service for the party. Before Tony Blair took office in May 1997, staff around him had helped with a similar operation.

As Cameron's Director of Strategy at No. 10, Hilton acquired a reputation for eccentric behaviour, dressing down and walking around without shoes, and sometimes behaving rudely. One of his major contributions to the Cameron policy platform was the agenda that came to be known as the 'Big Society', which partly involved engaging the public in the delivery of public services.

This emblem of the Cameron premiership met with considerable resistance within Whitehall. Hilton's other proposals included radical measures aimed at stimulating growth, such as abolishing maternity leave. He pursued ways of reducing regulation and the official application of economic 'nudge' theory to achieve socially desirable behaviour. Gus O'Donnell, Cabinet Secretary and head of the home civil service 2005–11, subsequently said it was not possible to implement some of Hilton's ideas because they would have been illegal. Hilton's view that the Whitehall bureaucracy was more powerful than ministers soon found its way into the public domain.

Some of Hilton's qualities can be detected in a number of earlier aides. Edmund Gibson, Bishop of London, used his informal position as an assistant to Robert Walpole to pursue plans for far-reaching changes in the organisation and values of the Anglican Church. Working out of an office on the site of the current Cabinet Office, Gibson made enemies along the way and acquired the nickname 'Walpole's Pope'. Both Frederick Lindemann (Lord Cherwell) for Churchill and Thomas Balogh for Wilson were outside imports to Downing Street, possessed of difficult personalities. They put forward policies some regarded as outlandish and often found themselves in conflict with the Whitehall machine. In his role as a strategist for Cameron, Hilton had other precursors. Aides, such as the historian Lord Acton for Gladstone, helped prime ministers develop their broad ideological outlook. John Hoskyns, who eventually became Thatcher's first Policy Unit head, pressed on her the need for systematic, integrated policy. Like Hilton after him and Balogh before him, Hoskyns came to see the bureaucratic machine as a barrier to necessary reform. The problem faced by such aides is they are dependent upon the same administrative institution they denigrate to achieve what they want. A tension Hilton shared with Thatcher's adviser Derek

Rayner was seeing his purpose as eliminating unnecessary rules and tiers of administrative machinery, though his very presence in Whitehall only added to the overall bureaucracy.

Andy Coulson

When he became the first Prime Minister, Walpole deployed a team of assistants to promote him in the media. They proved effective but became the subject of negative coverage themselves. Subsequent premiers have had similar experiences. Coulson came from a background in tabloid journalism, something that aligns him with Joe Haines for Wilson and Alastair Campbell for Blair. But unlike these two media aides Coulson had not been a political writer. His CV included being editor of the 'Bizarre' show business column in *The Sun* from 1994 to 1998, before becoming editor of the *News of the World.* In January 2007 he resigned from this post following the prosecution of its former royal editor for phone-hacking, not on the grounds that he was involved but because these actions had taken place on his watch. George Osborne, Cameron's most important ally, who became Chancellor of the Exchequer in 2010, was the chief advocate of recruiting Coulson as Conservative Director of Communications and Planning in July 2007. Coulson served as Chief Press Secretary at No. 10 from May 2010 until January 2011 but was forced to resign amid mounting press interest in his role in the phone-hacking scandal. The police subsequently charged him over alleged payments to public officials and for perjury.

The accusations against Coulson included that he had paid for the 'Green Book' which contained contact details for the royal household and that when giving evidence during the perjury trial of the former Scottish Socialist Member of the Scottish Parliament, Tommy Sheridan, Coulson had himself answered untruthfully when denying knowledge of or involvement in phone-hacking or other illegal activities. The latter claims related to a time when he was working at No. 10. These allegations arose from a set of police investigations with a far wider scope. Among the many media industry figures and public employees who were embroiled, Rebekah Brooks, formerly the chief executive of News International, the group which owned *News of the World*, was another with close links to the Prime Minister. A trial date in September 2013 was set for Coulson, Brooks and others for offences including conspiracy to commit misconduct in public office and conspiracy to unlawfully intercept communications. But Coulson was by no means the first prime-ministerial aide to attract allegations of wrongdoing. Francis Bonham, a political aide to Robert Peel in the 1830s and 40s, resigned his official post after the exposure of his inappropriate involvement in the award of railway contracts. Maundy Gregory was an informal patronage-broker for prime ministers including David Lloyd George. He became in 1933 the only individual ever successfully prosecuted for the sale of honours. But Coulson was potentially the most controversial of all.

The precise reasons for Coulson's initial recruitment have been a subject of interest and figured in attempts to unpick the relationship between the Conservatives under Cameron and Rupert Murdoch's media-empire. Not long before Coulson joined Cameron, the *News of the World* had run on its front page a story about Osborne, Coulson's main sponsor, with the title TOP TORY, COKE AND THE HOOKER. The presence of particular aides in prime-ministerial circles has caused puzzlement in the past. Ronald Waterhouse was a private secretary to Law, Baldwin and MacDonald – in some ways the prototypical permanent Principal Private Secretary. Yet his administrative abilities were apparently negligible. His contacts with the intelligence world and the royal family seemed of greater value to his prime ministers. The willingness of Wilson to tolerate the behaviour of his Political Secretary, Marcia Williams, has been another subject of speculation. Her explosive personality could cause chaos within his team and make his life difficult, yet for some reason he was unable or unwilling to do without her.

In opposition Coulson gave priority to organising the most professional media operation possible, with a view to winning the election. He supported both Cameron and the shadow Cabinet and, although once in office he assumed a cross-governmental function, his central concern was No. 10. He normally saw Cameron every day. A key challenge for Coulson was ensuring that, in accordance with Cameron's desired approach to the premiership, while departments were able to operate with a degree of autonomy, overall presentation, that is the public representation of the government, was coherent. Within No. 10, Coulson coordinated special advisers of both parties; he worked with career officials, but did not have management responsibilities over them. In this respect Coulson differed from Campbell, Blair's media aide, who was – like Blair's Chief of Staff, Jonathan Powell – integrated into the Whitehall hierarchy in 1997, while being a special adviser. Coulson even went on to identify his own replacement, Craig Oliver a BBC news editor.

Cameron's aides – outsiders

In spring 2012 Hilton announced he was leaving No. 10 for a sabbatical. By this time Coulson had left, as had James O'Shaunnessy, Cameron's Director of Policy in opposition and government. Cameron, perhaps sooner than he hoped, faced the challenge of replacing staff whose special personal link to him was difficult to replicate. Cameron had managed to bolster his team early in 2011 when Andrew Cooper, the founder of the Populus polling company, became Director of Political Strategy. As a polling

expert who had participated in the campaign to 'modernise' a
political party, Cooper was similar to Philip Gould for Blair,
though Gould never held a formal post at No. 10, and as a former
member of the Social Democrat Party (SDP), Cooper shared his
background with a number of others who assisted Blair: Andrew
Adonis, Roger Liddle and Derek Scott. Just as an ex-SDP presence in No. 10 under Blair caused raised eyebrows in the Labour
Party, so it did within the Conservatives under Cameron.

Ed Llewellyn, another special adviser brought in from opposition, is currently Cameron's Chief of Staff. His job title has long
antecedents. It existed – though perhaps only colloquially – in the
time of William Gladstone in the late nineteenth century. David
Wolfson, Chief of Staff to Margaret Thatcher, had a nebulous
position. He had no prescribed duties, but he was a useful figure
to have around, undertaking personal and political tasks for the
Prime Minister, and creating a relaxed atmosphere. He was also
wealthy enough not to need payment. Jonathan Powell was the
most powerful figure inside Tony Blair's No. 10, exercising the
legal authority to manage career officials. Since Powell, the Chief
of Staff has been a firmer part of the Prime Minister's team. Brown
revoked the management power Powell had enjoyed under Blair
but, despite Cameron not restoring it in 2010, Llewellyn is still
an important figure. He plays a significant role in foreign policy,
and in liaising with the Liberal Democrats to ensure the smooth
running of the coalition. The Deputy Chief of Staff, Kate Fall, is
another pre-2010 general election veteran, and knows the Prime
Minister from their time at Oxford. She has close personal access
to the Prime Minister and keeps his diary.

Stephen Gilbert is the No. 10 Political Secretary. He acts as
the link between the Prime Minister and the Conservative Party.
Premiers have needed ways of handling mass parties ever since
their rise in the nineteenth century, stimulated by the great reform

acts of 1832 and 1867. In the 1830s and 40s, Robert Peel, who disliked party business himself, devolved such work to Francis Bonham. Bonham's knowledge of the Conservative Party made him indispensable. Despite revelations about Bonham's business-dealings, Peel remained loyal to him. Gilbert's specific post can be traced back directly to Marcia Williams who was brought into Downing Street by Wilson in 1964 and met resistance from permanent officials, but was ferocious in her determination to establish herself. Her immediate successor, supporting Heath, was Douglas Hurd, who did not encounter the same difficulties. A Cameron appointment who is harder to categorise is Colonel Jim Morris, Military Assistant to the Prime Minister. Morris served in Afghanistan as Commanding Officer of the 45 Commando Royal Marines and received a Distinguished Service Order. He then worked for the Secretary of State for Defence, Liam Fox, before joining Cameron in October 2010. Morris advises Cameron on military issues in general and Afghanistan in particular. He is most reminiscent of the men in uniform Churchill liked to have around, especially Hastings Ismay, Churchill's crucial link with the Chiefs of Staff Committee. Various prime ministers of the 1920s and 30s welcomed the presence of the Cabinet Secretary Maurice Hankey, who came from a background as a Royal Marine artillery officer.

The Chancellor of the Exchequer, George Osborne, is a close ally of Cameron. From the early historic period of the premiership through to the mid-nineteenth century, prime ministers were normally in direct control of the Treasury. If they sat in the Commons, they held the post of Chancellor themselves, alongside that of First Lord of the Treasury. The Treasury was, in effect, the department of the Prime Minister. From the mid-nineteenth century the Treasury separated from the premiership and the Prime Minister has never had a proper department since, though the establishment of such an entity has been considered. Because the connection with financial and economic policy has weakened it is valuable if a premier can work closely with the political head of the Treasury, the Chancellor. When prime ministers are not able to do so, as has happened with Macmillan, Thatcher and Blair, severe problems can arise.

A key personal influence on Cameron is his wife Samantha. Earlier prime ministers have received various forms of assistance from their spouses –Mrs Gladstone sometimes carried out secretarial duties for her husband – and other family members have become involved in prime-ministerial support work. Gladstone, Law and Ramsay MacDonald all deployed their children in their offices. Prime ministers need personal and household support for their family life: providing meals, transport, carrying messages, enabling them to relax and be human. Those who do so may roam beyond such activities into matters of state or be suspected of doing so.

Cameron's aides – civil servants

When Cameron first became Prime Minister, alongside members of his existing entourage, another aide became crucial. Jeremy Heywood was already in place as Permanent Secretary to the Prime Minister's Office, a role created especially for Heywood by Gordon Brown in 2008. Previously the highest-ranking permanent official at No. 10 was the Principal Private Secretary. At least since the time of Henry Pelham in the 1740s every premier has had a private secretary (whether Walpole before him had one is unclear). The total number of private secretaries attached to the Prime Minister grew slowly over time, and they have included among their number an individual as illustrious as Edmund Burke, who worked for Lord Rockingham in 1765–66. Heywood's successor at No. 10 was Chris Martin, another career official, drawn from the Treasury, who took the title Director General placing him below a Permanent Secretary but above a Principal Private Secretary.

At the beginning of 2012 Heywood became Cabinet Secretary, an office which dates to late 1916, when Lloyd George decided he needed an official to take minutes at meetings of his War Cabinet to avoid confusion about what senior ministers had actually agreed to do. Holders of the Cabinet Secretary post are major players in government, and perhaps the most powerful prime-ministerial aide of all, Norman Brook, built up his authority from this position in the post-Second World War period. In his new post Heywood was based formally at 70 Whitehall, the address of the Cabinet Office headquarters next door. This building is in an area once known as the 'Cockpit' which has long been a centre for British administration and many prime-ministerial aides have worked there. Since the 1730s they have been able to access No. 10 through a connecting passageway, with no need to walk out onto Whitehall and round to Downing Street. But they are not as close to the Prime Minister as they would be if based at No. 10. Cameron does not see as much of Heywood as he did when the aide was his former Permanent Secretary, and Heywood no longer works exclusively for the Prime Minister.

Another career official, Sir Bob Kerslake, the head of the home civil service, supports Cameron on Whitehall issues. He attends Cabinet and meets with the Prime Minister every few weeks to discuss civil service reform. Kerslake simultaneously fills the post of Permanent Secretary to the Department of Communities and Local Government. Previous occupants of his civil service post have been among the most prominent of prime-ministerial aides. Warren Fisher, the first official head of the home civil service, combining the role with that of Permanent Secretary to the Treasury, was an influential voice for successive prime ministers for nearly the entire interwar period. Later, William

Armstrong, who held the post of head of the home civil service, was so important to the embattled Edward Heath in the early 1970s that he came to be known informally as 'Deputy Prime Minister'. Eventually the pressure of his role drove him to a nervous breakdown.

Perhaps Kerslake's time will not prove as important or dramatic as such predecessors, but he is involved in a Whitehall reform programme of radical intent, which seeks to open up the policy-making process to outside groups, introduce private-sector practices to the civil service and give a greater role for ministers in determining who their senior Whitehall aides should be. These objectives are born partly from the frustration some prime ministers, including Wilson and Thatcher, have felt with the Whitehall machine. The career civil service, which developed slowly from the eighteenth century, adheres to the principle of impartiality. Its staff are not supposed to become attached to particular politicians or policies. From the point of view of premiers it may seem that aides of this kind, who keep their jobs whether a given government stands or falls, are not as committed to their success as partisan special advisers. It is certainly the case that party political aides tend to be more concerned with the immediate political consequences of decisions, the day-to-day popularity of the government and the winning of elections. At the same time, permanent civil servants will probably want policies to be successful, and their non-partisan perspective can be helpful to the analysis of options. Once, the divisions that now separate party-political and impartial official assistants did not exist. In the eighteenth century, 'men of business', as they were known, were able to work in both environments. Secretaries to the Treasury, the most important of prime-ministerial aides in this early period, could hold seats in the Commons, perform a role similar to today's Chief Whip, organise election campaigns and take an interest in partisan propaganda, while at the same time fulfilling functions which are today taken on by officials such as the Cabinet Secretary, head of the home civil service and Permanent Secretary to the Treasury, all as part of the same portfolio.

The Prime Minister and his support team, career officials and outsiders alike, operate in an environment more clearly defined and limited than that of previous eras. A number of codes, some with a legal basis, others of less firm status, set out principles and practices governing their activities. They include the Ministerial Code, the Cabinet Manual, the Civil Service Code and the Code of Conduct for Special Advisers. Aides run the risk of public criticism if they are construed as violating any of the stipulations in these documents and written submissions they produce may be made public under the Freedom of Information Act 2000. Persuading backbenchers of the governing parties to vote for legislative proposals they recommend is increasingly difficult. Policies are more likely than they once were to fall foul of judicial review, for instance because they are found incompatible with European law or the Human Rights Act 1998. The advent of devolution in Northern Ireland, Scotland and Wales has substantially restricted the impact of UK government in these areas. In some senses aides are working for the Prime Minister of England. If staff members become involved in controversial episodes, there is a reasonable chance a Prime Minister may feel obliged to establish a public inquiry of some kind. A greater willingness seems to exist on the police's part to investigate the activities of premiers and their aides. The power of the premiership has always been limited in its impact, and its actions likely to be subject to criticism, but now the constraints upon the office, sometimes taking a codified or fully legal form, are more tangible and the opportunities for negative scrutiny greater than before.

The purpose of this book

A large and burgeoning body of literature exists on the British premiership. Theories abound about its development and the way it exercises power. While there is disagreement about many features of this institution, it is the most important political office in the land. The holder of the premiership is the most prominent political figure within Britain, at the top of the greasy pole. But given the level of interest in the office and the importance ascribed to it, the gaps in our knowledge are surprising. Attempts to consider the entire history of the premiership are few, yet it is integral to the political history of Great Britain.[1] Almost since the formation of the state in 1706–7, the office of Prime Minister and the people who have held it have in one form or another been at the centre of events. We sought to begin the correction of this omission in an earlier work.[2] Another underexplored area, the subject of this present assessment, is that of the history of aides to the Prime Ministers. Analysis of the premiership from a contemporary perspective has given a reasonable level of attention to the staff attached to it, though there is scope for more work considering this subject in its own right. The real gap comes in assessing the past development of prime-ministerial assistants. Only two similarly titled works come into this category. The first is a collection of profiles of particular aides, covering a period from the 1860s to the 1940s, titled *The Powers Behind the Prime Ministers* by Charles Petrie. The second, *The Powers Behind the Prime Minister* by Dennis Kavanagh and Anthony Seldon, first published in 1999, describes the teams supporting successive

---

1 In this book, we use the term 'Britain' to refer both to Great Britain and the later state, the United Kingdom of Great Britain and Ireland/Northern Ireland.

2 See: A. Blick and G. Jones, *Premiership: The Development, Nature and Power of the Office of the British Prime Minister* (Exeter: Imprint Academic, 2010).

prime ministers, focusing on the period from 1970 but with background material starting, again, in the 1860s. The second work in particular is of great value and we draw on it here.

Our book covers new ground primarily because of the time-span it covers, starting with the rise to prominence of Robert Walpole – often regarded as the first Prime Minister – in the early eighteenth century. It considers both the people who worked for premiers and the structures they operated within. We balance accounts of overall trends with biographical profiles of key individuals. For any given period we have a number of interests. Who was important? What did they do? How did they interact with each other? What was changing? What past precedents were there for what was going on, and what precedents for the future were now appearing? How do developments in one era fit into the whole procession of history? We interpret the term aide to the Prime Minister broadly. Our interest is in whether or not some-one mattered to a premier, even if providing this assistance was not part of an official role. At the same time we are concerned with the formal support-structures surrounding the premiership and the overall constitutional environment.

We focus on individuals who were subordinate to the Prime Minister more than those who tended to wield power on their own accounts, such as deputy prime ministers. We emphasise the importance of proximity of various kinds: personal, physical and organisational. The terms of employment of aides – tempo-rary or permanent – and the rules applying to them, allowing party-political activity or requiring impartiality, are recurring themes. We consider what drove change when it occurred, and the different conflicts that were at stake over the operation of prime-ministerial aides and the public representation of them. We assess the part played by prime-ministerial assistants in key events in British history.

The chapters divide into five time periods. First is 1721–1868. At the beginning of this era, Robert Walpole began his 21-year stint as First Lord of the Treasury, during which he made the most important early contribution to the development of the office of Prime Minister. The cut-off point comes with the first general election to take place after the substantial expansion of the franchise brought about by the Representation of the People Act 1867. By this time the premiership was in a second phase of its own historical development. Where previously holders of the office were normally directly responsible for the Treasury, by the mid-nineteenth century this important early link had weakened. The second runs from 1868 to 1916. By the latter point it had become clear the routines of the late nineteenth century could not cope with the pressures of a world war. The third (1916–45) begins with the dramatic arrival of David Lloyd George at No. 10, and ends with the departure of another war leader, Winston Churchill. Both influenced the role and remit of prime-ministerial support teams. In the following period, 1945–97, Britain struggled to reverse perceived national decline partly through changes to the way prime ministers were supported and advised. The final period (1997–2010) covers the time when 'New Labour' held power, leading up to the current arrangements considered in this introduction. Tony Blair began some of the most substantial changes to the premiership and its staff ever seen, and his successor, Gordon Brown, struggled to find an effective approach of his own.

We draw on secondary sources as well as diaries, private papers and National Archive files. We footnote the key sources in the text and provide a list of further reading at the end. This project has benefited from a long period of gestation during which our subject has undergone significant development. We have conducted, over a period of decades, interviews with more than 100 members of the prime-ministerial staff, on and off the record. Their periods of service date back as far as the Asquith premiership at the beginning of the last century and as recently as the present Cameron tenure. We provide a list of the more formal interviews with dates at the end of the book. Arrangements are in hand to deposit our records in a research archive where others can access them.

CHAPTER TWO

AIDES TO AN EMERGING OFFICE, 1721–1868

When the British premiership began to emerge during the eighteenth century, its existence was uncertain and changing. But this developing political office had one definite and constant feature: the individual who filled the position needed help. Robert Walpole is commonly regarded as in practice the first Prime Minister (1721–42). He and his eighteenth-century successors deployed assistants whose roles would not be out of place in the present Downing Street: aides advised on policy and saw it was implemented; they leaned on MPs to vote with the government in Parliament; they helped make decisions about appointments to key posts; they sought to manage the media and manipulate the outcomes of elections. They could become controversial figures, with their activities subject to critical public scrutiny. These characteristics of the prime-ministerial staff have endured.

Like today's special advisers, early aides were committed to the political success of the particular premier they served. By the early nineteenth century a permanent civil service with less obvious personal and political attachments slowly started to appear. A further development involved the Treasury. At first, premiers could commonly use it as their own department, helping them achieve pre-eminence in the country, in Parliament and within their own governments. From the nineteenth century, however, the Prime Minister gave up direct responsibility for the Treasury.

This change severed premiers from a crucial power base and their role as chair of the Cabinet became an increasingly important source of authority. In later periods the earlier departmental incarnation of the premiership was largely forgotten. Subsequent prime ministers and their aides would sense the absence of a large-scale support staff and ponder the possibility of creating their own department.

Robert Walpole and the development of an institution
The office of Prime Minister has always had vague parameters, and is still not clearly defined to this day, in law or otherwise. Murkiest of all its history is the early period. The very idea of a Prime Minister was an affront to constitutional orthodoxy. According to established thought, no one single subject of the monarch should rise above others and it was believed the introduction of a premier would represent the inappropriate imposition of French administrative methods. The title 'Prime Minister' began as a term of abuse during the reign of Queen Anne (1702–14), applied to her successive Lord High Treasurers Sidney Godolphin (1702–10) and Robert Harley (1711–14), both of whom used the Treasury as a power base. The proposition that a single subject might become more important than all others was seen as wrong, an undesirable introduction of French constitutional practices. Each minister, according to orthodox thinking, should be responsible for his particular policy area directly to the monarch, who was her or his own premier. Given the hostility towards the very idea of a Prime Minister in the eighteenth century, and the circumspection it prompted, a precise archaeological history of the office is difficult to establish. Premiers denied the label applied to them even if it obviously did. It was not always clear who was the Prime Minister and there did not necessarily have to be one at all. Only by the mid-nineteenth century was the post

clearly established as a permanent and proper feature of government.[3] Formal recognition came later still, starting slowly from the 1870s. This long period of uncertainty around the early office clouds any study of the aides attached to it. The lack of a formal post of Prime Minister meant no official staff and an explicitly labelled 'Prime Minister's Office' did not appear until the 1970s. Yet the history of aides is as old as – and inseparable from – that of the premiers they served.

Public controversy, civil war and revolution during the seventeenth century led to a new power balance within the English constitution. Monarchs were now more dependent upon Parliament to provide them with money and enable them to pursue their desired policies. Furthermore, the House of Commons was gradually but surely establishing dominance over the House of Lords. Walpole, by exploiting the opportunities this new environment created – operating from a base in the Commons, not the Lords – made his crucial early contribution to the development of the office of Prime Minister. His aides both supported a particular politician who came to be regarded as a premier and helped establish an institution that others would inherit in future. Over the decades that followed, as subsequent prime ministers used and adapted Walpole's techniques, the role of being the single most important national political leader passed from the monarch to the Prime Minister.

Walpole rose to indisputable pre-eminence within government by 1730. He was the dominant figure within the House of Commons and the government, gaining royal favour and influencing the dispersal of patronage. Walpole provided a direct link between the Crown and the Treasury on the one hand and the

---

3   See: B. Kemp, *Sir Robert Walpole* (London: Weidenfeld and Nicolson, 1976); R. Pares, *King George III and the Politicians: The Ford Lectures 1951–2* (Oxford: Clarendon Press, 1953), p. 176.

Commons on the other. His task was complex and his position never entirely secure, as shown when he fell in 1742. Though Walpole's skill as a politician was immense, he needed help and part of his brilliance was in assembling and deploying a team in pursuit of his objectives. The extensive use of aides fitted well with Walpole's approach to government. He was disposed to dominate policy and did not feel obliged to discuss decisions with other ministers even if their immediate areas of interest were involved. After all, the Treasury, of which he was head, had to underwrite the cost of everything. Collective Cabinet responsibility as it was later understood had not yet developed. Government was more a disparate collection of individuals than a cohesive group and, while a full Cabinet numbering at least twelve existed, Walpole preferred to use smaller collections of allies.[4]

One basis for Walpole's power was the dispersal of patronage to secure political support and his methods were not dissimilar to those used in former Soviet states. Again his role as head of the Treasury was important. Walpole expanded his personal involvement in numerous decisions about who would benefit from the Treasury, with an eye on what could be obtained in return. He and his Secretary to the Treasury, John Scrope, oversaw the distribution of jobs and contracts and were able to spread their influence widely through the country, and buy support in Parliament.[5] Walpole also needed help with another function. His relationship with the King was vital and though Walpole could be persuasive he did not want to overplay his hand by impressing his views directly on the monarch too often. Walpole believed that the King would be more favourable towards an idea if he thought of

4   B. Hill, *Sir Robert Walpole: Sole and Prime Minister* (London: Hamish Hamilton, 1989); J. Plumb, *Sir Robert Walpole: The Making of a Statesman* (London: Cresset, 1957).

5   H. T. Dickinson, *Walpole and the Whig Supremacy* (London: The English Universities Press, 1973).

it as his own. Walpole paid George I's mistresses to help encourage the King's thoughts in certain directions and worked closely with George II's queen, Caroline, to similar ends. Informers provided Walpole with intelligence about who had proposed different courses of action. The most significant Walpole aide at court was John Hervey, who became a controversial figure. In 1735 the opposition poet Alexander Pope portrayed Hervey as an extension of the will of Walpole: 'as the prompter breathes, the puppet speaks'.[6]

Alongside the confidence of the monarch Walpole needed to ensure he had the support of Parliament. Part of his success in securing the compliance of the legislature was through his influence on its composition. If Walpole backed a particular candidate who secured entry into the Commons, the premier could expect the favour to be returned when the individual concerned voted (and perhaps when they spoke) in the House. Substantial payments, often drawn from the Secret Service fund, were used to win elections (which involved a tiny franchise and no secret ballot). Purportedly set aside for espionage, those using this money were accountable not to Parliament, but to the King. This fund acquired an unsavoury reputation as being a fund for political bribes. Those helping Walpole with elections included Scrope and other Treasury staff such as Richard Edgcumbe, a Lord of the Treasury who organised election campaigns in Cornwall. As well as influencing who was returned to Parliament Walpole deployed MPs to liaise with those currently sitting in the Commons.

Alongside organisational innovations, Walpole created the physical environment in which many prime ministers and their aides would operate in future. In 1732 George II proposed to give

---

6   J. Plumb, *Sir Robert Walpole: The King's Minister* (London: Allen Lane, 1960); Dickinson, *Walpole and the Whig Supremacy*, pp. 69–70; A. Pope, *Selected Poetry* (Oxford: Oxford University Press, 1994), p. 102.

him 10 Downing Street. The property had its attractions. It was in easy reach of the House of Commons, but the reconstruction and upkeep that would be necessary might make it a financial liability. To avoid these costs Walpole proposed that rather than receive it personally the property should become a permanent residence for the First Lord of the Treasury. After the King gave it over, Walpole put the architect William Kent to work on expanding and converting the No. 10 building. It was ready for occupation in 1735 and became the home and office of many premiers (though not all chose to live there) and their staff. Kent's contribution to British government did not end with Downing Street. The Treasury needed new premises following the fire of 1698 which had destroyed much of the Palace of Whitehall. By the 1730s the Treasury was based in an area known as the 'Cockpit', just north of Downing Street. The name 'Cockpit' had similar implications to 'Downing Street', 'No. 10' or 'Whitehall' today. These premises were in a sorry condition and the Treasury required a new building. Kent won this commission too and completed it by 1736. The 'Kent Treasury', as staff still refer to it, now forms part of the 70 Whitehall complex, which takes in the old Cockpit area.

As part of his building project Kent made an important contribution to the dynamics of the relationship between premiers in Downing Street and staff in what is now 70 Whitehall. He built corridors connecting No. 10 with the Treasury, 'thus creating the physical axis around which central government still turns'.[7] Walpole could walk through from No. 10 easily without having to go out onto the street. In the early period of the premiership it was natural that the First Lord, who was then directly responsible for the Treasury, should have immediate physical access

---

7   H. Roseveare, *The Treasury: The Evolution of a British Institution* (London: Allen Lane, 1969), pp. 100–102.

to its employees, who can be regarded as his aides. In 1963, 70 Whitehall became the headquarters for the Cabinet Office. Prime ministers were able in this later period to use the staff based there – but the relationship was more complicated because the Cabinet Office served government collectively (at least until the early twenty-first century), not just the premier.

Media management under Walpole

Like many politicians before and since, Walpole was concerned with the public's perception of him and his government – and sought to colour it. He endured powerful literary attacks in diverse media during his term of office, which he lacked the legal means completely to silence. Consequently, after a slow start, Walpole developed an increasingly sophisticated public-relations operation.[8] He sought to discourage criticism and promote his own case, and engaged various aides to assist with different parts of this project. While it was an impressive feat of organisation, his operation and key figures within it became a subject of criticism, providing further fuel to the same sources he had set out to combat.

During his long period of office, criticism of Walpole as a person and his policies appeared in various media, including journals, pamphlets, plays and poetry. Sometimes it was explicit, at others implied. Coordinated attacks came from the Scriblerus Club, a literary group of staggering combined ability, whose associates included John Gay, Alexander Pope and a young Henry Fielding. At the centre of Scriblerus was Jonathan Swift, who had worked for the prototypical premier, Harley, earlier in the century. Harley had developed propaganda systems in an environment created by

---

8   The account that follows draws on: T. Urstad, *Sir Robert Walpole's Poets: The Use of Literature as Pro-Government Propaganda, 1721–1742* (London: Associated University Presses, 1999). See also: T. Horne, 'Politics in a Corrupt Society: William Arnall's Defense of Robert Walpole', *Journal of the History of Ideas*, vol. 41, no. 4 (October–December, 1980), pp. 601–614.

the Licensing Act ceasing to have effect in 1695. No longer could governments simply stop criticism of them from being published. They had to find active methods of promoting themselves, hence the value to Harley of Swift and his colleagues.

With Walpole in office, Scriblerus was now an opposition group. Its members found some of their best material in their assault on the Prime Minister. Swift's *Gulliver's Travels* included a character, Flimnap, Treasurer to the Emperor of Lilliput, who was an oblique representation of Walpole.[9] Gay's celebrated comic musical *The Beggar's Opera* was first performed in 1728. It contains various allusions to corruption in the Walpole government, splits between different members of it and insinuations about the personal life of its head. One character, Robin of Bagshot, member of the highwayman Macheath's gang, has aliases including 'Bob Booty' – a nickname that stuck to Walpole for the rest of his career. Alongside a general tainting of the public reputation of Walpole, literary activities could help undermine specific policies. Media-driven U-turns were possible in the eighteenth century; Walpole dropped his Excise Bill of 1733 under pressure from the opposition press.

During the course of the 1720s attacks on Walpole escalated and he started to develop methods intended to thwart them. At first his approach was defensive. One course of action was to try and prosecute the critics but it was a difficult task and might backfire. Other methods were to use bribery to discourage the production of unhelpful literature, or prevent it from reaching its intended destination using control of the post office. In tandem with such efforts Walpole moved towards a more positive approach. Eventually he constructed a complete propaganda machine. He deployed writers, distribution mechanisms and

9   Jonathan Swift, *Gulliver's Travels* (Oxford: Oxford University Press, 1998), pp. 25–6.

outlets, all dedicated to damning his opponents and promoting and rebutting criticism of his government. Journals of which Walpole gained control included the *British Journal*, the *Daily Courant*, the *Flying Post*, the *Corn Cutters Journal* and the *Free Briton*.

There were three categories of pro-government writers: those for whom writing was their primary source of income; those with another job, often as politicians; and those whom Walpole already engaged in another capacity. Though they were never of the same quality as the Scriblerus Club, they were effective in their own way. Participants in Walpole's media activities often worked as a team. If Walpole discovered difficult accusations about to emerge, as in 1735 over his alleged participation in financial wrongdoings with the South Sea Company, his actions in stemming the tide of public opinion anticipated the media monitoring and 'rapid rebuttal' methods introduced under Tony Blair in the late twentieth century. They would assess the nature of the story that was unravelling and develop ways of countering it. Walpole had two main aides helping to coordinate his media operation: Thomas Gordon and Nicholas Paxton.

Thomas Gordon, previously the author of political pamphlets, took an interest in the literary content of the Walpole propaganda campaign. The exact details of his role and the length of time he served as an aide are unclear but Walpole appointed him First Commissioner of Wine Licences in 1723. The Wine Licence Office seems to have become something of a front for government publicity operations. By 1740 all five commissioners were Walpole placemen and three of them were involved in propaganda, though not as part of their official duties.

Paxton was more concerned with the mechanics. Contemporaries regarded him as an unsavoury figure. Paul Whitehead, an opposition poet, described him as 'yon fell Harpy

hovr'ring o'er the Press'.[10] Paxton, a lawyer by training, was
Solicitor to the Treasury. In this post he was responsible for identifying actionable published material. He was closely involved in
attempts to ban opposition propaganda or restrict its dissemination. His role invoked resentment. 'Dialogue II' from *Epistle to
the Satires* by Pope opens with the line: ''Tis all a libel – Paxton,
sir, will say.' Paxton had substantial funds at his disposal and
channelled payments to writers. This feature of his work attracted
further comment from Pope, when describing how each cheap
writer or 'hackney' received 'double pots and pay' from Paxton.[11]
The money Paxton disbursed had further uses: buying political
intelligence and shoring up the local electoral position of the
government.

Edmund Gibson (1669–1748)

Edmund Gibson, Bishop of London and nicknamed 'Walpole's
Pope', is a prime example of the creative use Walpole made
of aides, providing services that prime ministers find valuable,
including liaising with important groups, and advising on the
dispersal of patronage and policy. Gibson was a figure of intellectual, ecclesiastical and political substance, and studied at Queen's
College, Oxford. After dabbling with the idea of a legal career
Gibson entered the clergy. He became associated with the Whigs
and in 1714 gave a sermon against the Tories in support of the
Hanoverian succession. Gibson became Bishop of Lincoln in
1715, which provided him with a place in the Lords and cemented
his position as an increasingly prominent Whig. The twenty-six
bishops in the Lords comprised an important political bloc and
the Anglican Church was a powerful force in the land beyond

---

10   P. Whitehead, *Satires* (Los Angeles: The Augustan Reprint Society, 1984),
     p. 14.
11   Pope, *Selected Poetry*, pp. 120; 124.

Parliament. It had tended to display more Tory than Whig loyalties. In 1723 five bishops died, including Charles Trimnell, the Bishop of Winchester, who was the senior adviser to the Whigs on church matters. Consequently Walpole and his partner in government at the time, Charles Townshend, had both the opportunity to fill the new vacancies with amenable individuals and the need for a new ecclesiastical counsellor, whom they found in Gibson. Gibson was already advising Townshend at the time but claimed to be reluctant to take on this grand position. Yet Walpole and others sensed the ambitious nature lying behind his protestations. Gibson acquired an unpleasant reputation for flattering those above him and abusing those below.

The Bishop of Lincoln rose to become the Bishop of London. When Townshend fell from power in 1730, Gibson became closer to Walpole. Though often known as 'Church minister' and wielding substantial influence, Gibson played only an informal role. Working from an office in the Cockpit, Gibson's personal access to Walpole was critical. He helped build up a pro-Whig faction in the Church in general and among the bishops in the Lords. The people he recommended for posts were often politically reliable, but not so radical as to alienate the wider church. Gibson also managed the bishops in the Lords, acting as what would later be called a whip (a title adopted from hunting terminology as the eighteenth century progressed – a 'whipper-in' of men as opposed to hounds). His crucial contributions in this role included securing twenty-four votes in the 1733 debate on the South Sea Company that had threatened severely to damage the government.

Gibson was a conduit between government and clergy. An important adviser on church policy, Gibson had his own programme set out in long notes he sent to Walpole and Townshend. In general, he agreed with making the church more pro-Whig but Gibson sometimes objected to appointments made purely for such reasons. He

wanted to take into account intellectual abilities, personal values
and beliefs. Gibson did not succeed in his attempt to bring about
a full reorganisation of the church. In 1736 Gibson resigned, as
much as he could from an unofficial position, because he objected
to a government measure to increase the rights of Quakers. He
was not selected for appointment as Archbishop of Canterbury
when the office became vacant the following year. Gibson had
supposedly previously resisted this formal promotion because it
would mean losing day-to-day access to Walpole. Then as now,
physical proximity to the Prime Minister could at times trump
formal status. But now he wanted the senior post in the Church, it
was denied to the out-of-favour Gibson. After the fall of Walpole
his links with the Whig leadership grew stronger again and he
became an adviser once more, though perhaps not a direct prime-
ministerial support role in exactly the same way as before.[12]

Post-mortem of a government

When Walpole fell from power, his enemies saw the chance to
exact revenge. There followed swiftly an attempt in Parliament
to impeach him for corruption. Walpole's opponents tried to target
him through his aides; his contemporaries knew how important
his staff were to his system of government. Up to this point, legal
attacks followed by imprisonment or exile had been a standard
part of the repertoire of the partisan power struggle. But this time
the attempt to construct a case for prosecution was unsuccessful. In future, while attacks continued on later prime ministers

---

12   T. Kendrick, 'Sir Robert Walpole, the old Whigs and the Bishops, 1733–
     1736: a Study in Eighteenth Century Parliamentary Politics', *The Historical
     Journal*, vol. 11, issue 3 (1968); Andrea Soldi, 'Gibson, Edmund', *Oxford
     Dictionary of National Biography (ODNB)*; N. Sykes, *Edmund Gibson:
     Bishop of London* (Oxford: Oxford University Press, 1926); S. Taylor, 'Sir
     Robert Walpole, the Church of England, and the Quakers Tithe Bill of
     1736', *The Historical Journal*, vol. 28, issue 1 (1985); Plumb, *Sir Robert
     Walpole: The King's Minister*, p. 96.

and their aides, the means were political. The ultimate sanction against a premier was defeat through a vote of no-confidence in the Commons, a coup staged by other members of the elite, or a general election. Walpole's successful evasion in 1742 helped establish this change of practice – though in recent times more legal and judicial involvement in the No. 10 sphere has occurred with the 'cash for honours' police investigation, judge-led inquiries (instigated by prime ministers) and the rise of judicial review.

In January 1742, judging he had lost the support of the Commons, Walpole resigned. On 23 March 1742 Parliament passed a motion establishing a 'Committee of Secrecy'. Its twenty-one members consisted of both peers and MPs. Their task was to 'enquire into the conduct' of Walpole's government during his last ten years in office. The central interest was Walpole's management of elections through Secret Service money and granting of official contracts. However, the inquiry made no progress. The Commons Speaker, Onslow – who had himself received favour from Walpole – was able to place Walpole supporters on the committee. One of Walpole's senior electoral operatives, Richard Edgcumbe, received a peerage, which historian H. T. Dickinson writes 'put him beyond the reach of the committee'.[13]

Other aides to Walpole were called but they would not cooperate. On 13 April 1742 the Chairman of the Committee of Secrecy, Lord Limerick, reported to Parliament that Nicholas Paxton, placed on oath, had refused to answer questions. The committee moved to use the sanction of placing him in the custody of the Serjeant at Arms and the motion passed. The Committee of Secrecy could examine its prisoner as often as it wanted; Paxton appeared before it the following day. But on 15 April Limerick informed the House that Paxton had once more refused to

---

13   Dickinson, *Walpole and the Whig Supremacy*, p. 189.

cooperate so the committee resolved to move him to Newgate prison, where he would continue to be available to the committee for questioning.

The committee then chose to reveal details of its inquiry to convey the problems it was encountering with Paxton. It had uncovered evidence incriminating him in electoral irregularities and misuse of public money in the borough of Wendover in 1735. One witness, John Jones, had described how, when acting on behalf of the candidate, John Boteler, he delivered to Paxton a letter requesting money. According to Jones, after reading it Paxton asked Jones to see him the following day at Roger Williams's coffee house. At this meeting Paxton gave Jones 'a parcel of money'. Most, if not all of it, was in bank notes. Jones estimated the amount to be £500. When handing it over Jones recalled Paxton telling him, 'here is your answer'. Paxton confirmed to the committee that he knew both Jones and Boteler. But when asked if he had passed money to Jones to help Boteler he repeatedly refused to answer the question 'as it may tend to accuse myself'.

Despite incarcerating Paxton, the Committee of Secrecy failed to break him. One report complained of his 'obstinate and contemptuous' behaviour and recorded that he appeared to have been directly or indirectly involved in most of the transactions it had investigated. The committee noted concern at the huge sums placed at the disposal of Paxton when he was Solicitor to the Treasury without the presence of any proper means of ensuring his accountability. Such laxity, the committee believed, permitted practices detrimental both to the liberty of the nation and to parliamentary independence.

In June 1742 the Committee of Secrecy called Walpole's Secretary to the Treasury, John Scrope, to explain the use made of the £1,052,211 that was tracked back to him and Walpole. When adjusted for inflation, this sum would easily exceed £150 million today. To refuse to respond to questions about it from Parliament would be an act of audacity – not something beyond Scrope. He refused to take the oath on the grounds that questions might arise which he was determined he would not answer and also added that he could not give information about Secret Service money without permission from the King. He held that such funds by their nature required secrecy and that those disposing of them were answerable only to the monarch, who could not allow him to disclose details about them.[14] Scrope reportedly told the committee that, as an octogenarian, he did not mind if he spent what remained of his life in the Tower and would betray neither the King nor Walpole. (In fact he survived another decade and remained in office until his death.) The committee abandoned its attempt to extract information from him.

Opponents of Walpole, realising they were not getting anywhere, introduced a bill that would make those who gave evidence against Walpole immune to prosecution themselves. The Commons passed it but the Lords vetoed it. The Committee of Secrecy dragged on in its efforts to put together a case against Walpole, but could not manage to do so. In December 1742 there was an attempt to set up another committee but it failed. Yet while it did not get the cooperation it sought, the inquiry nevertheless revealed exorbitant outlays of cash carried out with the help of aides. Walpole had distributed more than £50,000 in the final ten years of his period in power for propaganda ends alone.[15] As his government crumbled, a final financial scramble had occurred. In its last six weeks more Secret Service money was drawn than in the three years up to August 1710. Treasury staff

---

14   *Cobbett's Parliamentary History of England*, vol. 12 (London: 1812), cols 586; 626–30; 637; 626.
15   Urstad, *Sir Robert Walpole's Poets*, p. 9.

down to the level of messengers, as well as officials from other departments, assisted Walpole in his covert operations, surely benefitting personally in the process.

The Place Act of 1742 was a further parliamentary reaction to Walpole's political management operation. It determined that a series of officials including Treasury deputies and clerks were precluded from sitting in the House of Commons. Advocates of the Act saw it as a means of preventing governments such as Walpole's from corrupting and dominating Parliament. A number of the officers excluded from the Commons by the Place Act had under Walpole been not only his parliamentary placemen but worked as his aides. Never again could prime ministers have as many support staff rooted in the legislature, voting or sometimes speaking on their behalf. This law was an important early stage in the development of an administrative machine distinct from the competitive political environment of Parliament. But it should not be concluded that after Walpole there was a cessation of the use by premiers – assisted by aides – of official resources for murky ends.

The Prime Minister and Treasury staff

In the eighteenth century, though there could be no formal department of the Prime Minister, premiers were usually directly responsible for the largest and most important office of government: the Treasury. Nearly all early premiers held the office of First Lord of the Treasury. The First Lord was the head of the Treasury in both name and practice. If the First Lord sat in the Commons, he simultaneously held the office of Chancellor of the Exchequer. That early premiers were in charge of the Treasury is central to any understanding of the development of the office of Prime Minister – and of the aides attached to it. The Treasury was a power base that helped facilitate the emergence of the British premiership. After the role of chief minister became more established in its own right, the association with the Treasury weakened. The post of Chancellor of the Exchequer became more distinct and grew more powerful, carrying with it the senior responsibility for the Treasury and finance once attached to the premier.[16] Before these developments, prime ministers received support in tasks ranging from policy development to parliamentary and electoral management from the staff of the Treasury, who can be regarded as their aides at that time.

A significant Treasury official for some early prime ministers was the Solicitor to the Treasury. In this position Nicholas Paxton had helped Walpole with the application of patronage and provided advice on rebutting criticism of the government. Paxton's successor, John Sharpe, was important to Henry Pelham (1743–54) in his premiership. One of his tasks was the distribution of large amounts of money. In 1747 and 1748 he disbursed a minimum of £105,000 in compensation to those who had suffered as a consequence of a cattle disease, a task that reflects the level of responsibility that prime ministers could entrust to their Treasury staff.[17]

Of all aides, the secretaries to the Treasury were the most important to the early premiers yet still the origins of this post are uncertain. In an article from the 1930s, Dora Clark described how the role descends from the sixteenth-century assistant to the Treasurer of the Exchequer, and up until 1711 there was only one Secretary to the Treasury, at which time a second was added. Initially a senior secretary remained in post permanently while a junior resigned when the First Lord who had recruited him

---

16   Hill, *Sir Robert Walpole*; M. Wright, *Treasury Control of the Civil Service: 1854–1874* (Oxford: Oxford University Press, 1969), p. 49.

17   J. Wilkes, *A Whig in Power: The Political Career of Henry Pelham* (Evanston: Northwestern University Press, 1964), p. 99.

left office. Then, between 1758 and 1782, a practice developed that when there was a changeover in the government both left. In this sense the role had become more clearly politicised. Previously the senior secretary had tended to carry out more work than the junior but the tasks were now shared more equally.[18] Normally secretaries held a seat in the Commons. As ever in eighteenth-century politics, many financial perks came with the job. Holders of government positions treated them as a form of property that they could exploit. Secretaries often went on to occupy more senior offices. A charge levelled at career civil servants in the twentieth century – that they were 'generalists', dabblers in such interests as the arts – could have been made against the secretaries to the Treasury, perhaps none more so than Richard Sheridan, the author of plays including *School for Scandal* and *The Rivals*, who held the post in 1783.

The wide range of tasks that fell to secretaries to the Treasury made the office increasingly demanding. As Members of Parliament secretaries provided essential knowledge of financial issues and the procedure of Parliament. They acted as prototypical whips, managing votes and applying discipline in the Commons. Secretaries helped organise elections, including attempting to predict outcomes across constituencies – equivalent to the opinion-polling of two centuries later. As well as being responsible for distributing the largest portion of the Secret Service money, they also managed the Treasury staff. Secretaries provided administrative support to the Treasury Board, including preparing and minuting its frequent meetings. They played a part in

---

18   The following passages on secretaries to the Treasury draw on: D. Clark, 'The Office of Secretary to the Treasury in the Eighteenth Century', *The American Historical Review*, vol. 42, no. 1, October 1936; J. Sainty, 'The Evolution of the Parliamentary and Financial Secretaryships of the Treasury', *English Historical Review*, vol. 91, no. 360 (1976), pp. 566–84; H. Parris, *Constitutional Bureaucracy* (London: George Allen and Unwin, 1969), p. 46.

implementing decisions and held the power of discretion in a number of areas. Because of these roles, and their personal expertise, secretaries were in a position to exercise influence on policy. To add to the gravity of their work, they had to be on hand personally to help the First Lord of the Treasury, a close attachment that highlights the link between premiers and their secretaries.

One important holder of the post of Secretary to the Treasury was John Scrope, whom we have already encountered as one of Walpole's most important aides. Born around 1662, he trained as a lawyer before becoming an aide to a succession of political leaders of different alignments. After working for the Godolphin and Harley governments he managed to survive when George I came to the throne and entered Parliament as an MP in 1722. When Walpole appointed him Secretary to the Treasury in 1724 he was already past the age of sixty and known as 'old Scrope'. Yet he served in the office for nearly thirty years until he died in 1752. Following the fall of Walpole in 1742 it was assumed Scrope – who had a close association with the outgoing premier – would have to leave his post. Other aides to Walpole made an immediate exit but Scrope possessed unique expertise about Treasury work and the drafting of bills and he had a reputation for personal reliability; later leaders could dispense with his talents no more than those previous.[19]

A prominent Secretary to the Treasury later in the century was George Rose, first 1782–3, then 1783–1801. During the second, longer stretch he was a key aide to William Pitt the Younger. After serving in the navy Rose had worked his way through various administrative appointments. He was appointed as the junior Secretary to the Treasury when Lord Shelburne was premier in 1782. Pitt the Younger was Chancellor of the Exchequer at

---

19   Parris, *Constitutional Bureaucracy*; Roseveare, *The Treasury*; A. Hanham, 'Scrope, John', *ODNB*; Wilkes, *A Whig in Power*, p. 99.

the time; when he became Prime Minister the following year he appointed Rose as his senior Secretary to the Treasury and they developed a close bond. His role as Secretary included the public presentation of the government and handling elections. Correspondence between Pitt and Rose shows the two of them were immersed together in the minutiae of government accounts. Rose helped prepare speeches for Pitt, and ensured that when the government dispensed patronage upon individuals those men were ready to repay the favour. Rose did not always share the policy preferences of Pitt the Younger, disagreeing with the premier's desire to see the slave trade ended. In a manifestation of the rivalry so often found in prime-ministerial inner circles, Rose harboured hostility towards Pitt's firmest Cabinet ally, Henry Dundas. Starting in 1784 the *Morning Herald* published in instalments verses parodying the Pitt government. Under the general heading 'Criticisms on the Rolliad', they included a portrayal of Rose as envious of the junior Secretary to the Treasury, Thomas Steele, and unable, despite 'all his votes, his speeches, and his lies', to 'shine in Billy's [Pitt's] eyes'. Rose – who was becoming tired of office – left when Pitt the Younger resigned in 1801; he subsequently held various public offices and worked to return Pitt to power in 1804.[20]

Separation of the functions of government

Secretaries to the Treasury such as Scrope and Rose were able and effective in the assistance they provided to prime ministers but the myriad of tasks they performed inevitably placed immense demands on them. As pressures on government rose, existing Treasury arrangements for helping the person at its head

---

20   G. Rose, *The Diaries and Correspondence of the Right Hon. George Rose* (London: Bentley, 1860), 2 vols; W. Hague, *William Pitt the Younger* (London: HarperCollins, 2004); R. Thorne, 'Rose, George', *ODNB*.

became unsustainable. The prime-ministerial support system had to change if it were to continue to function effectively. The developments which followed, though they improved the position, had unforeseen consequences: they helped initiate the appearance of a permanent civil service. In future, staff associated with this institution would not necessarily prove as obliging to the prime ministers they served as past aides had been.

As the eighteenth century progressed, central government came under strain, a turn of events that fell heavily upon the secretaries to the Treasury. Pressure came from many and new directions. The population was growing, along with the economy. Social strains and calls for political reform came to the fore. But most dramatic and urgent were the wars in America and with France. All these factors added to the burden of work falling upon the Treasury. The multi-tasking role of the Secretary to the Treasury became almost impossible – as the sad end of Edward Chamberlain suggests. Chamberlain was one of only a minority of individuals who worked their way up from a lower level within the Treasury to become Secretary. He obtained this appointment in 1782, during the second premiership of Lord Rockingham. The task he had taken on appeared formidable and Chamberlain resorted to defenestration and killed himself. The increasingly party-political character of the Secretary's role may have been particularly worrisome for him.[21]

A parliamentary commission of 1786 recommended that one Secretary to the Treasury should hold office permanently and not have a seat in the Commons. The Treasury did not find favour with this proposal at the time but in 1801, with stresses continuing to grow and conflict taking place in Europe, the political landscape shifted. The two secretaries to the Treasury each began

---

21   Parris, *Constitutional Bureaucracy*; Roseveare, *The Treasury*.

to take on more specific and distinct functions. One would become a 'Parliamentary' or 'Patronage Secretary' and help the First Lord of the Treasury in handling the Commons – the role would later be titled the 'Chief Whip'. The other would be the 'Financial Secretary', supporting the Chancellor of the Exchequer. Then in 1805 a Treasury minute of 19 August established a Secretary who could not sit in Parliament and was permanently in post. The title of this new post was Assistant Secretary and Law Clerk and the holder relieved the secretaries to the Treasury of many of their administrative duties. The major upheaval in the support system for premiers was completed in 1806 when specific provision was made for a secretary to the Prime Minister (in his guise as First Lord of the Treasury, with another secretary added in 1812). Not for the last time, war had quickened the pace of change at the centre of government.

Later in the nineteenth century premiers withdrew from direct involvement in the Treasury. Consequently the financial secretaries ceased to be their assistants, instead supporting the Chancellor of the Exchequer as the occupant of a distinct and prominent Cabinet office in its own right. The parliamentary secretary is the direct ancestor of the Chief Whip of later years, working for the Prime Minister in planning parliamentary business and enforcing discipline with a team of junior whips. Assistant secretaries to the Treasury became known as permanent under-secretaries – or more commonly permanent secretaries – from 1867. Once again, because of the First Lord's detachment from the Treasury, the permanent secretaries' attachment to the premier became less clearly visible.

Initially, assistant secretaries acted as personal counsellors to the First Lord of the Treasury. The first was George Harrison. From a financial law background, Harrison was favoured by Pitt the Younger, who advanced Harrison's early administrative career and made him the inaugural Assistant Secretary to the Treasury in 1805, a post Harrison remained in until 1826. His permanency was not absolutely beyond doubt but, like Scrope before him, he ensured he was too useful to remove. After Pitt the Younger, other premiers such as Spencer Perceval (1809–12) depended upon him. Lord Liverpool (1812–27) found Harrison especially useful, taking his advice on handling financial institutions and the organisation of the machinery of government. While the creation of the post of Assistant Secretary was intended as a means of managing the government workload more effectively, the demands upon Harrison were still immense. A Treasury minute from 1815 suggests he possessed considerable delegated authority. It provided for a payment to him 'upon whom … so much of the detail of the conduct of the business has devolved', and described how he had been employed in secretive and vital business that the war brought to pass. These tasks could only realistically have been entrusted to someone in 'constant attendance'. Here was the value of a permanent official not distracted by parliamentary and partisan duties.[22]

The reallocation of work within the Treasury was part of a broader trend. Secretaries to the Treasury were members of a class of political employee working for politicians, sometimes known as 'men of business'. The eighteenth century saw the slow beginnings of a process that would eventually divide their tasks and allot them to two different groups in British government. One group was that of party politicians.

With seats in the Commons, or peerages, they held ministerial offices temporarily, according to their personal fortunes and those of the government to which they belonged. The other group was that of officials – the civil service as they came to be

---

22   Roseveare, *The Treasury*; J. Sainty, 'Harrison, Sir George', *ODNB*; Parris, *Constitutional Bureaucracy*, p. 47.

known collectively – who occupied posts permanently, regardless of changes of government. They were not parliamentarians and came to maintain a distance from parties or political competition, usually avoiding attachments to particular ministers and policies.

Causes of this separation included a desire for greater efficiency through the division of labour, and parliamentary pressure for more accountable governance. The split was tentative in the eighteenth century, but accelerated in the nineteenth – with intellectual impetus coming from the famous report produced by Charles Trevelyan and Stafford Northcote in 1854 – and was most pronounced around the mid-twentieth century. Prime ministers were served by aides on either side of the divide. On the one hand there were parliamentary politicians, such as whips, parliamentary private secretaries and ministers with special responsibilities. On the other hand many permanent civil servants supported premiers. From the 1920s through to at least the 1960s they came to dominate administrative activity at No. 10 and were the most numerous among the senior prime-ministerial aides, able to provide Harrison's 'constant attendance'.

There were drawbacks. One of the tasks of premiers is to connect administration with competitive politics. Aides able to operate in both environments can be invaluable. In the eighteenth century, secretaries to the Treasury had provided prime ministers with such an overlapping service. Even as the separation of bureaucracy from the partisan struggle was at its earliest stages, some provisions exempted secretaries to the Treasury from any such distinction. Under The Place Act of 1742, Treasury clerks were prohibited from sitting in Parliament, but the Act specifically did not apply to secretaries to the Treasury. Furthermore, upon being appointed, secretaries to the Treasury who held places in the Commons were not subject to an obligation to resign and recontest their seats, unlike those who were newly placed in senior ministerial offices. But the position of secretaries to the Treasury became increasingly anomalous and in the end unsustainable. Premiers would have to look elsewhere for the sort of support these aides had previously provided.

As career officials disengaged from the partisan interests and individual fates of prime ministers, a constitutional convention emerged that such involvement was inappropriate. This tendency could be undesirable for premiers, who might doubt the commitment of such staff. One episode from 1843 suggests that, even in its relatively tentative stages, the development of a permanent official staff could bring difficulties for prime ministers. In this year Charles Trevelyan, the Assistant Secretary to the Treasury, enraged the premier, Sir Robert Peel, after returning from a journey to Ireland. Trevelyan had briefed Peel and Sir James Graham, the Home Secretary, on his visit but included the same information he had imparted to them in a letter to a pro-opposition newspaper under a pseudonym. Peel learned what Trevelyan had done, and also that the Secretary had acted in the belief that his disclosure was in the interests of a higher good. The Prime Minister wrote to Graham expressing bemusement at the actions of the Treasury official. Peel found Trevelyan's attitude beyond comprehension and concluded he 'must be a consummate fool'.[23]

Francis Bonham (c.1785–1863)

While the permanent civil service was beginning to develop, there was still a need for prime-ministerial aides who could fulfil both administrative and partisan requirements. In particular, premiers had to maintain contact with mass parties, which they needed to achieve and retain power. During his premierships (1834–5; 1841–6) Peel benefitted from assistance in this area from Francis

---

23   Parris, *Constitutional Bureaucracy*, pp. 41; 94–5.

Bonham. The aide was neither a career official nor was he primarily a parliamentary politician. Hovering between different environments, he made himself indispensable to Peel, helping him with numerous decisions and tasks. His unusual position attracted attention and placed him in the political line of fire as proxy for the premier.

In his 1851 biography of Lord George Bentinck, Benjamin Disraeli referred to the 'unseen management of [Peel's] party', describing the decisive contribution to its success from a man who possessed knowledge of human nature and opinions, was hardworking, well connected and resourceful, but 'was spoken of only in a whisper and moved behind the scenes'. Without naming him, Disraeli was referring to Bonham. The aide was valuable to Peel partly because the premier was not enthusiastic about the idea of political parties. Bonham helped with work that, whatever Peel's qualms, was essential. The nineteenth century saw the rise of the party as a defined, disciplined entity within Parliament and throughout the country. Here was another political force upon which prime ministers now depended. It required careful management, hence the value of Bonham being able to help with the task.

Bonham was another aide who first qualified as a lawyer and then served as a Tory MP from 1830 to 1831 and 1835 to 1837. He began his parliamentary career as assistant whip in 1831, and from 1832 to 1837 acted as the foremost election specialist for the Conservatives – though whether he ever formally held such a position is not clear. This latter job was not entirely new. Managers of parliamentary contests – sometimes working for prime ministers – were a feature of British politics before Bonham was born; the nature of his task was different. The Great Reform Act of 1832 meant a larger franchise, and registering voters became a crucial task. Bonham developed methods to meet the new challenge. Working mainly out of the Carlton Club (of which he was a founder member) Bonham accumulated a comprehensive body of information that helped facilitate the Conservative election victory of 1841. He combined this role with acting as a personal political adviser to Peel, keeping him informed about developments within the Conservative Party and beyond.

During both Peel premierships Bonham's official post was Storekeeper to the Ordnance. It involved little work, leaving time for him to carry out party duties for Peel. Bonham was neither the first nor the last prime-ministerial aide with a misleading job title. In 1834, when he first appointed Bonham to the post, Peel explained he could not have accepted the post of Prime Minister without help from Bonham, whose office enabled him to provide that very assistance. Bonham was no longer an MP when Peel formed his second government yet he was reinstated to his previous post and advised on a wide range of issues in Peel's longer – and more significant – second term. They included the construction of his government in 1841; choosing MPs to speak on particular occasions in the Commons; and appointing people to positions of power and prestige in the church and at universities. Bonham also helped handle the owners of newspapers. Politicians courted him, recognising his significance to Peel.

Bonham should be regarded as a partisan official – committed to and working for the Conservatives in general and Peel in particular, employed within the government as a consequence of their obtaining power, but not, after 1837, sitting in Parliament. In modern terms he was a provider of support rather than a minister. He is similar to later aides such as special advisers or the Prime Minister's Political Secretary. Bonham did not relish speaking or receiving attention of any kind when he was an MP, and did not pursue a parliamentary career with vigour. Not being dragged into the daily business of an MP was an advantage, enabling him to take an overview of party concerns which he might not otherwise have possessed.

The unusual status of Bonham, along with his personal short-comings, encouraged opponents of Peel to single him out as a target. In 1844 Mr Divett, a Whig MP who disliked Bonham, tried to force his removal, drawing attention to the disparity between his formal position and his actual activities. This move against Bonham was doomed since Divett could not even find a seconder for his motion. Next, Disraeli sought to oust Bonham; he claimed that the aide had participated in a subversive plot decades before. Disraeli's accusation arose from a case of mistaken identity. Peel made a powerful defence and Disraeli was forced to withdraw the claim. But enemies of the government sensed that Bonham could be vulnerable. In June 1845 it emerged that, nine years previously, as an MP he had played an inappropriate part in seeking to influence the award of railway contracts. This time Bonham resigned, though Peel supported him in the Commons. Leaving office did not make a significant difference to his activities as an aide to the Prime Minister – he continued in his role for the remainder of the Peel premiership, and beyond.[24]

Prime ministers' secretaries

A common feature of many political leaders through history and across different cultures is a reliance on one person or a small group of individuals in close physical, organisational, and often personal, proximity to them, helping with their day-to-day functions. In central government many individuals have the term 'secretary' in their job title. A number of them have been aides to premiers. Though possibly not as high powered as secretaries

---

24   N. Gash, 'F. R. Bonham: Conservative "Political Secretary", 1832–47', *The English Historical Review*, vol. 63, no. 249 (October 1948); N. Gash, 'Bonham, Francis Robert', *ODNB*.

to the Treasury, the private secretaries to the Prime Minister have had a special role. They have operated in a highly confidential area where the political and the personal overlap, and have done so for an unbroken period longer than any other aide or group of aides to the premier.

The precise genesis of the role of private secretary to the Prime Minister is uncertain. Unlike his successors, Walpole did not have a private secretary attached to him in his capacity as First Lord of the Treasury. But debate exists about whether Henry Bilson-Legge supported him in his role as emergent Prime Minister. Legge, a son of the Earl of Dartmouth, met Walpole in 1733 through his friend Edward Walpole, son of the Prime Minister. Three years later Robert Walpole made Legge his private secretary in his capacity as Chancellor of the Exchequer. But Legge's was largely a sinecure post and it does not follow necessarily that Legge consequently worked as an aide. In 1739 Walpole placed him as Chief Secretary to the Lord Lieutenant of Ireland; then in 1741 as the second Secretary to the Treasury.

From Pelham onwards it is possible to identify those individuals who might be termed a Prime Minister's private secretary, usually serving the First Lord of the Treasury. Generally, secretaries were appointed by and left office with a particular premier. Originally it fell to prime ministers to provide for their own secretaries. In 1806 – perhaps prompted by the early death of Pitt the Younger, which appears to have been brought on in part by overwork – the Treasury introduced an allowance of £300 for a private secretary to the First Lord. The same provision was added in 1812, allowing premiers to take on a second such aide.[25]

Being a secretary to a senior politician meant more than merely carrying out functions such as writing, copying and filing – even

---

25   'Private secretaries to the prime ministers 1743–1868', paper supplied to authors by Sir John Sainty.

though these tasks were part of the work required by premiers. The job entailed involvement in the confidential business of the employer. There was a relationship of trust and mutual dependence, sometimes lasting many years, between secretaries and prime ministers. The former discreetly performed delicate duties for the latter, and were well compensated for their work. This type of connection is illustrated by the career of possibly the first such secretary, John Roberts.

Roberts first began working for Henry Pelham as a tutor to his son and then became his private secretary. He provided support to Pelham as Prime Minister from 1743 until Pelham died in office in 1754. His tasks included helping oversee the distribution of Secret Service funds. As was usual in eighteenth-century politics, Pelham received generous financial compensation for his efforts in the form of appointments and payments. When Pelham died, his brother, the Duke of Newcastle, not only succeeded him as premier but took on Roberts as his secretary. Roberts supported Newcastle during the elections held in 1754 and 1761 and continued to be responsible for the Secret Service money until 1756. However, Roberts had difficulty establishing as strong a link with Newcastle as he had with Pelham.[26]

Private secretaries after Roberts continued to perform sensitive roles. Working for George Grenville as premier from April 1763, Charles Lloyd took responsibility for patronage. One task was to act as a go-between. Private secretaries helped premiers such as Lord Bute deal with much of their political work and conduct business that arose from their Treasury role. Lord North's biographer records William Brummell helping organise for him a meeting with the leading opposition figure Charles James Fox, which was supposed to be revealed only to George

---

26   M. Powell, 'Roberts, John', *ODNB*; Wilkes, *A Whig in Power*.

III.[27] In the following century, as private secretary to his father the Earl of Aberdeen, Arthur Gordon was a significant liaison with the Peelites. Evelyn Melbourne Ashley performed for Palmerston diplomatic and intelligence functions in an informal capacity. There were limits, however, to the amount of work that a single private secretary could or would be expected to take off the hands of the premier. In his biography of William Pitt the Younger, John Ehrman notes the restrictions on available help. As was normal at the time, Pitt the Younger was constrained by the expectation that he would carry out much of his own correspondence; while his private secretary could see less important people for him, he had to deal with the major business himself.[28]

Research by Sir John Sainty[29] reveals the types of individuals who were private secretaries to prime ministers. Up to 1812, four were staff drawn from the Treasury and another was formally attached to the Treasury when recruited; three were clergy. Two were officials from the offices of the secretaries of state and three were MPs at the same time as supporting premiers. From 1812 the practice developed that one generally came from the Treasury and one from somewhere else. This pattern was not rigidly adhered to – for his final year in office neither of the two private secretaries supporting Lord Melbourne came from the Treasury; while from 1841 to 1846 – the duration of Robert Peel's second premiership – both of his were. For at least some of his first term of 1846–52, Lord John Russell, who had three private secretaries, obtained two of them from the Treasury. As before 1812 some private secretaries were official staff but from parts of the government other than the Treasury. Two came

27   H. Butterfield, *George III, Lord North and the People: 1779–80* (London: G Bell & Sons, 1949).
28   J. Ehrman, *The Younger Pitt: The Years of Acclaim* (London: Constable, 1969), p. 578.
29   Sainty, 'Private secretaries to the prime ministers 1743–1868'.

from the Home Office and two from the Foreign Office. In the
period 1812–68 seven private secretaries served jointly as MPs.
Such an arrangement was more common for Whigs or Liberals –
Earl Grey (1830–34), Lord Melbourne (1834, and 1835–41) and
Palmerston (1855–58 and 1859–65) were each served by two
aides with this dual role – while only Lord Derby (1852, 1858–59
and 1866–68) of the Conservatives had a solitary secretary who
served in the Commons as well. There was a contingent from military backgrounds. The Earl of Derby was served by three soldiers
during his time as Prime Minister. In part, the post of private
secretary to the Prime Minister was an employment scheme for
an assortment of family members, friends and out-of-wedlock
offspring of premiers and their associates. There existed in the
nineteenth century an extended family network from which aides
to Whig and Liberal prime ministers were drawn.

Most private secretaries maintained low public profiles while
they held the post. However, there were some exceptions. One
who received extensive attention for unfortunate reasons was
Edward Drummond. From a background as a Treasury official, Drummond was secretary to four Tory and Conservative
prime ministers – Canning (1827), Ripon (1827–28), Wellington
(1828–30 and 1834) and Peel. Wellington even praised him in
the House of Lords for the assistance he had given. Drummond
unwittingly provided the ultimate service for the last of his
premiers while walking along Whitehall on 20 January 1842. A
man called Daniel M'Naghten shot him in the back from close
up, having mistaken Drummond for Peel. Five days afterwards
Drummond was dead, his parlous state perhaps exacerbated by
inadequate medical care. M'Naghten was found 'not guilty by
reason of insanity'. He remained in an asylum until his death in
1865. The case set an international legal precedent, leading to
the introduction of the so-called 'M'Naghten rules' in Britain and

the US. There has been some speculation subsequently that he was a paid political assassin.[30]

Private secretaries were significant because they provided valuable assistance to premiers and were privy to some of their innermost secrets. Some are obscure, others more notable – either for their achievements after service as private secretaries or primarily for their attachment to a Prime Minister. Two fall into these second and third categories respectively – Edmund Burke for Lord Rockingham (1765–66 and 1782) and George Pretyman for Pitt the Younger.

Edmund Burke (1729 or 1730 to 1797)

Burke became one of Britain's most significant political philosophers and practitioners. In his career he was both a prominent Whig and a substantial influence on Conservative thought. His service for Lord Rockingham during his first 1765–66 premiership pre-dated such greatness and was a crucial step towards it. Yet initially he did not appreciate the opportunity presented to him and nearly had it taken away.

Before becoming private secretary to the premier, Burke occupied the margins of the worlds of politics and literature. At first he had tried to progress as a writer but achieved only limited success. From the late 1750s he began an association with a politician, William Gerard Hamilton, who became Chief Secretary to the Lord Lieutenant of Ireland, for whom Burke performed a secretarial role. In July 1765 Rockingham was forming a government but his swift procession to the premiership had caught him off balance and he had not identified an appropriate private secretary.

---

30   J. Hamilton, rev. H. Matthew, 'Drummond, Edward', *ODNB*; N. Gash, *The Life of Sir Robert Peel after 1830* (London: Longman, 1972), pp. 364–5. M'Naghten is also known as McNaughtan or Mcnaghtan. R. Moran, 'McNaughtan [McNaghtan], Daniel', *ODNB*.

His assistant, George Quarme, did not normally undertake political functions, though Rockingham obtained the counsel of John Roberts, previously secretary to Pelham and Newcastle, on constitutional issues.

After taking advice from William Fitzherbert and Lord John Cavendish, who became junior Lords at the Board of Trade and the Treasury respectively, Rockingham decided to recruit Burke, a move that Fitzherbert helped to set in motion. The appointment was made around 10 July 1765 but little is known of the exact details; in retrospect, it was a momentous occasion. It marked the beginning of Burke's full transition to a political career and considerable celebrity, yet at the time Burke lamented not having a more attractive opportunity. It is hard to credit today that the post of private secretary to a premier could be regarded with such indifference, but Burke wrote to a friend on 11 July 1765 that he had obtained a 'humble enough' sort of job that could perhaps be exploited to his benefit in some way. He thought that Rockingham was a decent man with whom he could get on well.

Burke soon began to realise the true nature of the opportunity he had been afforded. There followed an attempt to remove it from him that it is tempting to say was founded in envy. In a letter of 16 July 1765 he referred to 'this little gleam of prosperity' which had 'fallen' on him, as well as noting a recent failed attack by his 'Enemies'.[31] The assault Burke referred to was an attempt by the Duke of Newcastle to displace him. In proposing Burke to Rockingham, Cavendish sought to reduce the influence of Newcastle, who wanted to place his own man in the private secretary role. Newcastle then attempted to undermine Rockingham's confidence in Burke, alleging that the aide was a Catholic and a

---

31   T. Copeland, *The Correspondence of Edmund Burke*, vol. 1, *April 1744–June 1768* (Cambridge at the University Press, 1958); Burke to Charles O'Hara, 11 July 1765, p. 211; Burke to David Garrick, 16 July 1765, p. 211.

Jacobite sympathiser. Burke offered to leave on the grounds that he could not work for someone who did not have absolute faith in him, a statement that greatly impressed Rockingham. Those lacking first-hand knowledge of the post – such as Burke before he held it – regarded the private secretary-ship as a relatively minor appointment. But Newcastle – a former Prime Minister (1754–56 and 1757–62) – regarded it as worth securing for a client, perhaps because of the opportunities for personal further- ance or influence associated with it.

No specific salary came with Burke's role. However, Rockingham made discretionary payments, possibly from the Secret Service money initially, then from his own funds. One of Burke's functions was facilitating communication between the government and a significant group of outside commercial trad- ers, from whom he acquired details about their business. He also helped solicit and arrange submissions given to the 1766 House of Commons American Committee. On one occasion Rockingham used his private secretary to liaise with William Pitt the Elder, who was outside the government. By December 1765 Burke had secured a seat in Parliament. He soon made a spectacular impact. In a letter dated January 1766 he complained of the demands of combining his parliamentary and secretarial duties.[32] He contin- ued as a private secretary to Rockingham, who made payments to Burke for the next decade and a half. The precise significance of Burke as private secretary to a Prime Minister is difficult to establish. There is a temptation to ascribe his eventual greatness to his early career also. Though not many at the time saw him as powerful, a notable exception was the Earl of Buckinghamshire, who described Burke as not just the right hand of Rockingham

---

32   Copeland, *The Correspondence of Edmund Burke*, vol. 1, Edmund Burke
     to Richard Burke, 14 January 1766, p. 230.

but 'both of his hands', claiming he had come from a garret to head the government.[33]

George Pretyman Tomline (1750–1827)

An instinct of many prime ministers when they take office is to recruit to their staff people with familiar faces. When Pitt the Younger first became Prime Minister he turned to George Pretyman (later known as Tomline) to be his private secretary and operate within his innermost circle. Pretyman was an early mentor of the future premier, an aide during his time at No. 10 and present with Pitt the Younger at the end of his life. Pretyman – whose outside career had benefited from this association – went on to become the official guardian and promoter of the legacy of the deceased politician. But Pretyman had detractors, and his relationship with Pitt the Younger was not always harmonious. The private secretary's main contribution to the memory of his former chief, as his biographer, met with derision.

Pretyman attended Pembroke College, Cambridge where he later became tutor to Pitt the Younger, helping to develop the future Prime Minister politically and intellectually. Pretyman's biography of Pitt suggests close involvement in his studies (though the book tells us little else about the relationship between the two). He notes that the future premier took particular interest in comparing speeches, arguing in different directions on the same topic, considering how speakers set out to make their case and attack that of their opponent. Pretyman regarded this task as appropriate to the training of a lawyer or

---

33   P. Langford, *The First Rockingham Administration: 1765–1766* (Oxford: Oxford University Press, 1973), p. 21; F. Lock, *Edmund Burke*, vol. 1, *1730 – 1784* (Oxford: Clarendon Press, 1998); S. Ayling, *Edmund Burke: His Life and Opinions* (London: Cassell, 1990).

politician.[34] Pitt the Younger displayed great oratorical ability from the beginning of his career, which he owed partly to the guidance of Pretyman.

After Pitt became Prime Minister late in 1783, he appointed Pretyman as his private secretary though the premier did not use this title for fear it might harm Pretyman's prospects for church advancement. Nonetheless, Pretyman moved to No. 10 and began continuous attendance on Pitt, doing his best to adapt to the Prime Minister's untidy working methods. Pretyman was part of an intimate support unit around the premier. His wife was close to Harriot, the sister of Pitt the Younger; the Prime Minister never married and Harriot became his hostess in 1785, also living in No. 10. In 1787 Pitt obtained for Pretyman appointment to the bishopric of Lincoln. George III objected but the premier pressed his case, stressing his personal indebtedness to his private secretary. Pretyman then ceased to provide immediate support to Pitt, though the two remained in contact with each other and Pretyman advised Pitt on certain policy issues. In 1801 Pretyman let Pitt know he disagreed with Pitt's support for Catholic emancipation (as part of a package that included union between Great Britain and Ireland) and stressed the need to support Protestantism and resist popery. In 1805 Pitt tried and failed to secure for Pretyman the office of Archbishop of Canterbury. While still in office in 1806 Pitt became mortally ill. Pretyman seems to have been the closest person to him towards the end and took on responsibility for Pitt's papers. In 1820 Pretyman became Bishop of Winchester.

The importance of Pretyman to Pitt the Younger, both in his early career and during his premiership, is clear. But assessments of the aide must take into account his negative qualities. He

---

34   G. Tomline, *Memoirs of Life of the Right Honourable William Pitt*, vol. 1 (London: John Murray, 1821), p. 7.

became unpopular both because of his perceived arrogance and his proximity to Pitt. Opponents of Pitt publicly attacked him, among others in the Pitt circle. Even Pitt himself may have found his aide tiresome at times; perhaps the act of securing the appointment of Pretyman as a bishop was an attempt by the premier to rid himself of his private secretary.[35]

Functions of aides

No specific allocation of distinct functions to prime-ministerial staff existed in this period but the aides at the regular disposal of premiers, including their private secretaries and Treasury staff, sometimes supplemented by further assistants, were able to carry out many different tasks. In the early stages of the premiership the office may have lacked the firm footing it gradually gained, but this uncertainty meant there were less clearly formed conventions about what prime ministers and their staff were and were not allowed to do. The limitations upon aides were less strict than they later became, though certain functions required their rapt attention. It is possible to find some kind of precedent for virtually any activity carried out in subsequent eras.

As Walpole used propagandists, so his successors did the same. Charles Lloyd, private secretary to Charles Grenville (1763–65), wrote various pamphlets in support of the government, and continued to defend its record in opposition. Charles Long was Secretary to the Treasury under Pitt the Younger and was also an accomplished political author. In 1792, Long helped set up the *Sun* newspaper, the purpose of which was to counteract

---

35 Ehrman, *The Years of Acclaim*, p. 14; G. Tomline, *Memoirs of Life of the Right Honourable William Pitt*, vol. 1 (London: John Murray, 1821); Hague, *William Pitt the Younger*; R. Reilly, *Pitt the Younger* (London: Cassell, 1978); J. Jackson, 'Tomline, Sir George Pretyman', *ODNB*.

growing criticism of the government within the press. George Rose, also Secretary to the Treasury under Pitt the Younger, published propaganda informed by his policy expertise. In 1799 he wrote a detailed work setting out to prove that thanks to government measures the national economy was a success.[36]

When in the twentieth century the permanent civil service had developed fully and career officials occupied prime-ministerial support roles regardless of the premier, they provided continuity and awareness of established practices and confidential information to premiers. In the eighteenth and nineteenth centuries there was little provision of this sort, but it could be found. John Scrope served as a repository of official knowledge. Private secretaries could also play a part in the transition to a new Prime Minister. Before his death in office in 1754 Pelham had given an instruction to his private secretary, John Roberts, requiring him to gather and secure his papers, then sift them and pass them on as suitable to whomever his successor might be. Pelham's brother, the Duke of Newcastle, became the next premier and used Roberts as his secretary. In the following decade Roberts served yet another Prime Minister, acting as a kind of living institutional memory. He was appointed a Lord of Trade when Rockingham took power in 1765. Beyond this ministerial role he had a specific use. He was one of few members of the government who had previously held office. As such he became a counsellor to the premier on how to observe appropriate conduct. In December 1765 he advised Rockingham on who he should choose to give the speech that was made at the Cockpit the night before Parliament met, based on how this decision had been made in the days of Walpole and Pelham. Possibly

---

36 G. Rose, *A Brief Examination into the Increase of the Revenue, Commerce, and Manufactures of Great Britain from 1792 to 1799* (London: J. Wright, J. Hatchard, J. Sewell, 1799).

Roberts also gave guidance on proper etiquette and issues of political tactics.[37]

In the nineteenth century the young Queen Victoria came to feel dependent upon Lord Melbourne. At the 1841 general election, Melbourne lost control of the House of Commons to Peel. The constitutional wisdom was that Melbourne had to go but the formal position remained that the monarch made such decisions about appointments. Victoria was reluctant to see her mentor leave office. Fortunately, Melbourne's former private secretary George Anson had been appointed to support Victoria's husband, Prince Albert. Anson acted as an intermediary between Victoria, Melbourne and Peel, both before and after the election, with Peel's private secretary Drummond contributing to the relationship as well.[38] This association can be seen as a precursor to the arrangement which eventually emerged for delicate changeovers, for instance elections leading to no overall majority in the House of Commons. It centred on the 'golden triangle', comprising the monarch's private secretary, the Principal Private Secretary to the premier and the Cabinet Secretary, the stable, continuous core of the British constitution.

Before the conventions of collective Cabinet government had fully developed, and when premiers were still directly responsible for the Treasury, there were fewer restrictions on their playing a primary policy-forming role – indeed there was a requirement for them to do so. Staff such as secretaries to the Treasury were on hand to help them and aides made significant contributions that could prove decisive. Thomas Whately was Secretary to the Treasury under Grenville. He came to be poorly regarded in

37   Wilkes, A Whig in Power, p. 213; Powell, 'Roberts, John'; G. Keppel,
      J. Roberts and J. Tyler, 'John Roberts, MP and the First Rockingham
      Administration', English Historical Review, 67, 265 (1952), pp. 547–560.
38   D. Cecil, Melbourne (London: Constable & Co., 1965), pp. 502–3; 505;
      520–21; Gash, The Life of Sir Robert Peel after 1830, p. 274.

what was then the American colony for his prominent part in the Stamp Act of 1765. This measure aggravated tensions, which eventually ended in revolution. In 1844 George Arbuthnot, private secretary to Peel, was significant to the Bank Charter Act. Arbuthnot's involvement with and commitment to this legislation are underlined by his writing a detailed pamphlet supporting it more than a decade after its implementation.[39]

Richard Price (1723–91)

Pitt the Younger was a dynamic Prime Minister who was at the vanguard of his government's policy programme. To assist him he utilised not only staff directly involved in the administrative machine such as secretaries to the Treasury, but others who might be deemed 'outsiders'. Richard Price comes under this latter category. In his varied career Price was connected to two prime ministers. Though his role was informal, he was a forerunner of the politically committed, expert adviser upon whom prime ministers drew during the twentieth century in order to provide assistance of a sort not otherwise available to them. As with a number of these later aides who had connections with think tanks, Price was a member of a wider intellectual circle associated with a premier, which had helped form his ideas before holding office.

Price came from Glamorgan. He became a dissenting minister and developed wide interests, including philosophy, politics, demography and probability. Not shy to express controversial views, Price even voiced public support for the American rebels in 1776. Price was a protagonist in one of the great intellectual debates of world history, with another prime-ministerial aide his opponent. In 1789 Price's positive response to the French

---

39   G. Arbuthnot, *Sir Robert Peel's Act of 1844, Regulating the Issue of Bank Notes, Vindicated* (London: Harrison & Sons, 1857), p. 3.

Revolution in its early stages spurred Edmund Burke to make a definitive statement of conservative philosophy, *Reflections on the Revolution in France*. He specifically attacked Price in the text. Burke's work in turn prompted Thomas Paine to publish *The Rights of Man*, an assertion of republican principles and the right of a people to determine their own destiny.

During the 1770s Price and Lord Shelburne (later Prime Minister from 1782 to 1783) developed a close intellectual, political and personal association. For both men there were possible benefits. Shelburne partly hoped to use Price to influence dissenting opinion, while Price saw in Shelburne a route to public impact. Alongside these calculations they became friends. Shelburne obtained from Price briefings on numerous political issues, including financial policy. During the 1770s Price influenced Shelburne in the reform ideas he developed and proposed while in opposition. As an associate of Shelburne, Price was part of the so-called Bowood Group, an informal intellectual circle often convened at Bowood House, Shelburne's home in Wiltshire. Its members included Joseph Priestley and, later on, Jeremy Bentham. Bowood was in a sense an early think tank, ensuring Shelburne was connected to intellectual developments and outlooks from different parts of society. Had he held office for longer Shelburne's proclivity for the company of notable intellectuals might have been a defining characteristic of his premiership; it is possible that an earlier, less formal, version of Lloyd George's Prime Minister's secretariat, Churchill's Statistical Section, Heath's Central Policy Review Staff or Wilson's Policy Unit could have developed. Possibly Shelburne sought to recruit Price as his private secretary when he became premier in 1782, but Price declined the offer.

Though not taking on a more specific post, Price advised

Shelburne as premier in a less regular fashion, putting forward a variety of financial proposals. In November 1782 Shelburne sought the views of Price on the King's speech, which included Price's ideas on how to redeem the national debt. Price advised Pitt the Younger as Chancellor of the Exchequer on raising loans. Their relationship became more significant in the future. Overall Price's influence on Shelburne may have waned when compared with the pre-government period. Any potential for a radical premiership was not realised and Shelburne retained office for less than a year. Some of the policies he might have pursued were taken on by Pitt though – as in time was the advice of Shelburne's counsellor, Price.

Price was a longstanding proponent of the potential benefits of compound interest for the national wealth. The Shelburne government had planned to establish a sinking fund for this purpose but did not have sufficient time to introduce it. As Prime Minister, Pitt returned to the idea; in January 1786 he wrote to Price and enclosed papers on the subject, seeking his opinion on them. He asked Price to see him at his convenience. Price offered his thoughts and Pitt the Younger valued this contribution. When announcing his sinking fund policy – one of Pitt's most celebrated at the time – he made no mention to Parliament of the assistance Price provided. After Price's death his nephew and disciple William Morgan publicly attacked Pitt for the failure to credit Price and – inconsistent with the first complaint – for not properly implementing his ideas.[40]

---

40   J. Ehrman, *The Younger Pitt: The Consuming Struggle* (London: Constable, 1996); D. Thomas, *The Honest Mind: The Thought and Work of Richard Price* (Oxford at the Clarendon Press, 1977); J. Norris, *Shelburne and Reform* (New York: Macmillan & Co, 1963); D. Thomas, 'Price, Richard', *ODNB*; W. Morgan, *A review of Dr Price's Writings on the subject of the Finances of this Kingdom: to which are added the Three plans communicated by him to Mr Pitt in the Year 1786, for Redeeming the National Debt* (London: G. Stafford, 1791).

By the mid-nineteenth century the potential for direct policy intervention of the kind Price facilitated was more restricted. At the outset of his second premiership in 1841, Robert Peel made an important decision. He opted not to combine the post of First Lord of the Treasury with that of Chancellor of the Exchequer, delegating the latter post to a subordinate minister. Peel intended to enhance his impact over government as a whole. By relinquishing responsibility for the more detailed day-to-day work of the Treasury, he would make more time available for other business. When he wanted to, he could play a more direct role in the Treasury, even taking over the delivery of Budgets from the Chancellor. The longer-term consequence of Peel's act was different: in time, Chancellors of the Exchequer became top-level Cabinet ministers in their own right, with responsibility for the Treasury and its policy portfolio. By 1856 prime ministers had lost direct responsibility for the Treasury. Premiers' relationship with this institution, which had previously been their key source of support, changed irrevocably. The size of the prime-ministerial staff was drastically reduced and the nature of its activities changed. Prime ministers no longer generally possessed a specific policy brief. Their role as an overall coordinator of government became far more important. It rested on their position as chair of Cabinet, which had become more clearly established as the supreme decision-taking committee in British government. In this sense the office of Prime Minister and the aides attached to it had passed from a stage of development in which the premier was a 'finance minister plus' to a second non-departmental phase, in which a smaller staff supported a more general role.

The early years considered
The office of Prime Minister is occupied by one individual but the exercise of the role has always been a group activity. Aides

were not only essential to prime ministers in the performance of their duties from the very outset of Prime Minister as a concept but were also instrumental in the establishment of the institution itself, through the support they provided to Walpole and his successors. Three of the most active premiers of this period who also did much to shape the development of the post of chief minister were Walpole, Pitt the Younger and Peel; all made notable and innovative use of staff. Each did so in accordance with their particular characteristics and objectives. For Walpole the possession of power seems to have been an important end in and of itself. He deployed assistants to curry favour with potential supporters as well as to cultivate a favourable public image for himself and his government. Pitt the Younger used a collection of aides, sometimes drawn from beyond more regular administrative circles, to develop policy programmes. In Francis Bonham, Peel selected someone to handle interactions with the increasingly important national party organisation – a task he did not relish himself – and provide partisan, focused assistance.

Assistants were always liable to criticism from parliamentarians and others. The idea of there being a premier at all was controversial and therefore, by extension, aides were seen as illegitimate. Prime ministers could not be alleged to have used aides to supplant the Cabinet – as they later would – when, in much of this period, no such concept of collective government existed. Nor had the idea of a distinction between the use of official funds for government and for partisan purposes clearly appeared. But attacks upon the staff of Walpole and Peel demonstrate the existence of objections to the use of public post-holders and money as a means of maintaining a government in power. Complaints in later years that aides are not properly accountable to Parliament echo those of the Committee of Secrecy of 1742.

Functions associated with the support teams of later premiers

– such as media management, the provision of policy advice and partisan counsel – are not new. The use of patronage has been critical to the occupant of No. 10 from the outset. Exercising it effectively has always involved aides – both helping to decide whom to reward and processing business, a task which seems often to have fallen to private secretaries and secretaries to the Treasury. The vital responsibility for ensuring the implementation of decisions – sometimes afforded less interest by observers than the more glamorous process of making them – was taken on to a great extent by secretaries (then after 1805 assistant secretaries) to the Treasury.

To govern effectively, premiers had to reckon with various social groups and establishments. Their aides assisted them in dealing with different interests including the monarchy, other ministers, Parliament, the established church, the legal system, commercial interests, the media, the electorate, mass parties and the administrative machine. Some were long established and their influence would fade (but not disappear completely) – such as the monarchy and the church. Others – commercial interests and the electorate – were in the ascendant. Relationships with bodies such as Parliament and the emergent civil service were complex; while prime ministers enjoyed authority within or over both, they possessed varying degrees of autonomy. Some of these groups were heterogeneous – most notably the media. Dealing with some of them properly could require staff with specialised training; as a result legal qualifications, for example, were common among aides. The adoption of particular functions was often reactive to developments – like Walpole's use of staff to counteract public attacks upon him – which shows that the use of aides can sometimes be a crutch rather than a proactive force, as much indicative of vulnerability as a source or symbol of strength.

Aides were appointed by patronage – as with special advisers today, though, unlike the latter, in practice some could not easily be removed against their will, even with a change of government. There was no concept of open recruitment or equal opportunities, let alone legislation or commissions to enforce them. While the Civil Service Commission was established in 1855, its role was initially more circumscribed than it became. It was unthinkable that someone would even question the monopolising of aides' positions by Anglican males. Beyond denomination and gender, it is harder to make generalisations about social profile. English domination was not absolute – for instance Rose was a Scot. Many nineteenth-century prime ministers – especially Whigs and Liberals – happily placed relatives in secretarial posts. Yet it seems ability was – and had to be – a criterion, alongside personal and political connections and trustworthiness when making selections for such posts as Secretary to the Treasury. In later periods, teams at No. 10 have not become models for ethnic or gender diversity. The enduring preponderance of Oxford and Cambridge graduates is more understandable in the period up to 1827, when there were no other universities in England.

The eighteenth century was a golden age for prime ministers' aides. They could wield great authority and receive considerable rewards of wealth and preferment. Vast sums of money might flow through – or into – their hands. Among them were formidable historical figures such as Gibson, Burke and Price. One who exploited the opportunities open to aides was Charles Jenkinson. He became an under-secretary to Lord Bute when the latter was appointed Secretary of State in 1761, and entered the Commons shortly afterwards. When Bute (1762–63) took on the premiership he appointed Jenkinson his private secretary. The following year Grenville succeeded Bute and Jenkinson rose to be a Secretary to the Treasury. He went on to a later career as Secretary at War, President of the Board of Trade and Chancellor of the Duchy of

Lancaster. Eventually he was created the first Earl of Liverpool, and founded a political dynasty, with his son serving as Prime Minister from 1812 to 1827.

The constitutional fluidity of the eighteenth century afforded aides a certain freedom of action. There were fewer constraints upon premiers governing with their assistance, rather than always seeking advice from senior ministers. The numbers used could vary according to the deployment of patronage. Simultaneously they could sit in Parliament and play administrative roles. The tortuous attempts of the twentieth and twenty-first centuries to regulate the activities of staff – with distinctions between serving a government and the party in office, and rules about who could issue instructions to whom – had yet to be made. But the discretion, which could be used as leverage by aides, did not last. Parliament, partly through its response to the power wielded by Walpole, which it found so objectionable, campaigned for a separation of the bureaucracy from party politics. The pressure of work that arose out of the French revolutionary conflicts from the 1790s encouraged a more efficient division of responsibilities. Like later reorganisations of the support available to prime ministers after the First and Second World Wars, perceived national decline from the 1950s, and international terrorism from 2001, administrative change was a response to crisis and increased workload.

The separation of administrative and ministerial functions, and the rise of Cabinet government, imposed even greater limitations upon aides and the scope of their work. The nineteenth century saw various functions move away from the immediate remit of prime ministers and their staff. First, as Cabinet became more established as an entity of collective government, premiers lost some of the latitude they had previously enjoyed to determine the course of their governments with the assistance of personal aides. Second was the ceding of responsibility for the Treasury. This change relieved premiers of burdens and helped them concentrate on their roles as overall heads of government. It meant they no longer had a central policy function and a large staff to help perform it, or the ability to authorise huge expenditure, as enjoyed by Walpole. Third was the tentative emergence of a large permanent civil service with, in practice, a degree of autonomy. It would eventually take on many of the administrative tasks previously performed by staff closer to the Prime Minister.

CHAPTER THREE

A DIMINISHED OFFICE? 1868-1916

By the final third of the nineteenth century the British premier-ship was a far leaner institution than in the eighteenth. It generally lacked the direct policy role it had once possessed. Treasury staff were no longer a regular part of the official team and all that remained was a small private secretariat. But the role of Prime Minister, though different, was still of paramount importance, as was that of the aides attached to this office. The holder was responsible for coordinating a government at the centre of the largest empire in world history. While collective government was a more established principle, premiers could still use staff to help them pursue their own personal policy objectives and missions. It remained possible – though less common – for premiers, if they chose, to take direct charge of a department and its personnel. Prime ministers might oversee the work of aides in close – even obsessive – detail, or be more relaxed and delegate responsibility to them. When they wielded, or tried to wield, power drawn from their connection with the premier, assistants risked generating resentment and the perception they were overreaching themselves. The political content of the media continued, as ever, to be a concern to which aides, at the behest of prime ministers, attended. A tendency remained for some prime ministers to draw on help from beyond the more established circles. They were at the centre of a support network more complex and sophisticated than a focus on the more official structures might suggest.

The premiership, which was once a disavowed institution, had become in practice an accepted component of government. In 1878 it began to receive official recognition. The Treaty of Berlin describes Benjamin Disraeli as, among other things, 'Prime Minister of England'. From the 1880s the list of government members printed in Hansard, the parliamentary record, started to use the title 'Prime Minister'. In 1900, after a Cabinet reshuffle, the *Court Circular* referred to Lord Salisbury as 'Prime Minister'. Internal Whitehall records used this term early in the twentieth century. Then on 4 December 1905 the premier gained a place – after the Archbishop of York – in the official order of precedence.[41]

The office of Prime Minister had progressed from a term of abuse to an official title. Similarly, the aides who supported the Prime Minister began to receive more neutral public portrayal than they once had. References came in the press and in fiction. In his 1876 novel *The Prime Minister* Anthony Trollope describes the Duke of Omnium, who is premier in a Liberal–Conservative coalition government, as 'surrounded by private secretaries'. Omnium receives assistance in shoring up his parliamentary position from whips representing the two parties: Mr Rattler and Mr Roby. Trollope refers to a 'man of business' who handles politics in a particular region, Mr Moreton. Omnium obtains further assistance from his wife.[42] Trollope had captured well the working of a political institution of his time. The job of Prime Minister had numerous dimensions to it, involving administration, politics within and beyond Parliament, and much else. Whoever held

41   A. Blick and G. Jones, *Premiership: The Development, Nature and Power of the Office of the British Prime Minister* (Exeter: Imprint Academic, 2010).
42   A. Trollope, *The Prime Minister* (Oxford: Oxford University Press, 1999).

the post, whatever their approach and the circumstances they encountered, they needed support.

Aides to William Gladstone

William Gladstone is acknowledged as one of the great prime ministers, alongside the likes of Robert Walpole, William Pitt the Younger, David Lloyd George and Winston Churchill. Like them he owed some of his success to the aides who served him. He held office for four separate terms (1868–74; 1880–85; 1886; 1892–4) and is renowned for his capacity for work. He created tasks for himself and his aides, whose activities he oversaw in intense detail. In the 1870s and 1880s Gladstone became the last Prime Minister to absorb the Treasury within his remit, taking on the post of Chancellor of the Exchequer. He used his team not so much as a way of reducing the pressure on him, but of getting even more done. The working methods he followed and imposed gave expression to some of his pronounced personal eccentricities. In the end, old age slowed down even Gladstone. He could not sustain his earlier methods and the activities of his aides changed to reflect this decline.

There was a great amount of affection between Gladstone and his staff. To Gladstone officials were an extended family, and his team included family members. When required, his wife could copy letters for him. He received further help with correspondence from his daughters Mary and Helen and his son Henry. Herbert, another son, acted as a link with the Liberal Party. More tenuous family connections existed. In 1872 Frederick Cavendish worked, without remuneration, for Gladstone, who was his wife's uncle by marriage. Spencer Lyttelton, who was Cavendish's brother-in-law, was a paid member of Gladstone's secretariat. Lyttelton served as a sort of personal assistant at various points from 1872 to 1894.

In general Gladstone pursued the principle of appointments to public service being made on merit rather than through personal favouritism, and successfully cultivated an image for himself as a promoter of this cause. But some tension existed between this perception and his approach to selecting personal staff. He tended to choose aristocrats, often on the advice of his ally Lord Granville. One purpose of such recruits was to help Gladstone handle his relationship with the Whigs, a group that played an important part in his government and whose members were further up the social scale than he was.

Gladstone placed a premium on trust within his team and as a result was able to speak freely with his staff. Like a later premier, Margaret Thatcher, he executed his decisions, once made, ruthlessly, but he often agonised over them beforehand. Consequently Gladstone needed to be able to discuss ideas at length with people he considered dependable, whether his private secretaries or other counsellors. Gladstone was an organised administrator. He devised numerous means of achieving efficiency in his office, which he himself followed rigorously and imposed on his staff as well, even down to how they should use paper clips. Gladstone maintained close and ongoing personal oversight of the work of his team. His secretaries used a detailed filing system and a 'Book of Knowledge', which his secretary William Gurdon produced in his first term, facilitating continuity of working methods. Edward Hamilton maintained it during the second Gladstone premiership before it disappeared sometime after 1885.[43] In some ways Gladstone was a streamlining force on the work of prime-ministerial aides. He was the

---

43   For a detailed description of working practices inside the Gladstone secretariat see: A. Godley, *Reminiscences of Lord Kilbracken* (London: Macmillan & Co., 1931), pp. 87–90. See also: G. Jones and J. Burnham 'Innovators at 10 Downing Street', in K. Theakston (ed.), *Bureaucrats and Leadership* (London: Palgrave Macmillan, 1999).

first to identify the need for a firm set of rules and procedures and to implement their introduction. Though it was not maintained by his immediate successors, his system was eventually accepted and became part of established practice. During his tenure some significant innovations took place: from 1892 to 1894 Gladstone's senior private secretary, Algernon West, was assisted by H. G. L. Shand, probably the first member of a prime-ministerial staff to use short-hand.

There was another side to Gladstone's deployment of his staff, which arose from his intricate but flawed personality. Gladstone was a man prone to obsessions: felling trees; reading and writing books at a phenomenal rate; an overwhelming religious commitment; a supposed compulsion to save prostitutes; and self-flagellation. He recorded all such activities to excruciating effect in a bare, matter-of-fact diary – the keeping of which – almost every day for seven decades – was itself an accomplishment suggestive of fanaticism. The way he functioned and insisted those around him operate gave expression as much to the irrational desire for organisation for its own sake as for the achievement of external goals.

To his staff, Gladstone's peculiarities were plain. West recounts how Gladstone was prone to scratching the back of his head while hitting the table. Those around him who found the habit irritating prevailed upon West to raise it with him. West in turn told the Dean of Windsor, who was good friends with Gladstone and tactfully but successfully hinted to the Prime Minister that his habit was a problem. Gladstone scheduled the whole of his life to maximise efficiency; he was, in modern jargon, a workaholic. He could not tolerate the idea of wasting even a minute. If he had to wait ten seconds without a paper to deal with, he began to fidget. The task of his private secretaries was as much to keep Gladstone busy as to relieve him of burdens. A further fixation was on avoiding financial inefficiency. Yet another was his detailed interest in church appointments. His secretaries dreaded the news that an ecclesiastical post had become vacant.

His aides became involved in the undesirable task of protecting the premier from one of his more problematic flaws. Gladstone's proclivity for associating with prostitutes was widely known though not openly publicised. Potentially it could have wrecked his career. He indulged most during the mid-1840s and early 1850s and the prospect of his starting again was never far away. Understandably people around Gladstone were worried. In February 1882 Lord Rosebery, the Liberal politician and future Prime Minister, visited his friend from Eton, Edward Hamilton, Gladstone's private secretary, to tell him that Gladstone was 'walking in the streets at night'. After further discussion Rosebery reluctantly raised the subject with the premier. Rosebery and Hamilton were initially hopeful that Gladstone had now decided to stop, but he continued. Gossip soon spread through London society. In May a worried and annoyed Hamilton confronted Gladstone, who once again seemed to accept the warning. On 13 June Hamilton learned from the Director of Criminal Investigation at Scotland Yard, Howard Vincent, that there had been no more reports of incidents involving Gladstone.[44]

Another characteristic of Gladstone was his desire as Prime Minister frequently to take an active policy role. He enlisted aides to help him with his hands-on approach. Twice during his premierships Gladstone temporarily reversed the separation of the office of Prime Minister from the Treasury, becoming his own Chancellor of the Exchequer 1873–74 and 1880–82. When he first attempted this arrangement in 1873, *The Times* commented on 8 August that, though he was returning to past practice, the

---

44   D. Bahlman (ed.), *The Diary of Sir Edward Walter Hamilton: 1880–1885*, vol. 2, *1883–1885* (Oxford at the Clarendon Press, 1972).

business of government had become complex in the intervening period. He would 'need help and support'. Gladstone relied on junior ministers in the Treasury and expanded his secretariat at No. 10 from two to four. When Gladstone took on this dual role again in 1880 Hamilton expressed concern that the burden would be too great for him; Gladstone must have agreed for he passed some of the strain onto his private secretaries. George Leveson-Gower found the workload heavy and the subject matter unfamiliar and complex. Gladstone as ever was demanding, though still capable of showing some consideration. Under these burdens Leveson-Gower felt 'regularly seedy'. Yet however hard his staff worked they could not significantly lift the pressure upon Gladstone. Reassuming direct control of the Treasury, an act that marked the beginning of the second phase of his premiership, was not sustainable in practice. If becoming Chancellor of the Exchequer was not enough, Gladstone took on an Irish Land Bill. Hamilton believed the Conservative Party hoped the Prime Minister would have a breakdown. By April 1882 work was overwhelming Gladstone and he started suggesting he would relinquish the Treasury, something he finally did in December.[45]

Though pushing himself to a collapse more than once earlier in his career, Gladstone managed to occupy the post of Prime Minister past the age of eighty. In 1870 he told a private secretary that he would soon be able to retire. He was still Prime Minister nearly twenty-five years later. By 1885, West had formed the opinion that the older Gladstone became, the less he was willing to consider giving up. Gladstone asked the opinions of staff and allies on this subject on various occasions; they encouraged him to stay on. Perhaps they sensed he wanted them to respond in

---

45   Bahlman, *The Diary of Sir Edward Walter Hamilton, 1880–1885*, vol. 2;
      G. Leveson-Gower, *Years of Content: 1858–1886* (London: John Murray,
      1940).

this way. As Gladstone aged, his diminishing competence left a
vacuum, one which some individuals close to him (friends and
family members) – whose possible motives included a sense both
of duty and the opportunity to wield power – sought to fill. The
way West expresses himself in his diary from his time as private
secretary in the 1890s suggests he felt he could impose particular
courses of action upon Gladstone, and that to do so was appropriate. As might be expected there had long been intrigue and
competition within Gladstone's entourage. As Gladstone grew
older the tensions increased. In March 1893 Hamilton wrote of
his belief that, while Gladstone was inclined to leave office that
year (as Hamilton thought he should), 'the petticoat influence'
– by which he seems to have meant his female relatives – might
oblige him to stay on. Measured against his own exceptional
standards in his final term of office, Gladstone was slowing
down. Working for Gladstone became more difficult. He grew
reluctant to face up to dealing with difficult issues. Hamilton
regretted the following February: 'It is the old, very old man.'
Aides and other supporters took an interest in ensuring Gladstone
ended his career in a fitting manner. When Gladstone finally
decided to resign, West helped stage-manage the revelation to the
public, taking part in drafting a misleading announcement denying the premier had any such intention.[46]

Algernon West (1832–1921)

West supported Gladstone from different posts throughout the
four premierships and was among the most important of all his
aides. At the beginning he was one of his private secretaries. He
then moved elsewhere within the government machine, in the

---

46   D. Bahlman, *The Diary of Sir Edward Walter Hamilton: 1885–1906* (Hull:
      University of Hull Press, 1993); H. Hutchinson (ed.), *Private Diaries of
      the Rt. Hon. Sir Algernon West, G. C. B.* (London: John Murray, 1922).

process helping Gladstone extend his prime-ministerial reach. Then at the very end he helped Gladstone as his leading private secretary. West spent his career inside the civil service assisting ministers of differing political complexions, yet he was a partisan Liberal supporter.

An Etonian, West initially planned a career in the clergy but became a clerk at the Inland Revenue in 1851. In 1868 he became a private secretary to the Prime Minister, Gladstone. Four years later he returned to the Inland Revenue, becoming Chairman of the Board of Inland Revenue by 1881. West retired as a civil servant in 1892, when Gladstone recruited him as his most senior but unpaid full-time aide for his final premiership.

In 1868 West moved into No. 10 with his wife. Gladstone preferred to stay in his house at 11 Carlton House Terrace, with a secretary present at Downing Street to deal with any issues that might crop up out of normal hours. West was aware of many personal associations he had with his new address. He was the third son of Martin West and Lady Maria Walpole, who was a great-granddaughter of Robert Walpole. In 1858 West married Mary Barrington. Her mother was a daughter of Earl Grey and she was born at No. 10 Downing Street when he was Prime Minister. The next person to live at the address was her brother, Charles Barrington, who was secretary to Lord Palmerston. Given these connections and the nature of his professional career, West took an interest in the history of No. 10 and the office connected to it. He was aware of the importance to Walpole of John Scrope as his Secretary to the Treasury. A brief outline West produced of Scrope's life described the loyalty Scrope had shown to Walpole despite being under pressure to give evidence against him. In studying the relationship between an earlier aide and a Prime Minister, West had acquired an historical sense of the role he performed for Gladstone. In this sense he was party to a collective memory.

He was personally attached to Gladstone and full of admiration for him. The two men had shared outlooks on various issues such as finance and from 1868 West and Gladstone established a firm bond, spending time talking over political issues when walking home together from Parliament in the early morning. As a private secretary, West worked alongside William Gurdon, who came from the Treasury. Gurdon handled Treasury business, the Civil List and the 'Royal Bounty'. West dealt with non-official political matters and, in particular, patronage. In this latter task he had daily contact with Lord Granville, Leader of the House of Lords, who helped manage both the Cabinet and the House of Lords. West had the multifaceted role that has been characteristic of No. 10 private secretaries. One feature of it involved patronage, discussing the granting of honours. Another was liaison, with prominent figures in the church. A further task involved counselling Gladstone on policy issues. West helped Gladstone in a practical sense with the effort to carry disestablishment of the Irish church through Parliament. When the Lords agreed to the legislation, West had to communicate the news to the Queen because Gladstone had gone through some kind of breakdown. Finally, West participated in liaising with the press.

West left No. 10 for the Inland Revenue in 1872 but was not cut off from the premier. He continued to communicate with Gladstone and his staff over party-political matters such as the dissolution of 1874. When in 1873 Gladstone took on the extra portfolio of Chancellor of the Exchequer, he drew on West as a source of information in support of his attempts to achieve more efficient government. In December 1873 Gladstone wrote to West asking for evidence of poor performance by the India Office. In using staff assistance to help him pursue a personal programme to improve the effectiveness of government Gladstone set a precedent for premiers including Churchill and his Statistical

Section, Thatcher and her Efficiency Unit and Tony Blair and his Delivery Unit.

West continued to assist Gladstone on revenue and political issues during his 1880–85 and 1886 premierships. In 1886 West helped Gladstone in his efforts to achieve parliamentary assent to Home Rule, including proposing the wording of a resolution to put before the House. Late in 1891 West, who was about to retire from the civil service, agreed he would be secretary to Gladstone once more. West wanted to keep a low profile and not create resentment about his role, so did not take an official title. But, in West's account, Gladstone wished to make it known in 1892 his aide was the 'chief of the staff'. The term had already been in colloquial use within the Gladstone team – in a letter written on 8 September 1881 Leveson-Gower referred to Godley as 'our Chief of the Staff'.[47] At West's suggestion an announcement of his title appeared in the *Pall Mall Gazette*.[48] He provides some precedent for this job title at No. 10, which became official around a century later, and became the most central figure in the Gladstone team. The aide counselled Gladstone on forming his Cabinet in 1892 and liaised with individuals involved. As he had done previously, West discussed many decisions with Gladstone and handled relations with the royal family. A party political role continued for West, including managing parliamentary issues. On 12 May 1893 he met with 'two pressmen loud in their praises of Mr Gladstone' – could it be he was trading access for support? West's diaries for the period 1892–4 seem to show he took part in arranging meetings of the Cabinet, and discussing with Gladstone what had taken place in them immediately afterwards. West wrote accounts of Cabinet meetings for the Prince of Wales,

---

47   Leveson-Gower, *Years of Content*, p. 198.
48   Hutchinson (ed.), *Private Diaries of the Rt. Hon. Sir Algernon West*, pp. 41–2.

presumably based on the notes Gladstone produced for the
Queen. Early in 1894, when Gladstone was in Biarritz, West
communicated messages between him and Cabinet members.
Tasks involving Cabinet fell to West partly because no specific
staff existed for supporting this collective body of government.
The following century would reveal this gap in the machinery of
government to be potentially harmful.[49]

Lord Acton (1834–1902)

Lord Acton was a celebrated historian whom Gladstone respected
as an authority on many different levels. He helped the Prime
Minister both to think and put his wishes into action. He provided
counsel and knowledge on a range of subjects and conducted
important liaisons for the premier. Acton studiously cultivated his
connection with Gladstone. He saw it as a route to personal influence. As his sense of importance grew, Acton behaved in ways
which undermined his own position and reduced his chances of
achieving his objectives. Consequently, though he was significant,
he was not ultimately as important as he hoped he would be, or
indeed thought he had been.

Acton, who was born in Naples, was from a multinational aristocratic background. He came to Britain after his father died. His
mother married the man who would later become Lord Granville.
With his connection to Granville, Acton found his way into the
Gladstone circle. He was a Roman Catholic and in the 1850s

---

49   A. West, *Contemporary Portraits: Men of My Day in Public Life* (London:
     Thomas Nelson and Sons, Ltd., 1920); Godley, *Reminiscences*; A. West,
     Political England: A Chronicle of the Nineteenth Century (London:
     T. Fisher Unwin Ltd, 1922); A. West, *Recollections: 1832 to 1886*,
     2 vols (London: Smith, Elder, & Co., 1899); A. Ramm (ed.), *The Political
     Correspondence of Mr Gladstone and Lord Granville: 1868–1876*
     (London: Offices of the Royal Historical Society, 1952); Bahlman, *The
     Diary of Sir Edward Walter Hamilton: 1885–1906*; Hutchinson, *Private
     Diaries of the Rt. Hon. Sir Algernon West*.

became a prominent Liberal Catholic, one who campaigned for greater freedom for intellectuals within the church. As an historian, Acton had difficulty finishing books and made his contributions in shorter formats. Probably for this reason Gladstone's family did not entrust Acton with the task of producing the former premier's official biography after his death.

Acton engaged in political activities alongside his religious and intellectual pursuits. He became a Whig MP for Carlow in 1859, though his career in the Commons lasted only until 1866. Gladstone encouraged Acton to be a more public figure but, like Francis Bonham, the aide to Robert Peel earlier in the century, Acton was more comfortable supporting a politician than placing himself in the front line. Acton and Gladstone had an enduring and close relationship and Gladstone valued spending time with him even during his spells as Prime Minister. Acton's erudition made him useful as a source of factual information. However their relationship was about more than detail. Gladstone drew on Acton to help him develop his broad overview of the political scene from someone who shared his moral outlook. Acton might today be regarded as a strategist, concentrating on the longer-term and helping provide an overall direction.

As well as advising Gladstone, Acton acted as his liaison officer. Acton attended the first Vatican Council of 1869–70; as a personal envoy for the British Prime Minister he lobbied without success to avert its decision to adopt the doctrine of papal infallibility. Both Gladstone and Acton were worried this principle could contribute to a conflict of loyalties for Roman Catholics. Demonstrating his capacity to obsess about an issue that others might not believe to be as significant as he did, Gladstone became more interested in developments in Rome than in domestic policy. He communicated the offer of a peerage to Acton while he was travelling to Rome, partly in order to give Acton elevated status in dealing with bishops. When in Rome Acton had a quasi-official status as a prime-ministerial representative, with the use of Foreign Office lines of communication with Gladstone by which he could send regular updates on progress to the anxious Prime Minister. In using Acton in this way Gladstone upset the Cardinal Archbishop of Westminster, Henry Manning, who disliked the position of influence Acton enjoyed with the premier. Gladstone was bypassing not only the Roman Catholic hierarchy but the Foreign Office, operating a private policy of his own that differed from the position of the Foreign Secretary, Lord Clarendon, who actually blocked the issue of an official statement of British opposition to the infallibility doctrine.

Acton is most remembered for his adage about the corrupting nature of power; his behaviour later in the career of Gladstone helps illustrate his point. He developed a growing interest in strengthening his political connection and deploying it for his own ends. Significantly, he formed a close friendship with Gladstone's daughter Mary in 1879. The historian Owen Chadwick argued this association changed the relationship between Acton and Gladstone. Acton was able to influence him through Mary, who subsequently took on secretarial duties for Gladstone. After Acton's career as an elected politician ended, he had spent considerable time abroad in France and Germany. From the mid-1880s Acton began staying in Britain more often, giving him proximity to Gladstone. By 1892 he was living at the Athenaeum, the famed gentlemen's club. Acton sensed an opportunity to gain influence, and perhaps obtain a public office which could help his financial position; he liked the idea of being close to the source of political authority. He circulated among leading figures of the Liberal Party during the campaign for the 1892 general election and in June assisted Gladstone in the drafting of the manifesto. When forming a Cabinet, Gladstone used Acton as a link with the most prominent Liberals and the Lord, in turn, influenced decisions about whom to appoint. The power intoxicated him. Acton seems to have believed he would receive a Cabinet position himself. Senior Liberals raised concerns about him and soon prevented him from coming to future high-level meetings.

Ultimately Acton was given the post of Lordship-in-Waiting to the Queen. There was good reason for the appointment. Gladstone had a bad relationship with Queen Victoria but Acton, on the other hand, was a good friend of the monarch and able to act as an intermediary. Gladstone wanted Victoria to be better disposed towards his government and encouraged Acton to spend time at Windsor. In tandem with this royal role Acton offered Gladstone advice on political tactics and on the appointment of diplomats. When Gladstone was at Biarritz in February 1894, Acton supplied West, who was with the Prime Minister, with information about the navy estimates.

The precise extent of the influence of Acton upon Gladstone is immeasurable. Victoria regarded his importance to the Prime Minister highly. Those who sought to pass on views to Gladstone used Acton for this purpose. Gladstone displayed a tendency to defer to the judgement of Acton, who was able to speak to Gladstone in terms few others could. Acton perhaps overestimated his importance, concluding that if Gladstone acted in accordance with a suggestion he had made it was because of him alone, and that other factors were not at play. The most dramatic claim Acton made involved Gladstone's policy of Home Rule for Ireland. Initially Acton believed he shared responsibility with John Morley, the Liberal politician and writer. In 1898 Morley denied to Acton that he believed he had played such a role. Acton concluded he could claim exclusive credit. Mary Gladstone recorded after Acton's death that she shared this view. But Gladstone did not achieve his place in history by allowing others, even those he esteemed to the extent he did Acton, to place ideas in his mind without thorough critical examination.[50]

Montagu Corry (1838–1903)

Gladstone's great rival, Benjamin Disraeli, took a different approach to aides. Unlike Gladstone, Disraeli had no interest in constant engagement in the minutiae of administration. Oscar Wilde described him as 'a man who could write a novel and govern an empire with either hand'. Disraeli delegated the detail to others within his prime-ministerial team, principally Montagu Corry, his private secretary. Throughout his time as premier Corry was crucial to Disraeli in many areas of his work, both domestic and foreign. The link between the two men received royal recognition and was so close as to prompt speculation about its nature.

Born in London, Corry came from aristocratic stock. Educated at Harrow and Trinity College, Cambridge, he became a lawyer. There is a frequently recounted anecdote about the first time Corry met Disraeli. In the summer of 1865 some young women at a party at Raby Castle, the home of the Duke of Cleveland, had persuaded Corry to perform a song and dance for them, when Disraeli unexpectedly looked into the room. Disraeli stood staring for some time. Later on that evening he told Corry, 'I think you must be my impresario.' In June the following year Corry wrote to Disraeli recalling the evening and enquiring about possible openings working for Conservative politicians, stressing his commitment to the party. At the time Disraeli was seeking a new

---

50   O. Chadwick, *Acton and Gladstone* (London: The Athlone Press, 1976); J. Altholz, 'Acton, John Emerich Dalberg', *ODNB*; R. Hill, *Lord Acton* (New Haven: Yale University Press, 2000); R. Schuettinger, *Lord Acton: Historian of Liberty* (La Salle: Open Court, 1976); E. Campion (ed.), *Lord Acton and the First Vatican Council: A Journal* (Sydney: Catholic Theological Faculty, 1975); J. Fears (ed.), *Selected Writings of Lord Acton*, vol. 3, *Essays in Religion, Politics and Morality* (Indianapolis: Liberty, 1988).

secretary and the two began a connection that developed into a close friendship up to the end of Disraeli's life in 1881.

Disraeli emphasised Corry's value to him in an 1878 letter to Queen Victoria in which he lamented the temporary loss of his aide because of illness and praised his aide's ability and character. Corry had become increasingly important following the death of Disraeli's wife in 1872. At that time, the aide began handling domestic as well as political work. Upon losing power in 1880 Disraeli was reported describing his greatest regret as being Corry's loss of office. In his opinion the aide was Cabinet material. At this point Disraeli proposed Corry for membership of the House of Lords and Corry duly became Lord Rowton. The outgoing premier was generally unenthusiastic about creating peerages, because of his deference to the aristocracy, but he made an exception for his assistant. Gladstone is reputed to have likened the elevation to Caligula making his horse a consul. Shortly after he left office Disraeli completed a novel, *Endymion*, containing a passage in which Disraeli gives insight into his bond with Corry. It describes how the relationship between a minister and his secretary should be of the finest possible degree. The confidence, forbearance or sympathy required was similar to that needed in a marriage. There was, Disraeli noted, a shared interest in such a partnership. Through various struggles, successes and failures it could develop into 'devotion'. A young secretary would feel enthusiastic about the person he served, who would in turn be careful to value properly an aide whom he found both able and personally reliable. Corry had recently provided Disraeli a reason to be grateful, negotiating an advance of £10,000 for *Endymion*, at that point possibly the greatest amount ever paid for a novel. When Disraeli died, Corry was with him.

Much speculation has surrounded the sexual orientation of Benjamin Disraeli – and by extension his relationship with Corry.

In his study of the life of the Prime Minister, William Kuhn argues his novels should be treated as partly autobiographical and highlights potential homoerotic content in them. He considers at length the close bond between Disraeli and Corry, describing how Disraeli once complained that a painting he had of Corry on display in his house had 'not given the golden light in Monty's hair'. After Disraeli's wife died, in some ways Corry took her place. In July 1878 after Disraeli returned from the Congress of Berlin, Victoria invited him to come to Osborne House for two days accompanied by Corry. Contemporaries were interested in the idea that the two were a couple of some kind. Kuhn describes how a representation appeared in *Vanity Fair* of Disraeli and Corry arm-in-arm, indeed, society coverage in the press included frequent references to them as a pair. But Kuhn judges that, while Disraeli loved Corry as much as he did 'anyone', 'no evidence' exists for a 'physical' relationship between them. Corry did not marry but he had a number of affairs with women and is reputed to have fathered a number of illegitimate children. The affinity between Disraeli and Corry reveals as much about the link between premiers and secretaries in general as it does about these two individuals and their sexual inclinations. In likening the relationship between minister and aide to a marriage Disraeli finds an echo in Gladstone. Soon after West became his secretary for the first time Gladstone told him how their respective roles could be fulfilled properly only if there were the degree of confidence between them as should form between husband and wife. While Gladstone's sexual proclivities have been a subject of interest, never was the notion embraced that he had a sexual relationship with West or any of his other private secretaries, or was interested in men at all in this way.

Corry was of substantial practical value to Disraeli when socialising in the upper echelons of society. Disraeli was from a Jewish (though not practising) middle-class background whereas Corry had been to Harrow and Cambridge, and was thus more comfortable mingling in the highest social circles and able to maintain contact with these groups. Corry kept Disraeli abreast of political developments, and brought aspiring MPs to his attention. The secretary helped Disraeli in his handling of Victoria and the three formed a close triangular relationship. Disraeli recorded late in 1878 that 'the Faery' – as he called Victoria – had attempted to make Corry head of the Royal Household, at £2,000 per annum. The Queen continued to take advice from Corry for some years after the death of her former Prime Minister.

As premier, Disraeli was not habitually a policy activist, but he played an important role in foreign affairs with the support of Corry. For example, he informed Victoria in January 1878 how Corry had assisted him in an effort to form an alliance with Austria. Later the same year premier and aide participated in the Congress of Berlin. Corry lobbied the Queen and Prince of Wales to ensure Disraeli was made the most senior British representative at the event. The Congress proved to be an important moment in the history of the premiership; this gathering was the location of the first semi-official use of the title 'Prime Minister'. Though he was a useful aide to Disraeli at Berlin, certain myths have exaggerated his role. Corry perpetuated a further legend about events of 1875. In this year the opportunity arose to purchase the Egyptian Khedive's shares in the Suez Canal Company. Parliament was in recess at the time so a private loan was needed. According to his account, when the Cabinet discussed the issue, Corry waited outside the room. Upon receiving a sign from Disraeli he proceeded immediately to see Lord Rothschild and request £4 million for the following day. He told Rothschild his security was the British government. Rothschild agreed. This story can be neither disproved nor verified. Possible embellishments aside, Corry mattered to Disraeli the person and the Prime Minister.

However, the burdens the premier transferred to his aide created great strain. Early in 1878 Disraeli informed Victoria that Corry had worked himself to a nervous breakdown and would have to take a foreign break. Lord Carnarvon, the Colonial Secretary, complained Disraeli 'detests details ... does no work' and asserted 'M. Corry is in fact Prime Minister'.[51] Despite such claims the real master was Disraeli and the authority Corry wielded was the product of the particular style Disraeli favoured. The secretary remained subordinate.

Private secretaries to the Prime Minister

Following the split from the Treasury the most important consistent source of support for the Prime Minister was the private secretariat. The job of private secretary had become widely recognised and renowned. When he learned Gladstone wanted to appoint him as his private secretary at the outset of his second premiership in 1880, Edward Hamilton noted in his diary on 24 April 1880 that it was the post he would have chosen of any in the entire civil service. West believed that after being a member of Cabinet the most attractive possible position was to be private secretary to a leader such as Gladstone. These attitudes contrast sharply with the initial lack of enthusiasm Edmund Burke felt

---

51   G. Buckle, *The Life of Benjamin Disraeli, Earl of Beaconsfield*, vol. 4, *1855–1868* (London: John Murray, 1916); G. Buckle, *The Life of Benjamin Disraeli, Earl of Beaconsfield*, vol. 6, *1855–1868* (London: John Murray, 1916); M. Wiebe, 'Corry, Montagu William Lowry-, Baron Rowton, *ODNB*; West, *Contemporary Portraits*; W. Kuhn, *The Politics of Pleasure: A portrait of Benjamin Disraeli* (London: Free Press, 2006), p. 333; West, *Recollections*, vol. 2 (Smith, Elder, & Co., London, 1899), p. 27; C. Petrie, *The Powers Behind The Prime Ministers* (London: MacGibbon & Kee, 1958); R. Blake, *Disraeli* (London: Methuen, 1969), p. 543; J. Ward, 'Derby and Disraeli' in D. Southgate, *The Conservative Leadership: 1832–1934* (London: Macmillan, 1974).

about his appointment when Lord Rockingham recruited him over a century earlier in 1765. The secretariat was a gradually growing group, mixing civil servants and outside appointments. But wherever they came from and whatever they went on to do, all had a firm connection to the premier they served.

Nonetheless, the allure of the role could be misleading. Although these aides might be influential, they were still, of necessity, subordinates. Appearing in *The Times* on 8 June 1916, the obituary of Maurice Bonham Carter – private secretary to Asquith 1912–16 – described the perception of him as 'a player of second fiddles', including in his role supporting a Prime Minister. No. 10 was not an ideal working environment. Another secretary to Gladstone, George Leveson-Gower, described his 'queer little room' which had the appearance of having been rapidly created to fill a space. On the ground floor of the building it looked out onto a garden that was actually more of a gravel track with some trees and a small grass area. In warm weather the heat became unbearable. In August 1880 Leveson-Gower wrote to a friend warning he might become ill. There was a terrible smell on the stairs, the drains were not working and a large cesspool had appeared in the garden. But, because the present government had taken office with a pledge to execute a retrenchment programme, nothing could be done to correct these problems.

The number of publicly salaried secretaries grew slightly. It was supplemented further at different points by unpaid aides, who included MPs and relatives of the premier. Since 1812 the First Lord of the Treasury had been allowed two secretaries paid from official funds. Taking on the extra post of Chancellor of the Exchequer in 1873 entitled Gladstone to two more. He retained Hamilton from the previous Chancellor and recruited Spencer Lyttelton from outside. When Benjamin Disraeli succeeded Gladstone as Prime Minister in 1874, he did not take

on the post of Chancellor of the Exchequer, but employed three
secretaries instead of reverting to two. An important shift had
occurred. When Gladstone came to office again in 1880 he took
on the added role of Chancellor once more, and increased the
number to four. But the regular figure for paid private secretaries – until the 1920s when it rose to four – was three. Despite the
complications it is possible to observe a slight upward trend in
numbers, perhaps because of a perceived rising workload. John
(known as Arthur) Godley observed the amount of business
and the associated responsibilities had increased significantly
between his first spell as a private secretary in 1872 and his
second from 1880.[52]

At this time the secretariats of prime ministers comprised a
combination of individuals drawn from inside and beyond the
administrative machine. By the end of the period, in the premierships of Henry Campbell-Bannerman (1905–8) and Asquith
(1908–16), the settled position was: one senior private secretary from outside, an official from the Treasury and a further
appointment whose origin could vary. An exception arrived in
1907–8 when the Treasury had no representation. Insiders seem
to have been particularly valuable for their knowledge of official procedure, while the irregulars often provided contact with
the party-political world. The concept of a permanent body of
staff supporting different governments was taking hold. So too
was the connected principle of party-political impartiality, but
it did not apply rigidly. Party politics and administration, once
thoroughly intertwined, began to separate. But they were at this
stage like two cells divided by a semi-permeable membrane. It
was still more possible than it would later become to move from

---

52   West, *Recollections*, vol. 2; Leveson-Gower, *Years of Content*; Bahlman
     (ed.), *The Diary of Sir Edward Walter Hamilton: 1880–1885*, vol. 2;
     J. Godley, *Reminiscences.*

one world to the other and often such transitions involved a spell on the prime-ministerial secretariat.

Patronage fostered personal interests on the part of staff, both irregulars and insiders. As well as the former type of recruit, the latter might possess or develop open partisanship. William Gurdon was a Treasury clerk and served Gladstone as a junior to West from 1868. When West left in 1872 Gurdon succeeded him, returning to the Treasury at the end of the first Gladstone premiership in 1874. Following his retirement from the civil service in 1899 Gurdon became a Liberal MP. Movement in the other direction could occur also. Godley became a private secretary to Gladstone, who was a family friend, from beyond the administrative machine in 1872. He remained in the post until the end of the Gladstone government in 1874. Gladstone recruited Godley as his senior private secretary when he returned to the premiership in 1880. Godley then became a commissioner of the Inland Revenue in 1882 and subsequently Permanent Under-Secretary for the India Office.[53]

Another private secretary whose career passed through the civil service and party politics was Arthur Ponsonby. He served in the Foreign Office until 1902 before joining the Liberal Central Association and later becoming the senior private secretary to Campbell-Bannerman when he became Prime Minister. As a career official who then joined a party headquarters and served as the pre-eminent member of a prime-ministerial staff, he was a precursor to Tony Blair's Chief of Staff, Jonathan Powell, who served in the Diplomatic Service before joining Blair in opposition and accompanying him into power in 1997. After

---

53   H. Matthew, 'Godley, (John) Arthur' *ODNB*. See also: G. Jones, 'The Prime Minister's Secretaries: Politicians or Administrators?' in J. Griffith (ed.) *From Policy to Administration: Essays in Honour of William A. Robson* (London: Allen & Unwin, 1976).

Campbell-Bannerman passed away in 1908, Ponsonby secured election to his old parliamentary seat. Ponsonby later joined the Labour Party, serving as a minister in 1924 and 1929–31.

Private secretaries – whether from within the machine or outsiders – all had a firm association with the specific Prime Minister they served. It was the general practice when a new incumbent took office for the predecessor's secretaries to leave and the incoming premier to appoint his own. Exceptions were few. George Murray was kept on by Rosebery when he succeeded his fellow-Liberal Gladstone in 1894. Asquith inherited Vaughan Nash from Campbell-Bannerman in 1906 and retained him, a decision that was completely at the Prime Minister's discretion – he could have jettisoned the aide post-haste had the inclination taken him. Another secretary to serve two different prime ministers, though with an interval between them, was J. F. Daly. He worked for Disraeli between 1874 and 1880 and Salisbury from 1886 to 1887. Possibly the first private secretary to survive the transition to a premier of a different political bent was Malcolm Ramsay, a Treasury official inherited by Campbell-Bannerman from Arthur Balfour. Though Ramsay was an obscure figure, in retrospect his retention was a significant precedent for the later development of a No. 10 staff dominated by career officials.

Before Salisbury became Prime Minister, the Treasury (and the department attached to it, the Inland Revenue), had developed a monopoly on posts in the prime-ministerial secretariat filled by staff from within the administrative machine. As Prime Minister Salisbury – reflecting his policy priorities and pressing concerns of the time – took on the additional post of Foreign Secretary (1885–6, 1887–92 and 1895–1900). He was First Lord of the Treasury only in 1886–7 and Lord Privy Seal 1900–1902 – a title assumed presumably for the precedence it brought. While he was First Lord in 1886–7 Salisbury was served by one aide from the Treasury – J. F. Daly – but afterwards no more. For the remainder of his premierships the Treasury was excluded. What was exceptional about Salisbury's premiership was not that his private secretaries from within the civil service were from the Foreign Office, but that Salisbury held the portfolio of Foreign Secretary – a role from which the use of aides of this type flowed naturally. From 1902 Balfour appointed, alongside outsiders, only Treasury officials – Frederick Parry in 1902 and Malcolm Ramsay from 1902 to 1905 (though Ramsay had been a clerk in the Foreign Office before transferring to the Treasury). Under the Liberal prime ministers Campbell-Bannerman and Asquith at least one Treasury official was normally present. But the Foreign Office gained a more regular position on the staff of the premier, one not dependent upon him holding the post of Foreign Secretary, and premiers obtained assistance for their involvement in external policy during a time of rising international tension.

From the perspective of the aide's home department it conferred influence and prestige to have someone placed with the Prime Minister. For the premier it meant gaining effective contact with a particular part of government and knowledge of its working practices; expertise was not guaranteed, however. Treasury officials were often generalists. An exception was Henry Higgs, a notable economist, who served Campbell-Bannerman 1905–8. Serving a Prime Minister could be a stage in a successful administrative career: Frederick Leith-Ross joined the Treasury in 1909 and served as private secretary to Asquith 1911–13. He later became Chief Economic Adviser to the government (though lacking in economic expertise), Director-General of the Ministry of Economic Warfare in 1939 and for five years from 1946, Governor of the National Bank of Egypt.[54]

---

54   R. Middleton, 'Higgs, Henry'; 'Ross, Sir Frederick William Leith –', *ODNB*.

Prime ministers continued to appoint soldiers and those from legal backgrounds as secretaries. Henry Manners was an army officer and Leicestershire landowner. He was Salisbury's senior private secretary in 1885–6 and 1886–8, when he became a Conservative MP. The tendency for military connections is demonstrated by Manners's successor as aide to Salisbury, Schomberg 'Pom' K. McDonnell, who went on to serve for a short time in the Boer War and as an intelligence officer during the First World War. He died in action on the front in Flanders in 1915. When Gladstone appointed Godley in 1872, he was studying for the Bar. In the same way, both Montagu Corry (for Disraeli) and Bonham Carter (for Asquith) were barristers. Outside recruits to the secretariat often went on to parliamentary careers, or followed them at the same time.

The proximity of prime ministers and their team members was such that personal and professional relationships could often become virtually indistinguishable. As we have seen Gladstone's secretariats were almost surrogate families and included actual relatives within them. Bonham Carter, a good friend of the Asquith family, married Violet, the daughter of the Prime Minister, in 1915. The connections within the Asquith circle could be problematic. Asquith had a well-documented, possibly unconsummated, affair with Venetia Stanley. From 1915 Stanley was married to Edwin Montagu, formerly an aide to Asquith (performing the then emerging role of Parliamentary Private Secretary), and close to both the Prime Minister (who had guided his career) and Mrs Asquith. This complex involvement strained the relationship between Montagu and Asquith. Matters became worse when, in early 1917, Montagu joined the Lloyd George government, which had replaced Asquith's at the end of the previous year.[55]

---

55   'Sir Maurice Bonham Carter', *The Times*, 8 June 1960; C. Kaul, 'Montagu, Edwin Samuel', *ODNB*.

Nepotism often played a part in the appointment of secretaries. Lord Salisbury's team included members of his own family and of others in his aristocratic social circle. He used his son Robert Cecil and his nephew Evelyn Cecil for unpaid secretarial support through his premierships. Manners became the Duke of Rutland, and Salisbury's staff included the sons of the Earl of Antrim (Schomberg McDonnell), the Earl of Bradford (Lord Newport), the Duke of Richmond (Walter Gordon-Lennox) and the Earl of Warwick (Sidney Greville).

Within the secretariat there was a senior member. The title 'Principal Private Secretary' was used in *The Times* to describe Arthur Godley, aide to Gladstone as premier, on 27 August 1880, but the phrase did not appear in official lists during this period. Both outsiders (such as Montagu Corry for Disraeli) and regulars (including Algernon West for Gladstone) could be the highest-ranking secretary. One who provided significant service for Prime Minister Salisbury was Schomberg ('Pom') K. McDonnell. Like so many other senior officials and politicians – both now and then – McDonnell attended Eton College, before going up to University College, Oxford. He became Salisbury's senior private secretary in 1888. At the time, Salisbury warned McDonnell he could not offer job security, since if the premier lost office then so too would the aide, although clearly the role was interesting and not excessively demanding. McDonnell decided the benefits outweighed the job insecurity and at the age of twenty-seven he became the youngest person to hold this office; he went on to be the longest-serving in it, too, eleven years in all. His support for Salisbury continued until the point when the premier was about to retire in 1902; McDonnell helped liaise with the Conservative Party. Alongside the more regular activities associated with a secretary, McDonnell provided political advice, handled relations with the Prince of Wales, passed messages to foreign diplomats, organised events, monitored the press and dealt with requests for honours. McDonnell is credited as the counsellor closest to Salisbury.[56]

The disbursal of favour continued to be a central component of the premiership. By this time Secret Service funds were significantly restricted, and the use of patronage in official posts was becoming more limited as the Civil Service Commission, first established in 1855, became more powerful. But the Prime Minister was the main adviser to the monarch on many decisions about patronage. Honours could be a shadowy business. Leveson-Gower gives an account of how he was approached by 'an unknown Australian' attempting to purchase a title, offering the secretary a personal share of the proceeds.[57] Secretaries might help premiers with their parliamentary and legislative work, and advise on and help implement policy. Record-keeping and the conduct of communications continued to be central to secretarial work. Secretaries played a part in the management of relationships between the premier and other Cabinet members. The premiers' secretaries processed incoming information, such as diplomatic despatches, often summarising them for digestion by the premier. An important role was to act as 'buffer', fending off individuals with whom the Prime Minister did not wish to deal. Private secretaries also fulfilled a security function. Leveson-Gower describes how one of his tasks was carrying out a sweep of the Cabinet room after it had met to ensure that any paper containing an indication of discussion was destroyed. Secretaries took some responsibility for the personal safety of the premier. At various times there were fears that the Prime

---

56   D. Huddlestone, 'McDonnell, Sir Schomberg K. McDonnell', *ODNB*; A. Roberts, *Salisbury: Victorian Titan* (London: Phoenix, 2000); G. Cecil, *Life of Robert Marquis of Salisbury*, vol. 4, *1887–1892* (London: Hodder and Stoughton, 1932).

57   Leveson-Gower, *Years of Content*, pp. 167–8.

Minister might be assassinated by Fenians. Gladstone resented the presence of security guards. Leveson-Gower describes once having to inform detectives from the Home Office of the Prime Minister's likely movements. Concern for the Prime Minister was associated with a broader interest in security. Terrorism was a concern in the nineteenth century as it is today and during 1892–4 West kept himself informed about bombing campaigns by Irish nationalist terrorists.

John (Jack) Sandars (1853–1934)

The Prime Minister is both the public face of the institution and the most important person within it. Yet particular incumbents will always choose to pass on tasks to varying extents and in different ways. For reasons that included his health and his personal approach to the job, Arthur Balfour delegated extensively to one aide above all. John Sandars's role caused concern about whether the kind of authority he exercised was appropriate and legitimate. But it was Balfour, not Sandars, who brought about this arrangement: Sandars was simply enabling Balfour to operate within government in the way he wanted.

Sandars was the son of a colliery and estate agent, who became a friend of Arthur Balfour's brother, Cecil, while at Magdalen College, Oxford. After practising law he became in 1886 a private secretary to Henry Matthews, the Home Secretary. Sandars ran as a Conservative parliamentary candidate in 1892 but was not elected. He then became secretary to Arthur Balfour, who was First Lord of the Treasury and Leader of the House of Commons. Sandars's role for Balfour became pivotal. It involved providing personal advice, handling party and patronage issues, and dealing with the Liberal Unionists. Sandars continued supporting Balfour in his role of Prime Minister (1902–5) and subsequently of opposition leader.

Accounts of Sandars's impact during the Balfour premiership depict him exercising unprecedented authority for an aide. With Balfour often absent because of illness or holidays, Sandars performed tasks that might otherwise have fallen to a premier to carry out in person, or later on to the Cabinet Office. He is said to have been able to organise meetings of ministers in pressing circumstances and pass details of the discussion on to Balfour in Scotland. He had the authority to issue rebukes to members of the Cabinet on behalf of Balfour. Sandars is reputed to have been willing to prevent the despatch of letters Balfour had written. The Sandars family historian, J. Edward Sandars, as well as claiming his ancestor was able to convene Cabinet meetings on his own account, states that on one occasion he brought about a meeting of Parliament a week earlier than scheduled without previous discussion with either the Prime Minister or the monarch.[58] But the Conservative Party historian John Ramsden found little grounds for the view that Sandars wielded 'undue influence' over Balfour. Ramsden emphasised Balfour's tendency to delegate tasks to his aide that he found tedious or distasteful.[59]

There seem to have been objections to Sandars, including some from the King. Charles Petrie describes a specific incident from 1903. Sandars proposed continuing what he believed was an established practice, for the premier's private secretaries to pass on to the press the broad outline of the contents of the monarch's speech at the opening of Parliament, the day before it took place. Edward VII insisted he was firmly opposed to any such arrangement. He thought it occurred in no other country, even the US. He felt such briefing made a mockery of the event.

---

58   J. Sandars, *The Sandars Centuries* (privately printed, 1971), p. 64.
59   J. Ramsden, *The Age of Balfour and Baldwin: 1902–1940* (London: Longman, 1978), p. 29.

He thought that Sandars represented something new and sinister.[60] Sandars was involved in various covert disputes between Balfour and Edward, but the monarch realised Sandars was useful as a means of communicating with his often absent Prime Minister.[61]

Henry Campbell-Bannerman's team

When assessing the support provided by Corry to Disraeli and by Sandars to Balfour a focus on individual private secretaries is inevitable. In other cases group profiles are more appropriate. Henry Campbell-Bannerman was the first premier during the period of reforming Liberal governments that began in 1905. Though he helped inaugurate this era it was not through his dominance as a leader. Two of his key aides were his private secretaries: Arthur Ponsonby and Vaughan Nash. In theory, Ponsonby was the senior partner, but in practice the hierarchy was inverted. They worked together as a diverse, effective unit, pursuing radical objectives. Campbell-Bannerman afforded them considerable discretion in how they went about their jobs. But a Prime Minister so relaxed about the activities of his aides proved equally difficult to utilise as a means for Ponsonby and Nash to achieve their own objectives.

After his time at Balliol College, Oxford, Ponsonby had, as noted, joined the Foreign Office, then in 1902 the Liberal Central Association. He developed socialist inclinations but the Liberal Party was the only viable party for him at this time. When the Liberals took office late in 1905 Herbert Gladstone, the Chief Whip, recommended Ponsonby as the senior private secretary to the new Prime Minister. In becoming a private secretary at the highest level in British society, Ponsonby was continuing a family

60 Petrie, *The Powers Behind The Prime Ministers*, pp. 68–9.
61 H. Langley, 'Sandars, John Satterfield', *ODNB*.

trade. His father was secretary to Queen Victoria, a post which involved continual contact with his son's predecessors. The initial plan was that Ponsonby would combine this role with a seat in Parliament, but he was unsuccessful as a candidate the following year. Campbell-Bannerman informed Ponsonby that he could not feel sorry about this reversal since it guaranteed his secretary would be fully available to him.

Ponsonby's colleagues in Campbell-Bannerman's prime-ministerial team were Henry Higgs and Vaughan Nash. Nash served as a secretary both to Campbell-Bannerman 1905–8 and then to Asquith until 1912. When he died he was chiefly remembered for having performed this role. By background he was a radical journalist writing on labour issues for the *Daily Chronicle*, *Daily News* and *Manchester Guardian*, and as such had an excellent range of knowledge. He began assisting Campbell-Bannerman when the Liberal leader was in opposition and soon showed himself to be effective at handling people discreetly. Ponsonby, who became a firm friend of Nash, noted that Nash was not interested in personal publicity or credit. Yet because of this self-effacing quality, as Ponsonby noted, it is difficult to tell what precisely his impact was. One area in which Nash had significant influence involved party-political developments. He was part of a group within the Liberals that put to the Liberal Chief Whip, Herbert Gladstone, the proposal not to run in about thirty seats in the general election of 1906, thereby opening up the field for Labour contestants. From 1906 onwards Nash lobbied for a change in the law to make it more possible for trade unions to operate. Through his stance in support of organised labour, Nash helped facilitate the rise of a movement that eventually eclipsed the Liberal Party. Given his journalistic background Nash played a role in presentation and press relations. He helped with speech-writing for Campbell-Bannerman and performed a royal-liaison role for Asquith.

The motive for placing Ponsonby and Nash together in Campbell-Bannerman's team was the hope that their diverse qualities would complement each other. Formally Ponsonby was the more senior. In practice Ponsonby took on more junior tasks such as writing letters and fixing meetings. Nash, older with more experience, handled presentation and policy. It seems he did not resent Ponsonby entering the Campbell-Bannerman orbit after him and assuming, theoretically, the chief post. While Nash was nervous about the new social surroundings of Downing Street, Ponsonby, who grew up in Windsor Castle, was familiar with such an environment, though he disliked moving in elite circles. Between them they discussed overall political strategy with Campbell-Bannerman. Nash and Ponsonby hit upon the practice of meeting in places other than No. 10. Not being in the office must have allowed freer discussion, and made it possible to avoid the distractions of more regular work. The political style of Campbell-Bannerman afforded them significant latitude, but it could make it more difficult for them to achieve what they wanted. Ponsonby expressed frustration at the premier's lack of dynamism, though he respected him as an employer, recognising that his more consensual political style had merits. When the Prime Minister's health was declining, Nash and Ponsonby took part in concealing his deterioration.

Ponsonby's biographer, Raymond A. Jones, describes how Nash and Ponsonby contributed to a great change in British constitutional history. The House of Lords still possessed the legal power to veto all legislation. While there was a vague acceptance that the House of Commons possessed primacy over the Lords, this principle was protected by convention, which had no direct legal

force. This constitutional position was a problem for a reforming Liberal government since there was a majority against it in
the Lords. In 1907 Nash and Ponsonby devised a reform plan to
remove this brake on the Liberal legislative programme, separat-
ing it from the even more difficult issue of the composition of the
Lords – which remains unelected to this day despite numerous
reform efforts. To achieve their objective of curbing the powers
of the second chamber, the two aides sought to exert influence
on Campbell-Bannerman and other ministers. Cabinet seemed to
adopt their plan on 31 May 1907, though as officials they could
not attend to hear the actual discussion. Nash and Ponsonby
maintained pressure on Campbell-Bannerman. In June 1907
Nash helped write a parliamentary speech on the subject for the
Prime Minister. Eventually, the initiative of Nash and Ponsonby
became the basis for the 1911 Parliament Act.[62]

Beyond the private secretariat

While the secretariat was now the most important component
of the prime-ministerial team, premiers had other sources of
support. Whips helped them manage within Parliament and party
officials dealt with their national machines. If a Prime Minister
held a departmental portfolio, as Salisbury did the Foreign Office,
a large body of staff came with it, focused on the particular area
concerned. Civil servants who had a personal connection with
a premier might provide assistance that did not arise directly
from their official role. Other individuals who had no position
in Parliament, in a party or in the administrative machine, could
still take on significant tasks when required. Prime ministers who
wanted a particular kind of help had ways of finding it.

---

62   R. Jones, *Arthur Ponsonby: The Politics of Life* (London: Christopher
     Helm, 1989); 'Mr Vaughan Nash', *The Times*, 19 December 1932; 'Mr
     Vaughan Nash', *The Times*, 21 December 1932.

Salisbury in the late nineteenth century deployed a team concerned with party issues. He was the last Prime Minister to lead his government from the House of Lords (though the convention that a premier had to be an MP did not become fixed until the 1960s). Prime ministers who sat in the Commons had a direct connection with the elected chamber, which held them to account and of which they were leader. While Salisbury was not a member of the Commons, he still needed his government to maintain its confidence. Aretas Akers-Douglas was Chief Whip through the first two Salisbury premierships of 1885–6 and 1886–92. Akers-Douglas, who came from Kent, was from a colonial farming and slave-owning family background, and attended Eton. He became an MP in 1880. In the second, longer, Salisbury tenure as Prime Minister a particular challenge was managing the relationship with the Liberal Unionist MPs with whom Salisbury was in alliance. This arrangement could be tense but Akers-Douglas was effective at keeping Conservative MPs on board. As Chief Whip he was a talent-spotter, identifying, promoting and working with another Salisbury aide, Richard Middleton.

Like Akers-Douglas Middleton had a Kent connection and the two were among the main players in a Conservative group labelled the 'Kent Gang'. The party management role he played for Salisbury was crucial because successive reforms in the nineteenth century had enlarged the size of the electorate and introduced the era of the mass party. Middleton – known as the 'skipper' because of his navy background – worked successfully as a party manager in Kent and then became head of Conservative Central Office in 1885. From this post, which he held until his retirement in 1903, he oversaw major changes to the party organisation, increasing the professionalism of agents and rationalising the arrangement of geographical units. A particular skill was in predicting the outcome of by-elections. Middleton was a career apparatchik. The post he held was not for him a means of building a parliamentary career; it was, like for other aides such as Francis Bonham for Peel, the main contribution he wanted to make. In pursuing this task he worked together with Akers-Douglas and McDonnell. This kind of support structure was useful because Salisbury had a detached personal style and was generally more interested in foreign and imperial affairs. People were needed who could handle some of the domestic politics for him. Salisbury did not always do what this group of aides wanted. Sometimes they had difficulty in ensuring when speaking from the platform he did not say something that contradicted their efforts. But though not always in keeping with their plans, Salisbury appreciated their importance and the contribution this team made to his electoral success.[63]

When Gladstone and Salisbury combined prime-ministerial remits with those, respectively, of the Treasury and the Foreign Office, the size of the staff answering to them increased significantly. Salisbury made use of individuals he trusted within the Foreign Office.[64] In his role as an imperial Prime Minister he relied heavily on Philip Henry Wodehouse Currie who was Permanent Secretary at the Foreign Office from 1888. From this position he provided vital support to Salisbury when combining the foreign secretary-ship with the office of Prime Minister in 1885–6 and 1887–92. In contrast to a more micro-managing administrator

63   Viscount Chilston, 'Lord Salisbury as Party Leader (1881–1902)', *Parliamentary Affairs*, 13 (1960), pp. 304–17; J. Ridley, 'Douglas, Aretas Akers', *ODNB*; R. T. Shannon, 'Middleton, Richard William Evelyn', *ODNB*; D. Southgate, 'The Salisbury Era 1881–1902' in Southgate, *The Conservative Leadership*; E. Alexander, *Chief Whip: The Political Life and Times of Aretas Akers-Douglas, 1st Viscount Chilston* (London: Routledge and Kegan Paul, 1963).
64   For a description of the organisation of the Foreign Office during Salisbury's final term there, see: Z. Steiner, 'The Last Years of the Old Foreign Office, 1898–1905', *The Historical Journal*, vol. 6, no. 1 (1963), pp. 59–90.

like Gladstone, Salisbury tended to provide general guidance to his staff, as opposed to precise orders. Currie, who had been private secretary to Salisbury as Foreign Secretary from 1878, was able to ascertain what Salisbury wanted from his diplomats without the premier having to provide exact details, and put it into action. This quality of an aide can be advantageous, if it enables prime ministers to achieve more without a counterproductive immersion in detail. At times Salisbury ran crucial imperial policy from a small personal cabal, which included Currie within it. For instance, in 1887, Salisbury took personal charge of negotiating a prospective treaty with Italy, from which the Cabinet and the wider Foreign Office were excluded. Currie was one of only a few who were aware of the activity taking place.[65]

Edward Hamilton (1847–1908)

Prime ministers could obtain support from officials outside their secretariats even if they were not in direct control of a department. Gladstone (1886, 1892–4) and Lord Rosebery (1894–5) received such support from Edward Hamilton. He advised Gladstone on presentation and political management, and on policy, including an initiative that bypassed Cabinet. For both Gladstone and Rosebery he seems to have taken an interest in identifying and even forestalling the possible occurrence of public scandal. When operating in this area for Rosebery he came close to events which figure in one of the great conspiracy theories associated with prime-ministerial staff.

'Eddy' Hamilton entered the Treasury in 1870 and eventually became Permanent Secretary in 1902, holding the post jointly with George Murray, another Gladstone aide earlier in his career. Hamilton first became a private secretary to Gladstone, a friend of

---

65   Z. Steiner, 'Currie, Philip Henry Wodehouse', *ODNB*; Roberts, *Salisbury*.

his father, the Bishop of Salisbury, when the Prime Minister took on the post of Chancellor of the Exchequer in 1873. Hamilton rejoined Gladstone's secretariat from 1880 to 1885, becoming the senior member in 1882. From 1885 he continued to ascend the Treasury hierarchy, serving chancellors of different parties. In 1886 Hamilton helped Gladstone pursue a policy that excluded the Cabinet. Hamilton recorded in his diary for 9 March 1886 a long meeting with Gladstone about his plans for Irish Home Rule. While the public might believe the Cabinet was creating the policy as a group, Hamilton noted, Gladstone was keeping the process under his own control. Only a small group of ministers were consulted, and infrequently. In 1894 Hamilton received advanced knowledge of Gladstone's retirement and played a part in the succession, dealing with the private secretary to the Queen. Hamilton gently pressed the cause of his old friend Rosebery, who, he seems to have believed, was the most plausible person to become premier after Gladstone. Once Rosebery secured the role of premier, Hamilton maintained his status as an important prime-ministerial aide. The official provided advice to the premier on policy, managing the Cabinet and the monarch, and writing speeches. Hamilton was not only a counsellor but a conciliator of relations within government, trying to achieve greater harmony between Rosebery and his Chancellor of the Exchequer, William Harcourt. This work had a clear party political dimension, despite Hamilton being a permanent civil servant. Rosebery sought Hamilton's views on his government's first Budget and the possible political impact it would make.[66]

Just as he once did for Gladstone, Hamilton became involved in protecting Rosebery from implication in a scandal. His diary entry for 10 March 1895 records a case that had come before

---

66   Bahlman, *The Diary of Sir Edward Walter Hamilton: 1885–1906*; Brooks, *The Destruction of Lord Rosebery*.

the magistrates the previous day. The Marquess of Queensberry objected to the relationship between one of his sons, Lord Alfred Douglas or 'Bosie', and the playwright Oscar Wilde. Queensberry left a public message about Wilde wherein he referred to his sexual orientation. Wilde decided to bring a libel action against the unhinged aristocrat. The authorities arranged a trial. On 4 April Hamilton noted hearing about the emergence of 'horrible disclosures' about Wilde, meaning active homosexuality. Hamilton realised the defamation case against Queensberry would not be successful. The prosecution withdrew its case the following day, and Queensberry was found not guilty. That afternoon the police arrested Wilde.[67] At the first attempt to prosecute him the jury could not reach a verdict. A second effort followed. Hamilton referred on 21 May to the existence of a perception that the cessation of the previous trial had taken place to protect important individuals. He consulted with public prosecutor Hamilton Cuffe, who assured Hamilton this theory was groundless, and that having read 'every word of the case', Cuffe knew no notable name occurred in it.[68]

In pursuing this inquiry Hamilton presumably had Rosebery's interests in focus. Lord Drumlanrig, Queensberry's eldest son, had been private secretary to Rosebery while he held the post of Foreign Secretary and then, from 1894, Prime Minister. Queensberry believed that not only was 'Bosie' having an affair with Wilde, but Drumlanrig was in a similar relationship with Rosebery. Then in October 1894 Drumlanrig died in a hunting accident. The trauma of this event may have driven Queensberry to make his fateful attack on Wilde. Evidence that Wilde's lawyer

---

67   D. Brooks (ed.), *The Destruction of Lord Rosebery: From the Diary of Sir Edward Hamilton, 1894–1895* (London: The Historians' Press, 1986), diary entry for 10 March 1895, p. 225; diary entries for 4 and 5 April 1895, p. 236.

68   D. Bahlman, *The Diary of Sir Edward Walter Hamilton: 1885–1906*, diary entry for 21 May 1895, p. 298.

submitted to the libel trial included a letter in which Queensberry made an unflattering reference to Rosebery. Eventually the attempt to prosecute Wilde was successful. Speculation from that time has combined with other unreliable testimony to encourage certain theories about the Wilde case involving Rosebery and Drumlanrig. According to these conspiratorial interpretations, Rosebery was a homosexual; Drumlanrig did not die by accident but committed suicide to save Rosebery from exposure of their relationship; and the government singled out Wilde for persecution to pacify Queensberry and shield the Prime Minister, about whom Queensberry was threatening to make public allegations. Hamilton apparently was concerned that Queensberry might publicly denounce Rosebery, but his diary does not state that any accusations he might have made would have been true, and Cuffe told him there was no threat.[69]

Alfred Austin (1835–1913)

Alfred Austin was an informal adviser operating beyond both the regular prime-ministerial team and the administrative machine. He was both reminiscent of the poet-propagandists of the eighteenth century and a precursor of the 'spin doctors' of the twentieth and twenty-first. Austin courted the powerful and liked to imagine he was a great influence upon Salisbury and that he had an impact on policy as well as presentation. How seriously Salisbury took him is debatable but the Prime Minister certainly regarded him as useful. Eventually Salisbury rewarded the services of his aide in a brazen and controversial fashion.

Presentation and handling the media were concerns for premiers and their aides from the outset of the office. By the later nineteenth century, establishing a press operation similar to Walpole's was

---

69   See: L. McKinstry, *Rosebery: Statesman in Turmoil* (London: John Murray, 2005) pp. 348–67.

no longer possible, since Secret Service money was now strictly limited. But the public presentation of prime ministers and their governments remained an important concern. With these ends in mind secretaries such as Algernon West included in their work dealing with journalists. Similarly, Hamilton took an interest in press coverage of Rosebery's government. He wanted the representation to be favourable, but like many assisting prime ministers before and since he was often unsatisfied with what he read. In March 1894 – with Rosebery newly installed as premier – Hamilton complained that George Buckle, editor of *The Times*, who had previously suggested he was a supporter of Rosebery, was not taking the opportunity to prove it. Rather his paper was producing unhelpful coverage of the accession of Rosebery. Under Salisbury, too, staff performed a press-handling role. One task of Schomberg McDonnell for Salisbury was to explain to editors why government members might have fallen out of favour: a surreptitious briefing role that remains familiar today. Zara Steiner describes how in the late 1890s Salisbury's private secretary and the Foreign Office Permanent Secretary performed tasks such as making journalists aware of official announcements and attempting to influence the way they depicted certain countries.[70] In Austin, Salisbury secured media assistance from a less formal source.

Austin, born to a Roman-Catholic family, had inherited wealth which gave him the financial freedom to become a poet. Alongside creative writing and criticism Austin was a journalist with a strong attachment to the Conservative Party. He wrote for the *Standard* from the 1860s to the 1890s and was a founding editor of the partisan *National Review* in 1883. He ran as a Conservative parliamentary candidate on two occasions, though was not elected.

---

70   Steiner, 'The Last Years of the Old Foreign Office'.

Austin liked to mix with important people. Building his social network, he managed to cultivate a friendship with the Queen, swapping gifts with and dedicating work to her. In 1878 Austin was in Berlin covering the Congress for the *Standard*. Before leaving Britain, Disraeli contacted Austin via Montagu Corry requesting his presence at Downing Street. The Prime Minister wanted Austin's views on Bismarck. Disraeli then encouraged Austin to follow his own career path, one which began in literature and progressed into politics. Austin was reluctant to contest winnable parliamentary seats, but he was happy to campaign for the Conservative Party. He socialised with Disraeli towards the end of the former premier's life and established the *National Review* partly at the behest of Disraeli. His later relationship with Salisbury, successor to Disraeli as Conservative leader, was closer still. Austin applied his customary and – to the neutral observer – excruciating flattery to the would-be Prime Minister and even went as far in his poem 'Mafeking' to refer to 'Gallant young Cecil!', rhyming the phrase with ''Gainst death could wrestle'.[71] Austin was frequently a visitor at Salisbury's home at Hatfield where they discussed foreign affairs – a specialism of both men – at length. In Austin's account they had a shared outlook, placing the greater good above their personal interests. The arrangement was mutually beneficial: Salisbury was able to exploit Austin as a public outlet for his views, who in turn benefited from his access to the Prime Minister. Such an implicit bargain underpins the briefing system at No. 10 to the present. Austin records that he never hid from the *Standard* editor that his agenda was promotion of what he saw as the public interest over achieving benefit for the newspaper. Salisbury's daughter, Lady Gwendolen Cecil, described how Austin was

---

71   A. Austin, *Songs of England* (London: Macmillan and Co., 1900), p. 93.

able, through anonymous articles, to promote features of the premier's policies that he could not highlight himself, though Salisbury may never have explicitly asked his friend to perform this task.

Alongside drafting helpful articles for the premier, Austin provided him with advice. In August 1892 Salisbury, at the end of his second premiership, wrote to Austin noting how useful had been his 'counsel and assistance' at a number of difficult points.[72] Austin asserted that the shared attitudes of the two enabled him to make proposals to Salisbury that might otherwise have been unacceptable and which Salisbury often followed. The premier heeded such advice, so Austin claimed, over appointments, selecting speakers for parliamentary debates, on honours and on the timing of the introduction of policies. Austin asserted he influenced Salisbury on the handling of problematic third parties during the Boer War.

Finding his friend's press links useful, Salisbury humoured Austin and made him feel that he had more direct influence on the Prime Minister than was actually the case. Salisbury may have found discussions about policy with Austin worthwhile, and perhaps attached some significance to his views on various issues and decisions, but the account of his role Austin provided in his memoirs overstates what was likely to have been his real impact on the actions of the premier, though Austin may well have believed he was being accurate. Salisbury probably encouraged further self-importance on the part of Austin by having him appointed Poet Laureate. The reward was recognition of political services rendered rather than of literary ability. Austin's verse had the reputation of being so bad as to be unintentionally funny. Aside from its low quality,

72   A. Austin, *The Autobiography of Alfred Austin: Poet Laureate, 1835–1910* (London: Macmillan and Co., 1911), vol. 2, p. 180.

his poetry was inappropriately opinionated for someone in his new position.[73]

The Prime Minister's Office at the onset of war

H. H. Asquith's reputation suffers from a perception he provided weak leadership during the First World War. Lloyd George supplanted him in 1916 and offered a different approach, considering prime-ministerial support-mechanisms as central to the failure of Asquith. Fortunately we have detailed views of Asquith's No. 10 provided by two successive Treasury private secretaries. The first exists in a published account; the second from the earliest serving prime-ministerial aide we have interviewed. They portray some short-lived arrangements and others that persisted into the twenty-first century.

Frederick Leith-Ross moved from the Treasury to become a private secretary to Asquith in 1911, staying until 1913. Though he had some limited previous contact with Asquith, the premier had not personally chosen him. The decision was made in what Leith-Ross depicted as the usual way, by the Permanent Secretary to the Treasury. An attraction of Leith-Ross was his junior status as a civil servant. His predecessor as Treasury private secretary at No. 10, Roderick Meiklejohn, had been too forceful in his interactions with others across government. Leith-Ross's position on appointment was not as senior as Meiklejohn's had been, and the new private secretary was therefore judged less likely to be inappropriately assertive. Leith-Ross does not specify what precisely Meiklejohn did wrong, but his account demonstrates that secretaries were expected to be restrained in their

---

73   W. Scheuerle, 'Austin, Alfred', *ODNB*; N. Crowell, *Alfred Austin: Victorian* (Albuquerque: University of New Mexico Press, 1953); Cecil, *Life of Robert Marquis of Salisbury*, vol. 4; Roberts, *Salisbury*; G. Searle, *A New England? Peace and War 1886–1918* (Oxford: Clarendon Press, 2004).

behaviour – though presumably the exercise of more subtle influence remained permissible.

When Leith-Ross joined the secretariat there were four aides. The senior member, who was usually an outside, party-political appointment, was Vaughan Nash (who had previously served Campbell-Bannerman), assisted by Maurice Bonham Carter. Eric Drummond came from the Foreign Office, alongside a Treasury secretary, Leith-Ross. Bonham Carter soon succeeded Nash. The external recruits dealt with political issues. As a group they got on well together. Leith-Ross became a good friend of Drummond, as well as of Asquith and his wife. Drummond mainly handled Foreign Office papers for the Prime Minister while Leith-Ross focused on patronage and Treasury business. Some work was difficult to classify and secretaries overlapped in their activities. Leith-Ross sometimes gave policy advice to Asquith, including over Irish Home Rule. The senior private secretary accompanied the Prime Minister to his office in the Commons when Parliament was in session. If circumstances required, another secretary would come. Asquith did not rely on aides for speech-writing.

Leith-Ross had an office in No. 10 next to the Cabinet room in the Treasury (now 70 Whitehall) side, which he shared with Charles Lyell, the Parliamentary Private Secretary. Despite his lack of seniority Leith-Ross was able to get to know most of the Cabinet and other ministers because they often waited in his office before seeing the Prime Minister. Drummond and the Principal Private Secretary were based on the other side of the Cabinet room. Leith-Ross saw this period in his career as an apprenticeship, training him in the ways of government. He suggested he was more involved in organising the office than actually making a contribution to wider matters. Late in 1913 Leith-Ross had the chance of a considerable promotion within the Treasury. Asquith tried to prevent him from leaving but in the end allowed it to happen. Leith-Ross was not happy to go because however demanding the job it was always stimulating, ranging across many different areas. Mrs Asquith wrote to him to let him know she was sorry about his departure, because of his efficiency and discretion.

Some features of the life of the prime-ministerial aide of the time now seem quaint. So-called 'levees' were held two or three times annually at St James's Palace. Private secretaries to the premier had to attend the first of the year. They walked up in turn to the King, who was sitting on his throne, and bowed. Top hats and morning suits were essential dress requirements and long holidays were enjoyed. Standard practice when Parliament was not sitting was for only one secretary to be on duty. In his spare time Leith-Ross wrote articles on foreign affairs and for *Vogue,* and produced poetry. Working practices were largely informal. Although the Treasury kept written records of all business, at Downing Street, staff kept notes of what went on to an absolute minimum and no files were passed from one premiership to the next. This absence of written material required the private secretaries to maintain the closest possible contact with each other. However, while this culture of informality would subsequently decline, it did not disappear. Almost a century later Jonathan Powell, Chief of Staff to Tony Blair was interviewed during the Hutton Inquiry into the death of Dr David Kelly, and revealed that many meetings were not minuted. In some areas, more modern practices were developing. Staff, for instance, had to be able to use telephones.

In the period immediately before the First World War the government faced numerous difficulties on the domestic and foreign fronts. They included disputes over Ireland, militancy among trade unions, protests by suffragettes, and a rise in international military tension. The period 1911–13 seemed to

Leith-Ross at the time to be in perpetual crisis, though in hindsight it was nowhere near as tumultuous as what was to follow. Asquith, Leith-Ross holds, was able to make decisions swiftly but was reluctant to act upon them before consulting senior members of his government. The premier was interested in all areas of policy but did not seek to supplant his Foreign Secretary. His preference was for discussing issues in Cabinet, not using his status to impose a position. A source of strength in such circumstances was that he was the only minister present at Cabinet permitted to make a note of discussion and interpret what the Cabinet had decided. Asquith's secretaries were charged with copying the reports he made of Cabinet meetings for the King: the only record of these discussions. Leith-Ross does not specify what was done with these duplicates – it is doubtful they were circulated to ministers. The secretary's description suggests they were more than simply dry accounts of discussions and conclusions, which later Cabinet minutes became. At times these records probably needed to be persuasive, otherwise the support of the King for more controversial action, for instance, in curbing the powers of the House of Lords through the Parliament Act 1911, might not be guaranteed.

No officials attended Cabinet. Ministers gave oral presentations in which they proposed legislation. The Cabinet then discussed it in principle and reached a general agreement. There was no mechanism for the formal communication of decisions or for seeing they were put into effect. (The senior private secretary was responsible in advance for circulating to Cabinet members notice of its meetings and relevant papers.) Departments consequently had substantial discretion. After reaching a conclusion, Cabinet left the minister concerned to prepare the legislation required and deal with the issues of detail, which in practice permanent civil servants tended to resolve. Officials then presented a final draft for their political chief to approve. Referring to the body he later served in after Lloyd George established it in 1916, Leith-Ross noted that the Cabinet secretariat brought about a radical change in practices.[74]

On 30 March 1975 Giles Pinsent gave us an interview discussing his experiences then six decades before and now a century ago. He provided his recollections of this period during his time as successor to Leith-Ross as the Treasury private secretary in 1913–14. Pinsent seems to have moved into the same room occupied by Leith-Ross, which judging by his description is the space that eventually in the Blair era became the 'den' adjoining the Cabinet room. He had a telephone. He recalled typists worked on the other side. Another match with the Leith-Ross account is that the two other private secretaries had a room each, adjoining, on the other side of the Cabinet room. Occasionally Pinsent went to the House of Commons where Asquith had an office, though Pinsent did not work there.

Pinsent's account suggested that the staff he joined was at a primitive stage of development. It did not even have a clear name. The title that the group of private secretaries and the rooms they were in later acquired – the 'Private Office' – was not yet in use. Pinsent said he did not feel part of a team. He got on with his work himself and dealt directly with the Prime Minister. Pinsent saw Asquith, with whom he sometimes went to a dinner or a garden party, as the boss. When he arrived, there was no written guide to his work though a system of some kind existed, which his predecessor transmitted to him orally.

Pinsent recalled for us his working patterns and duties. Typically his day began at 11 a.m. – though he had to work well into the evening because of late parliamentary sittings. He

---

74   F. Leith-Ross, *Money Talks: Fifty Years of International Finance* (London: Hutchinson, 1968).

handled correspondence and dealt with callers who came into the building. He could help deal with factual queries for the Prime Minister. An important part of Pinsent's work was consulting on the appointment of 'parsons'. He collected letters from and about candidates, considering recommendations. Pinsent canvassed the views of bishops, tending to engage more with those friendly towards Asquith, engendering a bias towards Liberal appointments. An important criterion was matching high and low church appointments to their congregations. Pinsent was an atheist, but saw his lack of faith as an advantage since it gave him an impartial perspective. He would prepare a summary of the case on the outside of an envelope and wait for an opportune moment to present it to Asquith for a decision. The Prime Minister worked in the Cabinet room and Pinsent could listen or look in on him from his office next door. Pinsent found Asquith accessible. He would either make a decision immediately or seek more information, possibly consulting others. Pinsent attended the induction of 'parsons' on behalf of the Prime Minister. He did not deal with the appointment of bishops, which were handled by the other private secretaries. The other main task for Pinsent was dealing with Civil List pensions, which he processed in a similar way as the appointment of churchmen. These pensions were paid to poets, artists, historians and scientists in unfortunate financial circumstances. These tasks might on the surface seem a curious use of the time of a private secretary – who made up a third of the core team of the chief minister in a government – but they involved the patronage role which had been central to the premiership from the early years, when Walpole built his authority through gaining control over the disbursal of favour in its various forms.

Assessing the period

Over the period 1868–1916 aides continued to assist premiers with achieving their basic objectives such as retaining power and furthering their partisan, ideological or personal causes. With prime ministers now 'without portfolio', the extent to which they relied on others within and beyond government had increased. Even more than before, their ability to secure outcomes depended upon exercising influence rather than direct control, of which they had little. For this reason the work of aides, especially private secretaries, primarily involved handling significant individuals and groups: the monarch, ministers, the administrative machine, Parliament, the party, the press and the electorate. The exercise of power by the premier became more remote in another way. Because of successive expansions in the franchise and other related reforms – combined with the restriction of Secret Service funds – the opportunity to substantially influence election outcomes through surreptitious means dwindled. The mass party became ever more important: hence the use of prime-ministerial teams to ensure coordination between different parts of the party, in government, in parliament and nationally.

Among the most regular parts of the work of private secretaries was dealing with correspondence and patronage: both crucial to the management of the premier's relationships and securing the cooperation or acquiescence of those who could be barriers to the achievement of the prime minister's objectives. Direct prime-ministerial policy initiatives were less common than in earlier periods. They still occurred – assisted by aides who might help develop a proposal, or see it carried through Parliament or in international negotiations. When premiers and aides engaged in such exertions, the strain on both could prove immense. Because their offices alone were not suited for such tasks prime ministers, pursuing agendas in this way, might draw on additional informal assistance from beyond their secretariats.

It was possible for prime ministers supported by aides to have a substantial personal impact on policy – for instance for Gladstone with disestablishment of the Irish Church or for Disraeli at the Congress of Berlin. There were limits to what they could achieve. While Gladstone was able to draw up a proposal for Home Rule for Ireland along the lines he favoured using personal aides and excluding Cabinet, for broader political reasons he never saw it implemented. As well as being instruments of prime-ministerial power, aides could be actors in their own right. West, Austin, Acton, and Ponsonby and Nash, all pursued personal agendas but they lacked the personal authority and legitimacy associated with ministers. They were dependent upon the premiers for whom they worked, who in turn were reliant upon others. In this sense staff were two stages removed from the actual site of formal decision-making: the department. There were dangers for aides who created the impression they were overplaying their hand – apparently like Meiklejohn under Asquith. Aides who seemed excessively important – such as Corry or Acton – could generate resentment. Most assistants did not have noticeable policy objectives of their own, being more interested in providing loyal support to a premier and going on to a successful career.

The small size of the prime-ministerial staff in this period may appear puzzling. The most senior politician in the leading industrial and imperial power of the time was supported by a professional secretariat of no more than four and did not head a department. The explanation of this mystery is that prime-ministerial effectiveness came about in part because of the compact nature of the team of aides, not despite it. There were no doubt powerful forces of convention discouraging an expansion in the staff of the premier, but its maintenance at such a low level cannot have been judged intolerable or some effort would have been made to enhance it.

Lean teams had a number of merits. They made it more possible thoroughly to vet all the members for reliability and compatibility. The value placed on recruiting staff prime ministers already knew, or who came on the recommendation of trusted people, is suggested by the preponderance of family members and personal connections in their teams. A full department was less suited to operating in the delicate fashion that was often crucial to the exercise of prime-ministerial power. Personal control of aides was important – and a few aides were easier to manage than many. Another source of strength for a premier was flexibility – the ability to range across government when deemed necessary – calling for a suppleness that a larger more unwieldy group of aides might lack. The need for flexibility seems to have influenced Robert Peel in his decision not to occupy the post of Chancellor of the Exchequer and avoid involvement in the daily running of a 'department'. To replace the Treasury with a large specifically prime-ministerial staff would have been to contradict the logic of Peel's decision and subsequent developments in the office. In 1916 David Lloyd George began to test the limits of the existing model through his expansion and reorganisation at the centre of government, launched in the desperate circumstances of war.

CHAPTER FOUR

AIDES IN WAR AND PEACE, 1916-1945

David Lloyd George came to the premiership in 1916 intent on winning the First World War and ensuring he had the team to help him do so. Possibly the most dramatic set of changes ever in support staff followed. Individually and collectively his aides made an immense impact but ultimately he did not forge them formally into a department of the Prime Minister. Some of the models Lloyd George introduced remain relevant today. After he fell from power in 1922 his successors sought to distance themselves from his approach yet they found some of his methods too valuable to do without. During the 1920s, and sometimes for dubious reasons, the permanent civil service became increasingly prominent within the prime-ministerial staff, marginalising other sources of support. Career officials, remaining in post regardless of changes in incumbency at No. 10, offered many valuable qualities. They provided continuity and were vital if premiers were to prove successful in harnessing the vast Whitehall machine. But when a particular permanent civil servant, Horace Wilson, became too closely associated with an individual Prime Minister, Neville Chamberlain, and his policy of appeasing fascism, problems arose. On his elevation to No. 10 in 1940 Winston Churchill decided the existing civil service set-up could not provide all his requirements, particularly expert advice. The consequent

shake-up in the team supporting the premier resembled that
brought about by his old friend and rival, Lloyd George.

The Lloyd George premiership

On 9 June 1922, towards the end of his almost six-year-long
premiership which finished in October of that year, David
Lloyd George and some of his entourage travelled in a car from
Chequers, the official country residence of the Prime Minister, to
London. The diary of the Cabinet Office official Thomas Jones
records conversation turning to the qualities of politicians. Lloyd
George said that rather than drawing on top-rate 'statesmen' a
Prime Minister should have good 'counsellors' around him. He
felt he could govern the British Empire through a series of aides:
the so-called 'Round Table group', Maurice Hankey and Thomas
Jones from the Cabinet secretariat, Frances Stevenson to identify
untrustworthy characters, and J. T. Davies to handle the press.[75]
Lloyd George's comment, light-hearted though it was in tone,
revealed much about his leadership style. As premier he wanted
a prominent part in many of the key decisions of his government and to reduce the role of its other members. Lloyd George's
personal dynamism and innovative administrative approach were
key parts of the platform on which he rose to the highest office in
December 1916. Once installed at No. 10 the use Lloyd George
made of his staff was a defining feature of his premiership. In
the end, however, his deployment of aides played a part in his
downfall.

As a politician Lloyd George embodied a substantial challenge
to established methods, ideas and structures. His attainment
of prominence from a relatively modest social background, his
political radicalism, and his willingness to stretch or even break

---

75   T. Jones, K. Middlemas (ed.) *Whitehall Diary*, vol. 1, *1916–1925* (Oxford:
     Oxford University Press, 1969), diary entry for 9 June 1922, p. 201.

with the existing party system, all reinforced his challenging approach throughout his public career. This quality made Lloyd George controversial and fascinating to both contemporaries and later observers. It is manifest in his use of aides. Before he became Prime Minister Lloyd George had displayed a proclivity for institutional innovation, including the establishment of an entirely new department, the Ministry of Munitions, and making use of aides drawn from beyond the customary Whitehall circles. At No. 10 the determination of Lloyd George to obtain the support he wanted in the way he wanted, unrestrained by convention, was exhibited again and again.

Lloyd George sought to provide the dynamic war leadership which he believed had been lacking under Asquith. Joseph Davies, an associate of Lloyd George who went on to become a member of the Prime Minister's secretariat, described how since early 1915 Lloyd George had become increasingly discontented with the way in which the Cabinet was directing the war. The procrastination was damaging. Lloyd George grouped the problems into two categories: first, the ungainly size of the Cabinet; second, the impotence of the Prime Minister, who failed either to provide a lead himself or to force Cabinet members to take decisions over urgent issues. Lloyd George resolved he would achieve an ambitious change in the control exerted from the centre and came to power partly because others shared his analysis and saw him as the best person to correct these perceived problems. He took office with the personal desire to take a markedly different approach from that of Asquith, and with an expectation and hope on the part of others he would do so.

Aides played a part in his new way of operating, as demonstrated by David Davies, an MP and close ally of Lloyd George who helped him attain the premiership. As a member of the prime-ministerial entourage Davies took it upon himself to harass the military departments into performing more effectively. He made the mistake of applying his blunt approach to his dealings with the Prime Minister, passing on criticisms that had been made of Lloyd George, and he was ejected from office in mid-1917. The way in which staff such as Davies functioned was important to the changed style of leadership that Lloyd George pursued, but of equal significance was the creation of a radically altered structural framework for aides to operate within.

Institutions

Such was Lloyd George's demand for assistants that he assumed control of already-established staff arrangements and even augmented them. He cared little for the administrative details, but simply wanted people he felt he could rely on to make sure he got what he wanted. During his premiership Lloyd George relied to some extent on existing institutional support-structures. He continued the practice of being assisted by private secretaries, though he was concerned to ensure they operated in the way he desired. Individuals he placed in these posts had close personal links to him. None of Asquith's secretaries was retained. This clear-out was not the severe break with convention it would have been later in the century and the acrimonious circumstances in which Lloyd George succeeded Asquith made continuity of personnel unlikely. But Lloyd George's team was his own to an exceptional degree. He had hand-picked them before he became Prime Minister. None of them could be regarded as a regular career civil servant, and he would probably have sought to take them all with him to the premiership regardless of both what the prevailing norms may have been or the precise way in which he had obtained the office.

Lloyd George's most senior private secretary was John T. Davies. Like many aides to Lloyd George (who sometimes

conversed with his staff in Welsh) he shared the Welsh national-
ity of the Prime Minister. A former school teacher, he had been
private secretary to Lloyd George as Chancellor of the Exchequer
(1912–15, a post held by Lloyd George from 1908), Minister of
Munitions (1915–16) and as Secretary of State for War (1916).
He remained with Lloyd George until 1922, when he was made
a director of the Suez Canal Company. Davies worked in an
office adjoining the Cabinet room on the St James's Park side.
Another private secretary, Frances Stevenson, who became tutor
to Lloyd George's daughter Megan in 1911, was based in the
office next to the other side of the Cabinet room. Stevenson was
Lloyd George's mistress and later his wife, and continued to
support him for the rest of his life. Correspondence between the
two illustrates the sometimes confusing dissolution of boundaries
between different categories of relationship which can occur in
dealings between prime ministers and aides. Lloyd George signed
off one letter, from August 1918, 'Father lover & husband all in
one'. Stevenson describes him in July of the following year as 'my
father & lover & brother & friend'. The previous October Lloyd
George played on the complex quality of their relationship with
a mock introduction of boundaries, insisting he was not writing a
love letter but a 'business communication or rather a minute from
a Chief to his Secretary'.[76]

The third member of Lloyd George's initial team of private
secretaries, William Sutherland, had first assisted Lloyd George
at the Board of Trade, when he was President (1905–8). He had
moved with Lloyd George to the Treasury in 1908, becoming a
private secretary to the Chancellor of the Exchequer and following

76   A. Taylor (ed.), *My Darling Pussy: The Letters of Lloyd George and Frances
      Stevenson, 1913–41* (London: Weidenfeld and Nicolson, 1975), Lloyd
      George to Stevenson, early August 1918, p. 23; Stevenson to Lloyd George,
      10 July 1919, p. 29; Lloyd George to Stevenson, 5 October 1918, p. 25.

him through his later posts. Sutherland was nicknamed 'Bronco Bill' and became notorious for his involvement in briefing the press and the distribution of honours as a means of fundraising. In the latter function he collaborated with Freddie Guest, the Liberal Chief Whip, and the intermediary figure, Maundy Gregory. Gregory operated during successive governments and became in 1933 the only person prosecuted to date under the Honours (Prevention of Abuses Act) 1925. In 1918 Sutherland became an MP and Lloyd George's Parliamentary Private Secretary. His replacement in his previous post was Ernest Evans, who was in turn succeeded in 1920 by Geoffrey Shakespeare. Our interview with Shakespeare gave a vivid account of the varied duties of the work of the private secretary. They included helping write speeches, conveying messages and helping Lloyd George to relax. On a regular working day Shakespeare, under the direction of John T. Davies, would brief a succession of journalists individually between five and seven o'clock in the evening. He would hint, suggest, and convey the atmosphere and the general position, trying to steer them in certain directions – but resist answering direct questions. A less regular role Shakespeare described was acting as an envoy for Lloyd George in the negotiation of an Irish peace treaty, including a secret trip to Ulster. In 1921 Lloyd George recruited from the Cabinet secretariat A. J. Sylvester, prized for his stenographic and typing skills. Sylvester was the only private secretary to remain at No. 10 after the departure of Lloyd George, serving Bonar Law and Baldwin before leaving to rejoin the former Prime Minister in opposition in mid-1923.

Alongside the use of the existing model of private secretaries, considerable administrative change took place in prime-ministerial support-structures in two ways: the establishment of the War Cabinet secretariat and of the Prime Minister's

secretariat. The first followed Lloyd George's decision to establish a small War Cabinet to achieve streamlined decision-making.
He attached to the War Cabinet a secretariat, responsible for
preparing the Cabinet agenda, arranging its meetings, obtaining and circulating relevant papers in advance, producing the
Cabinet minutes, and communicating decisions to departments.
The first home of this secretariat was 2 Whitehall Gardens,
across Whitehall from Downing Street. It was an extension of
the staff which had performed the same role in supporting the
Committee of Imperial Defence (CID) from its formal creation
in 1904. Maurice Hankey, previously a Royal Marine artillery
officer and Secretary of the CID since 1912, became Secretary
of the War Cabinet upon its establishment, supported initially
by ten assistant secretaries. Hankey was influential in Lloyd
George's decision to establish both the War Cabinet and the
new secretariat. During the course of the Lloyd George premiership this secretariat developed into the Cabinet Office. Hankey
became the first Cabinet Secretary in 1919 and remained in the
post until he retired in 1938.

Before the establishment of the secretariat the existing practice
was that, though papers might be circulated in advance, the only
written record of Cabinet meetings was the letter from the Prime
Minister to the monarch, providing an account of proceedings –
an arrangement that could lead to confusion as to what precisely
had been agreed. Because it facilitated the establishment of a new
formalised system of Cabinet government, the secretariat was of
considerable significance. It is an irony that such an important
systemisation of government should have been willed by an individual as chaotic in his personal methods as Lloyd George. He is
notorious for not being able to function within the confines of
any kind of structure nor even keep track of his own paperwork.
Hankey witnessed this characteristic of Lloyd George, noting

how he discussed 'every subject under the sun except what is on the agenda'.[77]

The secretariat had a further impact that extended beyond the way the government operated. While the War Cabinet secretariat was not specifically a policy-forming body, it could act as convenor and distiller of ideas, as demonstrated by an achievement early on in its existence. By 11 February 1917, after extensive consultation within Whitehall, Hankey completed for Lloyd George an important memorandum. It presented the case in favour of using convoys to protect supply ships against submarine attacks. Hankey had obtained the views of younger staff within the navy who did not share the opinion of senior admirals that such an approach was impracticable. This new idea became policy.

In as far as the Prime Minister was the chair (and dominant member) of the War Cabinet, the secretariat was partly a support mechanism for the premier. Sylvester, who worked under Hankey before becoming private secretary to Lloyd George, described how the work of the secretariat and No. 10 blended into each other during this period. Individual members of the secretariat became in practice important aides to Lloyd George. They included Hankey and another senior member of the team, Thomas Jones. Hankey helped the Prime Minister in numerous ways, such as discussing government appointments. With the return to full Cabinet after the war, Hankey facilitated 'Conferences of Ministers' which excluded certain Cabinet members. The dual task of providing support to the collective and to the premier could produce strains. Hankey found himself in a problematic position when Lloyd George told him to restrict the availability

---

77   J. Naylor, *A Man and an Institution: Sir Maurice Hankey, the Cabinet Secretariat and the Custody of Cabinet Secrecy* (Cambridge: Cambridge University Press, 1984), p. 51. See also: G. Jones and J. Burnham 'Innovators at 10 Downing Street'.

of information to ministers, who regularly complained to him about being kept in the dark over some matters.

The relationship of the War Cabinet secretariat to the premiership could be ambiguous but Lloyd George created another new body which explicitly supported him alone: the Prime Minister's secretariat. Vaughan Nash, who had been a private secretary to both Campbell-Bannerman and Asquith, provided advice that helped bring about the establishment of this institution. On 15 December 1916 Thomas Jones, who was helping establish administrative arrangements for the new Prime Minister, noted having had a useful conversation with Nash that morning about secretaries to the premier. Nash described the many tasks that had to be carried out on behalf of a premier and suggested the establishment of a small secretariat with a significant figure heading it. Jones arranged for Nash to brief Hankey on these issues on the telephone.[78]

Once established early in 1917, the base of the Prime Minister's secretariat was a collection of huts on the lawn at the back of Downing Street; it was nicknamed the 'Garden Suburb'. Staff members were responsible for overseeing particular policy areas and the departments responsible for them, and briefing the Prime Minister. Their functions included helping develop policy, chasing the implementation of decisions, assisting Lloyd George with speeches and maintaining contact with the press. Initially it was intended they would be responsible for the regular gathering of information, but this function was attached to the War Cabinet secretariat. In a paper from March 1918 by the head of the Garden Suburb, W. G. S. Adams showed a motive for its formation was the desire to achieve an active policy-forming premiership. The Garden Suburb had a role in the numerous

---

78   Jones, Middlemas (ed.) *Whitehall Diary*, vol. 1, 1916–1925, pp. 15–6.

areas where the Prime Minister was taking a lead. When he was working out the general outline of a programme, he wished to have different features of it considered and worked through. A function of the Garden Suburb was either to carry out the development of his ideas or at least maintain contact with those in the departments responsible for the task.[79]

A total of six people worked in the Garden Suburb over the course of its existence.[80] Adams, the 'Principal Secretary', was a social statistician and Gladstone Professor at Oxford. He founded the *Political Quarterly* journal, later relaunched in the 1930s, and he would later help establish the Politics, Philosophy and Economics course. He shadowed the Irish Office and the Ministry of Food. Philip Kerr was a protégé of the Unionist War Cabinet member Lord Milner and editor of the *Round Table* journal. Kerr was responsible for Foreign Office, Colonial Office and India Office business. David Davies was a wealthy industrialist and Liberal MP. He handled military issues, the War Office and the Admiralty, before leaving in June 1917. Waldorf Astor was the millionaire owner of the *Observer* newspaper, a Unionist MP, associate of the Round Table group and husband of the first female MP, Nancy. His areas of interest were the liquor control board, public health and local government. Astor acted as Parliamentary Private Secretary to Lloyd George. Joseph Davies was an expert on statistics, concentrating on mines, railways and shipping. He was a Liberal Lloyd George supporter. In May 1917 Cecil Harmsworth joined the secretariat. He became the replacement for David Davies. The younger brother of Lords Northcliffe and Rothermere, he was elected a Liberal Imperialist MP in

---

79   'Proposed Statement by Prof. Adams', 7 March 1918, Parliamentary Archives, Lloyd George Papers, LG/F/74/10/4.

80   The definitive work on this subject is: J. Turner, *Lloyd George's Secretariat* (Cambridge: Cambridge University Press, 1980).

1906. Harmsworth oversaw for Lloyd George the Ministry of Munitions, Ministry of National Service and the Labour departments. The Garden Suburb was wound down at the end of the war and only one of its advisers, Kerr, was kept on. Kerr's 1921 replacement was Edward Grigg, who remained in post until 1922.

As a newcomer to government the Garden Suburb was a potential subject of resentment because of its potential to upset established practices and relationships. Adams was keen to deny this possibility had become a reality. In his March 1918 paper he insisted that relations with Whitehall departments had been relaxed and informal. The Garden Suburb, Adams stressed, had not become a barrier between ministers and the Prime Minister and facilitated contact when necessary. Adams knew of no case, he claimed, of abuse of the confidence that existed between members of the secretariat and the departments. A less harmonious view of relations with the departments emerged from the account of another Garden Suburb member, Joseph Davies. In April 1917 he recorded how, after the War Cabinet had accepted a policy on wheat imports proposed in a paper prepared by the Garden Suburb, various departments called the secretariat about the intrusion into their remit that had taken place. At the time Davies noted Adams was concerned because in his view British government departments were powerful enough to bring down a minister or even a Prime Minister. This proposition proved to have some substance as Lloyd George's bypassing of the Foreign Office eventually helped destroy his government.[81] Some regular civil servants resented the staffing of the Garden Suburb by aides drawn from outside the administrative machine. In January 1917, having advocated that Adams become head of the Garden Suburb, Thomas Jones felt shunned for some days in the War

---

81   J. Davies, *The Prime Minister's Secretariat* (Newport: R. J. Johns, 1951), pp. 102–4.

Cabinet secretariat, speculating as to whether it was because of his supporting Adams rather than an inside appointment.

Did this collection of individuals have a substantial impact upon the course of the Lloyd George government? Discussion of this question often centres on the role of the Round Table group and the circle of Lord Milner, with which Astor, Kerr and Grigg were associated. The particular goal associated with the Round Table was federation of the British Empire. Kerr had been part of the group of young men, known informally as his Kindergarten, surrounding Lord Milner when he was British High Commissioner in South Africa (1897–1905). Portrayals of Milner after his return to Britain have him as the leading figure in a school of thought labelled social imperialism, which advocated welfare reform and the reinvigoration of the empire. The presence of Astor and Kerr within the Garden Suburb has figured in discussions about the extent to which the Lloyd George coalition – which included Milner as a member of the War Cabinet – should be regarded as social-imperialist in nature.[82]

Prime ministers have long been in contact with groups similar to the Round Table and the individuals within them. Richard Price, a member of the Bowood Group, advised Lord Shelburne, on whom Bowood was centred, and later William Pitt the Younger. Increasingly during the course of the twentieth and twenty-first centuries prime ministers recruited aides who were connected with think tanks, of which the Round Table can be seen as an early incarnation. That premiers should seek the support of particular people indicates they regard their contributions as in some way worthwhile, and it is possible those individuals will

---

82   J. Turner, 'The Formation of Lloyd George's "Garden Suburb": "Fabian-like Milnernite Penetration"?', *The Historical Journal*, 20, I (1977); R. Scally, *The Origins of Lloyd George's Coalition: The Politics of Social Imperialism 1900–1918* (Princeton: Princeton University Press, 1975).

go on to influence the course of government in accordance with their predilections. At the same time it is stretching plausibility that premiers would allow themselves to be captured by any particular agenda-driven group; the process of policy formation and implementation is too complex to be attributed wholly to a particular input from one or two aides at No. 10.

Although the influence of the Garden Suburb should not be overstated, it had specific impacts on policy. Adams helped establish the Irish Convention in 1917, which worked to achieve agreement in Ireland by acting as a contact between the chair of the Convention and Lloyd George. When the Convention failed in 1918, his importance diminished. Kerr contributed to the development of Lloyd George's ideological posture in the conflict with Germany. David Davies sought to inject greater efficiency into the war effort, though he became frustrated with a lack of progress. The Garden Suburb, John Turner found, promoted more cooperation across Whitehall, then a novel idea, and generally helped manage the complex and unfamiliar business of war. Turner concludes that while the Garden Suburb may have created the impression of a body intended to help Lloyd George operate as an 'omniscient dictator', a group of five relatively 'junior' staff supported only by 'clerks and typists' and lacking in 'executive authority' could not fulfil such a role. The true function was to help shore up the political position of the Prime Minister. Lloyd George, whose own Liberal Party was divided, depended on a coalition for parliamentary support. The Garden Suburb spent a large portion of time handling 'administrative' issues of a 'politically sensitive' nature that touched the 'special interests' of unpredictable parliamentary groupings, and Kerr devoted much effort to seeking support from the 'wider public'.[83]

---

83   Turner, *Lloyd George's Secretariat*, pp. 2–7; 191–2.

Adams hoped the Garden Suburb was an embryo for an even more dramatic administrative innovation. On 2 January 1917 the draft of a letter for distribution within Whitehall announcing the formation of what was eventually labelled the Prime Minister's secretariat (or Garden Suburb) was produced. It stated that the Prime Minister had decided to form a 'secretariat' connected to the office of the First Lord of the Treasury. The copy of this note in Adams's file in the Lloyd George papers is amended by hand, it can be supposed that of Adams, so that 'secretariat' reads 'department'. Private secretaries throughout the government received the changed version, which used the word 'department' twice in place of 'secretariat', on 5 January.[84]

Adams might have believed he had been successful in his attempt to describe his new body as a department. Many in Whitehall would have regarded such a move as constitutionally inappropriate and a threat to existing ministries, whose political heads might have been uneasy. As a consequence of such concerns the name eventually settled upon was 'secretariat'. On 10 January 1917 *The Times* reported that the Prime Minister had decided to establish an 'Intelligence Department at 10, Downing Street' that might eventually develop into a 'definite Prime Minister's department' responsible for coordinating the activities of the Whitehall departments. *The Times* then began to take a different tack, presumably following a changed briefing line from the government. In an article of 15 January it noted this body did not amount to a 'new department'. The Garden Suburb would have no impact upon the regular activities of the civil service; it would instead act as a 'clearing house' for the business of the departments, not as the 'super-department' some might perceive. For a short time

---

84   Lloyd George Papers, LG/F/74/2/3.

the Garden Suburb had been officially a 'department', though formally attached to the First Lord of the Treasury rather than the Prime Minister.

Simply describing the Garden Suburb as a department, though significant, was not sufficient to establish a fully-blown office of state. For Adams the Garden Suburb could be a stage in the development of a more substantial body of support for the Prime Minister. His March 1918 paper on the body he ran was a draft statement to an inquiry conducted by the Liberal politician and intellectual Lord (Richard) Haldane into the machinery of government. Adams stated he saw the Garden Suburb as a hesitant first step towards an outcome he felt was essential both because government was becoming more complex and the task of the premier more demanding. He noted the existence of a longstanding view among observers of central government – including himself – that there was a need for a 'Prime Minister's department'. Adams argued it should include the whips and a general intelligence staff liaising with other Whitehall departments and making suggestions to them and the Prime Minister, seeking both to create new policy ideas and improve the efficiency and organisation of the administrative machine. The entity Adams favoured would not be a body with executive powers of intervention across government, but would be intended to 'draw together for the Prime Minister the threads of the Administration'. It would not be large and would have close personal contact with the Prime Minister. It would assist him in overlooking all of government. Adams seems at first to have persuaded Haldane's committee of the value of his proposal. But – probably under the influence of Hankey, who took an opposing view – the position changed.

The final Report on the Machinery of Government by the Reconstruction Committee of the Cabinet, known as the Haldane

Report, appeared in 1918.[85] Haldane is celebrated for its advocacy of 'the duty of investigation and thought, as preliminary to action' in civil government, a statement that, in the decades that followed, came to be revered in Whitehall. A draft version of Haldane included further recommendations that might have become equally noteworthy, but were removed, perhaps because of internal objections. This earlier text, included in the Lloyd George papers, calls for the establishment of a new entity at the centre of government. It could be made directly answerable to the Prime Minister and labelled the 'Prime Minister's department', or to the Cabinet, and known as the 'Cabinet department'. Notably the term 'Prime Minister's department' not 'Cabinet department' was used thereafter, possibly suggesting the former was the favoured option of the authors at this point.

The paper argued the new body should have at least two functions. First was resolving territorial disputes between departments. Second was communicating to them both the broad outlines of Cabinet policy and specific decisions with implications for more than one ministry, to ensure a concerted effort to execute them. Further possible tasks were to exercise control of the civil service, and to supervise the organisation of the departments, including personnel policy. If all these functions were entrusted to the new entity, it ought to be organised on the standard model for a Whitehall department, with a Permanent Under-Secretary who ranked alongside the highest in the civil service using sufficient high-grade officials made wholly available to him. A 'Board of Efficiency and Economy' including Whitehall insiders and individuals drawn from the private sector would provide advice. The Civil Service Commission would become

---

85   Cd.9230.

subordinate to or part of the department. Finally there would be a 'Standing Consultative Committee' of all the Whitehall permanent secretaries to arbitrate in demarcation disputes and communicate lines of policy to ministers.[86]

This set of changes would have created a more interventionist Prime Minister's Office, driving policy and management from the centre. The threat to various departmental and ministerial interests – and perhaps even collective Cabinet government itself – was clear. Opponents in Parliament no doubt would have considered the innovation an unwelcome or sinister development. The British constitution would have taken a different historical path. But the final Haldane report was silent about how the Prime Minister specifically should be supported, simply recommending that peacetime Cabinets – which it held ought to be smaller in size than had been standard practice before the war – should continue to have the support of a secretary, as Lloyd George had introduced when he became premier in 1916. Ultimately, though it was briefly flirted with, a department of the Prime Minister did not appear.

Philip Kerr (1882–1940)

A student of history when at New College, Oxford, Kerr was interested in intellectual concepts and high ideals rather than the less reputable end of politics, though his experience of journalism had honed his propaganda skills. Kerr was crucial to the efforts of the Prime Minister to exert his authority over foreign policy, helping him consider issues strategically. His role produced resentment. Winston Churchill, as Secretary of State for War, complained in 1920 that Lloyd George had taken over the work of the Foreign Office with the help of Kerr, and that Kerr did

---

86   Ministry of Reconstruction, *Report on the Machinery of Government Committee*, draft report, pp. 24–5.

not have the status required to fulfil his role appropriately.[87] In a note of November 1922 Lord Curzon, the Foreign Secretary since 1919, denounced Kerr as having acted as a 'Second Foreign Office'.[88] Kerr contributed to the development of policy and its public presentation: two tasks which often cannot fully be separated. He acted as a personal diplomat for No. 10. Just as Kerr was important to the Prime Minister, working for Lloyd George was a turning point in Kerr's life. Kerr described his period at No. 10 as when he 'was almost as close to the centre of world affairs as it was possible for a man to be'.[89] Though Kerr had previously considered becoming a Unionist parliamentary candidate, the admiration he developed for Lloyd George when working at the Garden Suburb prompted a shift in his allegiance to the Liberal Party. He demonstrated how working for a Prime Minister could be an early stage in an even more successful career. In covering external policy for Lloyd George, Kerr tended to concern himself with the overall sweep rather than focusing on particular technical details, and took in areas which included imperial issues, relations with the US and Europe. He also considered Ireland. Alongside policy advice, presentation was important to his work. He helped draft speeches for Lloyd George and wrote articles anonymously for the *Round Table*, the journal associated with the Milner group which Kerr had edited before the war. Kerr edited with Adams the War Cabinet Report of 1917, an official account of how the government was handling the conflict, and

---

87   K. Morgan, *Consensus and Disunity*, p. 112.
88   Reproduced in J. Turner and M. Dockrill, 'Philip Kerr and 10 Downing Street, 1916–1921' in J. Turner (ed.), *The Larger Idea: Lord Lothian and the Problem of National Sovereignty* (London: The Historians' Press, 1988), p. 33.
89   Reproduced in J. Turner, *Lloyd George's Secretariat*, p. 60. This work, along with that cited immediately above, is the secondary source drawn on most heavily for this account of Kerr as aide to Lloyd George. See also: A. May, 'Kerr, Philip Henry, eleventh marquess of Lothian', *ODNB*.

its 1918 successor. Occasionally Kerr acted as a go-between with foreign states on behalf of Lloyd George. In July 1920 he had personal contact about Ireland with Colonel E. M. House, a man who performed a similar role as an aide to President Woodrow Wilson (although Wilson was more dependent upon House than Lloyd George ever was on a single assistant).

Kerr's precise personal impact is difficult to disentangle. Sometimes when involved in explaining policy, this activity could shape the way it was formed and the framework within which it played out. A particular submission to Lloyd George might represent Kerr's personal views but at the same time it could amount to a version of what he believed the Prime Minister wanted to hear. Usually in any given area many advisers expressed some similar views, of which Kerr's was only one. Yet it is reasonable to state Kerr was a significant influence on the development of war aims. He promoted to Lloyd George the idea of a peace founded in democracy and without annexations. A key moment for Kerr came as one of Lloyd George's most important aides at the 1919 Paris peace conference. Among other contributions he wrote the phrase 'by the aggression of Germany and her allies' into Article 231 of the Versailles treaty, which became known as the 'war guilt' clause. However, some of Kerr's attempts to influence policy failed. He worked for the 1917 Imperial War Conference to become a basis for a more integrated empire, but there was resistance from the Dominions, scuppering the plan – a failure for the Round Table programme.

Working for Lloyd George strained Kerr and he left in 1921 to become managing editor of the *Daily Chronicle*. We heard from staff working for prime ministers during this period that not until 1930, with the recruitment of Robert Vansittart from the Foreign Office as Principal Private Secretary, did an aide provide for such an active involvement in foreign affairs by the premiership. Kerr, who was from 1930 the eleventh Marquess of Lothian, went on to become a prominent advocate of world federalism, presenting Anglo-American integration as the crucial first step. His ideas were eventually influential with proponents of European integration, though their focus was more continental than Atlanticist. Kerr became associated, like other former Lloyd George aides including Astor and Thomas Jones, and like Lloyd George himself, with the movement in favour of the appeasement of Nazism. Though he was the author of the crucial war guilt clause contained within it he came to view the terms of the Versailles Treaty as excessively harsh towards Germany. Kerr subsequently reversed his position on how to handle Hitler. He became ambassador to the US in 1939 immediately before the conflict with Germany began. His time in this pivotal role was short. Though he had originally planned to become a Roman Catholic priest Kerr subsequently converted to Christian Science. He died in December 1940 after acquiring an infection for which his religious beliefs prohibited treatment.

Personality and power

Lloyd George deployed his assistants both as an expression and means of implementing his forceful individual will across government and beyond. At the same time, in employing an increased number of aides on an extended array of duties he expanded the premiership, threatening to dilute his individual presence within it. There was something of a desire within the Lloyd George team to moderate this tendency and ensure as far as possible that his staff amplified his personal role rather than smothered it. Adams noted in his March 1918 description of the Garden Suburb that it had deliberately been kept small to retain 'close personal touch with the Prime Minister'. Members were able to develop familiarity with the outlook of the Prime Minister and the course his thinking followed. It functioned in such a way as to bring urgent issues to the attention of the Prime Minister but avoid overloading him.

Lloyd George himself had various techniques intended to ensure his team remained under his personal control, performing in the way he wanted, rather than according to institutional dynamics that might not suit him. He worked his aides hard. Geoffrey Shakespeare described to us the dynamism of Lloyd George, his restlessness, and his lack of concern for the feelings of his aides. But at the same time, Shakespeare added, he could show gratitude and was 'terrific fun'. Shakespeare's experience was typical of Lloyd George aides. Members of his staff found themselves moving in and out of favour, being variously flattered or derided in staged displays of rage. The division of functions within the team was not always clear and subject to change. Sometimes the same task was given to different people without them knowing each was working on it. Lloyd George's methods contributed to a rivalry within his team sufficiently intense to outlive him. When interviewed half a century later, Sylvester complained to us that Stevenson was inefficient, did nothing at Versailles; an important purpose was for her to 'fuss around' Lloyd George. Furthermore, Sylvester believed Shakespeare – who 'swanned around' – was employed to please his father, an ally of Lloyd George. In handling his staff the overall purpose of Lloyd George – and he was conscious of what he was doing – was to create loyalty to him, by injecting insecurity and competition, ultimately to ensure that work was carried out in the way he wanted. Lloyd George avoided being distracted by work generated by his aides by focusing on one issue at a time, to the exclusion of all else, frustrating staff who sought to engage him elsewhere.

How far did aides to Lloyd George facilitate his exercise of power? They helped ensure that the body he chaired, the War

Cabinet, and later the regular Cabinet, functioned more effectively than Asquith's Cabinet, which lacked a secretariat. Staff
facilitated prime-ministerial involvement in or even dominance
over policy, as at the Paris peace conference. It could be argued
the way Lloyd George used his assistants contributed to successful outcomes, most notably victory in the First World War. Aides
helped Lloyd George manage a precarious coalition government
long beyond the end of the conflict which first prompted its
formation. Although they helped Lloyd George achieve certain
desired objectives over the course of his premiership, his staff
came increasingly to be associated with difficulties. They were a
component in a leadership style that provoked resentment and
may have led to problematic policy decisions such as support for
Greece in its conflict with Turkey in 1922. Aides were involved
in controversial activities, including the sale of honours. These
difficulties undermined the position of Lloyd George within and
beyond the government, contributing ultimately to his downfall.

Contemporaries portrayed the Lloyd George approach to the
premiership – and the role of staff within it – in dramatic terms.
In an article for the *Nation* that appeared in October 1920[90]
the socialist political-scientist Harold Laski argued that under
Lloyd George the premier had come to resemble more the US
President than the chair of a collective body. A system of 'personal
government' was in operation, with other ministers reduced to
subordinates. Aides figured prominently in Laski's thesis. The
Prime Minister required a means of monitoring and limiting
the departments, and the Prime Minister's secretariat provided
just that. While Laski conceded the introduction of a support
body for the premier, helping sift material, had been a desirable
development, Lloyd George directed it towards a more complex

---

90   H. Laski, 'Mr George and the Constitution', *Nation*, 23 October 1920,
      pp. 124–6.

purpose. The staff liaised with the press, manipulating public opinion through ambiguous briefings. They enabled the premier to maintain contact with public opinion and acted as intermediaries with members of the government. While the Garden Suburb had not officially replaced the Cabinet, it had taken on such an important role within government as to diminish the usefulness of the Cabinet. Laski depicted the media work of Sutherland as providing public exposure to compensate for Lloyd George's infrequent appearances in the House of Commons. This account of the Lloyd George approach to the premiership was indicative of an impression formed more widely among politicians and observers. They felt the Prime Minister had followed a path that was inappropriate and even constitutionally illegitimate; as a consequence Lloyd George's successors were eager to distance themselves from his methods, including his use of assistants.

Post-Lloyd George arrangements

After a premier as assertive as Lloyd George the time was ripe for a less forceful approach. But changes of style are not always matched fully by transformations of substance.

The Prime Minister who followed Lloyd George, Andrew Bonar Law (1922–3) took a less dynamic, more inclusive approach to the role, as did Law's successor, Stanley Baldwin (1923–4, and again 1924–9 and 1935–7). This shift was both a particular reaction against the methods of Lloyd George and the expression of a more general desire to revert to arrangements in place before the First World War.

Law sought to provide not just a different tone. In his election address of October 1922 he promised a structural transformation, singling out the administrative innovations of Lloyd George and calling for change at the centre of government. He proposed abolition of the Cabinet Office in the form that it existed, with the Treasury, the traditional central department in Whitehall, taking on its essential functions. Law had already transferred responsibility for the League of Nations to the Foreign Office, and in future he intended the Foreign Office to be responsible for arranging international conferences, even if the Prime Minister were attending them.

In applauding this speech *The Times* argued that of all the innovations of the Lloyd George government none was harder to justify than the introduction of the Cabinet secretariat. It had become in practice a 'prime-ministerial department', separate from, or even subverting, established practices and safeguards of the constitution. Yet less than four years previously, in December 1918, the same publication had expressed the view that Lloyd George's changes at the centre of government, including the introduction of a War Cabinet secretariat and what could be termed, as *The Times* put it, a 'Prime Minister's Department', that is the Garden Suburb, were so useful as to be indispensable. This earlier view proved to be partly correct, despite the efforts under Law to restore an earlier order. Ultimately Law scaled down the Cabinet Office substantially, but did not merge it into the Treasury. Why did the Cabinet Office persist? First Hankey fought well to keep his independence. Second the institution of which he was head was useful. The coordination it provided could be valuable to any government. Since it was attached to the Cabinet as a whole, it was not only a tool for a centralising premier. Indeed, it represented an institutionalisation of collective government, creating in a sense a bias against prime-ministerial government. Some in No. 10 were suspicious of a Cabinet Office attempt to absorb them, and for this reason preferred to retain their traditional formal classification as part of the Treasury.

There are further reasons to qualify the impression, which Law sought to convey, of a break with the Lloyd George premiership.

All but one of the Garden Suburb – Kerr, succeeded by Grigg – had left Whitehall following the end of the war. In not persisting with this arrangement Law was merely shedding one aide rather than the full team that had operated earlier in Lloyd George's tenure. Beyond the limited nature of the structural changes there was some continuity of personnel. One private secretary to Lloyd George, Sylvester, stayed on for a time until he rejoined his old chief in opposition. Hankey remained an important provider of support to prime ministers, alongside his duties to Cabinet as a whole. His career merits consideration. Despite Law's initial attacks on the Cabinet Office, Hankey soon established good relations with the new premier, similar to those he had enjoyed with Lloyd George, but he failed to form a close relationship with Baldwin. But even when he did not click with a particular premier, his role meant he still had regular – probably daily – access to discuss Cabinet business. In 1924 after initial concerns Hankey quickly decided he liked Ramsay MacDonald, who insisted on preserving the Cabinet Office and retaining its secretary. The tasks Hankey performed for MacDonald included advising him on Cabinet-formation after the general election success achieved by the National government in 1931. After his retirement, Hankey served in Neville Chamberlain's War Cabinet and as a minister under Churchill, who removed him after a disagreement in 1942.

Perhaps the most incongruous survivor of all from the Lloyd George era was Thomas Jones, whose personal attachment to Lloyd George did not stop him providing support to successive prime ministers that extended beyond his more regular Cabinet Office functions.

Thomas Jones (1870–1955)
Thomas Jones was a small man nicknamed 'the microbe', partly as a reflection of his ability to infiltrate. Jones was not a self-publicist

but his biographer, weighing his educational, philanthropic and administrative contributions, describes him as one of the three greatest Welshmen in public life in the twentieth century, in the company of Lloyd George and Aneurin Bevan.[91] Born in Rhymni, Monmouthshire, Jones graduated with a degree in economics from Glasgow University. In 1909 he became Professor of Political Economy at Queen's University, Belfast, returning to Wales in the following year. Jones was present in London to help Lloyd George gain power in 1916 and was appointed to the War Cabinet secretariat. Jones records telling Hankey that rather than being involved in the machinery of government he preferred the idea of being 'a fluid person moving about among people who mattered' and ensuring Lloyd George remained on the correct course as far as possible.[92]

Jones's formal position was as assistant and subsequently deputy secretary to Hankey, with responsibility for domestic affairs. Alongside the duties these positions entailed, which included minuting meetings of Cabinet and its committees, Jones became, in practice, an aide to not only Lloyd George but a further three prime ministers – Law, Baldwin and MacDonald, covering in total three different political parties. Among No. 10 staff we spoke to from the time there was a perception that he was an ambitious individual who sought to be retained. His role often included acting as a liaison with different groups, helping prepare speeches and advising on ministerial appointments. In working for all prime ministers he sought to promote what he saw as moral causes, such as the needs of those further down the social scale with whom his background gave him familiarity.

---

91   E. Ellis, *T. J.: A Life of Dr Thomas Jones, CH* (Cardiff: University of Wales Press, 1992), p. 539.

92   Jones, Middlemas (ed.) *Whitehall Diary*, vol. 1, diary entry for 12 December 1916, p. 15. See generally: R. Lowe, 'Jones, Thomas', *ODNB*.

Under Lloyd George Jones was the senior British official in talks, both official and informal, which eventually culminated in the Anglo-Irish Treaty of 1921. In this period Jones became involved with party-political business, for instance investigating Lloyd George's political prospects should he withdraw from the coalition. Jones was one of the aides with whom Lloyd George could speak Welsh, a technique that proved useful for confidential discussions. On 19 October 1922 the Conservative parliamentary party voted to end the coalition government. When Lloyd George saw Jones he said to him 'Rhyddid', meaning 'freedom'.[93] Their association continued long after Lloyd George's spell at No. 10 and Jones's career in Whitehall. Jones subsequently produced the first biography of Lloyd George, published in 1951.[94]

Initially Jones thought he was headed for the Board of Trade in October 1922 but on the 30th of that month the new Prime Minister, Law, summoned Jones to meet him in the Cabinet room, informing him that he wanted his services as an aide. The incoming premier seems not to have regarded the connection with Lloyd George as a problem but instead an advantage since it gave Law access to knowledge of how the previous Prime Minister had operated. Nor did Baldwin regard the Lloyd George attachment as ruling out Jones as an aide in 1923. Indeed it may have been a source of attraction for the new premier. Baldwin had an 'obsession' with Lloyd George and quizzed Jones about him. The importance of Jones increased over that of Hankey, who did not establish a rapport with Baldwin. There is no evidence of overt conflict between the two Cabinet Office officials, but comment appeared in the press about their shifting fortunes under Baldwin. Generally Law and Baldwin probably regarded Jones as useful

---

93   Jones, Middlemas (ed.) *Whitehall Diary*, vol. 1, diary entry for 19 October 1922, p. 212.
94   T. Jones, *Lloyd George* (Oxford University Press, Oxford, 1951).

because he had a range of contacts and an outlook different from other aides available to them; he was discreet and understood how the government machine worked.

Law apparently had wanted to move Jones into No. 10 and have him as an aide in the Kerr or Grigg model (calling further into question his supposed rejection of the methods of Lloyd George). But Jones opted to continue to be based in the Cabinet Office. He helped with prime-ministerial speeches, including those Baldwin (who felt Jones had a winning way with phrases) gave advocating tariff reform during the 1923 general election campaign, an idea to which Jones was personally opposed. Jones had to adapt to different prime-ministerial styles of working. Law baffled Jones because, when preparing for speeches, he did not write anything down. The Prime Minister explained to his aide that he arranged the order in his mind. Witnesses told us that Baldwin, by contrast, sometimes had Jones write speeches for him.

Staff working at No. 10 remarked in our interviews that, while Jones was personally inclined towards Labour, he did not get on with MacDonald as well as with the other premiers he served. While Law and Baldwin were comfortable with Jones's past service, MacDonald, who first became Prime Minister in 1924, was suspicious of someone who had been able to serve Lloyd George, Law and Baldwin, and he did not draw on Jones as other prime ministers had done. From August of 1924 the Labour government became embroiled in the so-called 'Campbell case'. This political affair centred on doubts about the part the government had played in the decision not to prosecute J. R. Campbell, editor of the *Workers' Weekly*. Campbell had run a message from Communist International to members of the British armed forces which arguably encouraged them to mutiny. At one point there seemed to be a danger MacDonald would make Jones a scapegoat, for supposedly producing an inaccurate Cabinet minute, to

distance himself from the controversy. When Baldwin returned to
No. 10 in 1924 Jones took on a political-assistance function once
again. He was a channel of communication for Baldwin with the
trade unions around the time of the General Strike of 1926. Jones
became closer to MacDonald following his return to office in
1929, but in 1930 he left office to concentrate on philanthropic
concerns. He maintained frequent contact with Baldwin and
worked on Baldwin's speeches for the 1935 general election.

Aides under the Conservatives, 1920s–1930s

In the 1920s Conservative prime ministers received support from
a sophisticated team that connected the worlds of administration
and party politics. Though Law retained some aides who had
supported Lloyd George upon moving to No. 10, there was a
significant turnover of prime-ministerial staff. Law's son, Richard
Law, performed secretarial duties on an informal basis, as did
Geoffrey Fry. Staying on under Baldwin, to whom he became
a close counsellor, Fry seems to have been an important figure.
Fry wielded personal influence – perhaps not on policy – with a
fluid role. His wealth enabled him to work unpaid. One specific
task which Fry took on was handling ecclesiastical appointments.
He attended party meetings and carried out work that was less
appropriate for career officials. In some ways he was similar to a
Parliamentary Private Secretary but without a seat in Parliament.
Staff in No. 10 described him as almost a personal and political secretary and he had a reputation for being effective and
hard working. Law's most senior private secretary was Ronald
Waterhouse, a political appointment. Patrick Gower was a career
civil servant from the Treasury who served as a private secretary to Law, Baldwin and MacDonald. Another private secretary
was Edith Watson, who had served Law since 1916 when he was
at the Colonial Office. She stayed on at No. 10 under Baldwin,

MacDonald, Chamberlain and Churchill, handling correspondence with the public and – her speciality – parliamentary
questions. She retired at the end of the Second World War, having
become an institution in her own right. Her knowledge made her
indispensable.

A key aide to both Law and Baldwin was J. C. C. (John Colin
Campbell) Davidson. By the time Law became Prime Minister in
1922 Davidson, who was an MP, had already served as an intimate
private secretary to both men. Davidson became Parliamentary
Private Secretary to Law, who immediately gave his aide the
task of dismantling the support mechanisms set up by Lloyd
George.[95] Staff at No. 10 told us how close the relationship was
between the two. Davidson acted as a medium between the Prime
Minister and the press, whose representatives treated Davidson
in his own later words as 'a power behind the throne', providing
information that could be relied upon because of his closeness to
Law. The following year Davidson played a subsequently much-
criticised part in Baldwin's becoming premier after the departure
of Law. Baldwin retained Davidson as an aide, and continued
to seek counsel and assistance from him in various forms until
Baldwin's retirement in 1937. During the 1926 General Strike
Davidson helped coordinate official information. In 1926–30 he
was chairman of the Conservative Party, where he was an effective if divisive force. During the final Baldwin premiership he
continued as an informal aide, and was a regular caller at No. 10,
forming part of the Prime Minister's inner circle.

As Conservative Party chairman an important appointment
Davidson made was Joseph Ball, whom he installed as director
of publicity. In 1927 Ball joined the Conservative Party from
the internal intelligence agency, MI5. His experience of covert

---

95   S. Ball, 'Davidson, John Colin Campbell, first Viscount Davidson', *ODNB*.

activities was a valuable asset in Davidson's eyes and he referred to Ball's knowledge of the 'seamy side of life and the handling of crooks'. Through a network of informers, Ball was able to obtain access to internal Labour Party reports and advance copies of its publications. As Davidson put it, he and Ball operated a 'little intelligence service of our own'.[96] In 1930 Ball became director of the newly formed Conservative Research Department (CRD). In this position he established a close relationship with Chamberlain, who as Prime Minister (1937–40) made use of Ball in pursuit of his policy of appeasing Adolf Hitler. Ball helped Chamberlain conduct diplomacy, circumventing the Foreign Office. Ball drew once more on his intelligence skills in tapping the telephone conversations of opponents of Chamberlain's foreign policy, including Churchill and friends of the former Foreign Secretary Anthony Eden. He was thereby able to keep the Prime Minister informed about the intentions of both men. Ball covertly ran for the Prime Minister a journal entitled *Truth*, the links of which to the government Ball concealed through front companies. *Truth* aggressively attacked opponents of appeasement, including Churchill, and contained anti-Semitic content.[97]

Civil service ascendancy

Various prime ministers from the 1960s onwards sought to expand the personal and political component of their staff, challenging more established constitutional norms. Yet while the principles they tested had developed over a long period of time, they only began to become clearly entrenched as recently as the 1920s and with motives that might not be regarded as entirely wholesome.

---

96   R. James, *Memoirs of a Conservative: J. C. C. Davidson's Memoirs and Papers, 1910–37* (London: Weidenfeld and Nicolson, 1969), pp. 139; 272.
97   R. Cockett, *Twilight of Truth: Chamberlain, Appeasement and the Manipulation of the Press* (London: Weidenfeld and Nicolson, 1989), p. 11.

During the interwar period, the permanent civil service became the pre-eminent provider of support to the premiership. Crucial to this development was the establishment of a permanent head of the civil service. Lloyd George created this office in 1919 and attached it to the post of Permanent Secretary to the Treasury. The head of the civil service was responsible for advising the Prime Minister on senior civil service appointments. More generally, heads would support premiers in executing their overall responsibility for the civil service. Holders of the headship – which has subsequently moved across various parts of Whitehall, combining with different posts as well as being free-standing from 1968 to 1981 – have been important prime-ministerial assistants.

The first occupant was Warren Fisher. The precise nature of Fisher's role was not clear from the outset; he did much to define it himself. From his dual position as head of the Treasury and of the civil service he wielded great influence. Rather than exercising day-to-day oversight of business, a key lever for Fisher was his role in Whitehall appointments. Prime ministers rarely turned down his recommendations. Some thought this power dangerous. In No. 10 staff believed Fisher sought to remove from them responsibility for honours. Lloyd George, Law and Baldwin treated Fisher as an all-purpose adviser, though MacDonald less so. A potential tension existed between his role as aide to both the Prime Minister and the Chancellor of the Exchequer. Another possible problem was the relationship with the Cabinet Secretary, Hankey, which began badly with the attempt by Fisher to absorb the Cabinet Office in 1922. Subsequently they formed a strong partnership. At this time the Treasury still occupied the old Treasury building, with its connecting door to No. 10, while the Cabinet Office remained on the other side of Whitehall at 2 Whitehall Gardens. Our interviews with No. 10 staff suggest they saw more of Hankey in their building than Fisher. In the end

Fisher overplayed his hand. He became increasingly concerned during the 1930s about the scale of German rearmament and took a pronounced interest in defence. The way in which he pursued his objectives alienated others, in particular within the Foreign Office, where a well-founded suspicion existed that he intended to bring them increasingly under his authority. He felt disgust at the Munich agreement with Hitler of September 1938, a stance that undermined his relationship with Chamberlain. Fisher's final period at the Treasury before retiring in October 1939 saw him excluded from areas of influence.

The establishment of the headship of the civil service was part of the move towards a unified home civil service, with the Treasury – building on longstanding practical reality – made officially the senior office of government. This shift helped produce a more cohesive civil service, whose members were increasingly aware they were part of a single institution. Fisher enthusiastically encouraged them in this consciousness – though the service was not always as one over policy and administrative issues, and disagreements could develop within and between departments. An implication of a more integrated civil service was that the staff (or a portion of it) upon which prime ministers depended became less personally attached to them and – though in theory officials are subordinate to ministers – in practice had power of its own. Whitehall was emerging as an entity more distanced from individual prime ministers. Yet premiers had to engage with the bureaucratic machine, and all the more so as it developed increasingly as a force in its own right. Indeed the civil service provided premiers with a professional body of staff which could, if handled effectively, help occupants of No. 10 achieve their objectives.

As it developed along these lines from the 1920s, the permanent civil service expanded its supporting role for the premiership, putting its pre-eminence in this task beyond doubt. The principle was established that the senior private secretary – later known formally from 1929 at the latest as the Principal Private Secretary – would always be a career official and would not be displaced with a change of incumbent at No. 10. The circumstances in which this change came about were not straightforward. In 1924 for the first time a premier took office and retained the most senior private secretary of his immediate predecessor despite being of a different party. The aide who achieved this feat of retention was Ronald Waterhouse. He served three premiers: Law (1922–23) and Baldwin (1923–24), and, crucially, Ramsay MacDonald (1924), the first Labour Prime Minister. Waterhouse then served Baldwin again from 1924 to 1928, when his public divorce case after an affair with Mrs Baldwin's personal secretary forced his resignation from office.

Though Waterhouse's career prepared the ground for civil service pre-eminence at No. 10, he was not a permanent official, and he makes a murky source for a constitutional orthodoxy. Waterhouse, the son of a shipowner, served in the army in Africa and India, then joined the Intelligence Department of the War Office. Davidson recruited him as secretary to Brigadier-General Sir Frederick Sykes, Chief of the Air Staff. In 1920, at the suggestion of Davidson, Waterhouse began work for Law, at that time Lord Privy Seal. He continued to serve Law's successor, Austen Chamberlain, for a time, and then was appointed equerry and private secretary to the Duke of York. This latter position gave him constant access to the royal family, which would prove useful in his later career at No. 10. Law is reported to have disliked Waterhouse when he served him as Lord Privy Seal but employed him again anyway when he became Prime Minister. Waterhouse was a studied courtier and owed his sustained presence at Downing Street to this quality rather than any ability or diligence as a secretary, both of which he lacked. Our interviews with staff at No. 10 suggest that, though charming and superficially impressive, he lacked substance. Waterhouse was prone to talking too much, wrote nothing and was not reliable. He was apparently just not up to the job. Waterhouse did not get on with Patrick Gower, his fellow private secretary in the early 1920s. Though Waterhouse was theoretically the senior private secretary, the usual tasks, other than liaising with the Palace, fell to Davidson, who was Parliamentary Private Secretary to Law.

When Law resigned in May 1923, Waterhouse played a part in the attainment of the premiership by Baldwin. On a visit to the King Waterhouse gave the monarch's private secretary a letter written by Davidson, purporting to set out the views of Bonar Law, favouring Baldwin over Curzon. But Law did not in truth have such a clear opinion as the letter conveyed. Baldwin had reason to keep on Waterhouse despite his lack of proficiency as an aide. On the surface the survival of Waterhouse as the chief private secretary at No. 10 when a Prime Minister of a different party, MacDonald, took office is harder to explain. It has been said that MacDonald, Baldwin and Waterhouse between them agreed to retain the entire secretarial staff at No. 10. It may be that MacDonald, because he was the first Labour Prime Minister and had never held office before, felt he needed an experienced team. Possibly Baldwin suspected MacDonald would not hold the premiership for long and hoped Waterhouse could provide the link between the previous Baldwin tenure and the next. While this degree of collaboration may be difficult to credit, in a sense the two prime ministers were defined less by their differences and more by their shared opposition to Lloyd George. MacDonald was at first unaware of the kind of work secretaries could carry out for him and received some guidance from Waterhouse, who gradually won the trust of the new premier. MacDonald came to make increasing use of Waterhouse, in particular in dealing with the Palace. In 1924 Baldwin again retained Waterhouse, who continued at Downing Street until his forced exit in 1928.[98] A view within No. 10 was that Baldwin had wanted to rid himself of Waterhouse, but was not good at sacking people. In the wake of the divorce case Waterhouse offered his resignation expecting it to be refused, but Baldwin welcomed the opportunity to remove his private secretary.

Although Waterhouse was not a permanent civil servant, his survival across premierships created a precedent, crucial within the British constitution and civil service, leading to the establishment of a convention that the private secretaries at No. 10 were career officials. They comprised what came to be known widely as the Private Office, a term which our interviews suggest may have first appeared in the Lloyd George period to distinguish the No. 10 private secretaries from the Garden Suburb staff. An inner core of permanent staff emerged, directly connected to the machine of which they were a part, more clearly distinguished from temporary partisan appointments. Waterhouse himself found this differentiation restrictive, but it became a defining feature of aides to the Prime Minister.

As one form of variety, between permanent and irregular staff, disappeared from the team of private secretaries to the Prime Minister, other distinctions appeared in its place. Hierarchical divergence became clearer in 1929 when the *Imperial Calendar*, a forerunner of the *Civil Service Yearbook*, began regularly stating who the Principal Private Secretary was in an office which by this point numbered four official appointments. The first to be so designated was Robert Vansittart. Contemporary staff told us his dynamism justified his elevated title. Vansittart came from the

---

98   See e.g.: N. Waterhouse, *Private and Official* (London: Jonathan Cape, 1942); Jones and Burnham 'Innovators at 10 Downing Street'.

Foreign Office to No. 10 in 1928 and became in 1930 Permanent Secretary at the Foreign Office. This promotion demonstrated how a spell as a private secretary at No. 10 could be part of a fast-track career, a pattern which would intensify in the period after the Second World War, through to the present. Vansittart and his successors – probably until the Tony Blair period – sat with the second secretary in the small office directly adjoining the Cabinet room, where prime ministers often worked, on the Whitehall/Treasury side. Three more secretaries sat in the next room along. The two rooms on the St James's Park side of the Cabinet room could provide a base for other aides: Rose Rosenberg and Herbert Usher for MacDonald; and Horace Wilson for Baldwin and Chamberlain.

Functional differentiation increased when a private secretary was appointed specifically to handle press relations either in 1929 or 1931 (the date is disputed).[99] The first holder of this post was George Steward, who had been carrying out information work at the Foreign Office since 1915. He provided MacDonald with accounts of press coverage, as well as briefing and liaising with lobby journalists, often mingling among them. Steward consulted regularly with the private secretaries about what particular line he should promote. His role necessitated access to confidential official papers. He was not a high-powered aide nor the main conduit with the press on behalf of No. 10. Yet while prime-ministerial aides had from the days of Walpole been concerned with managing the media, the appointment of Steward marked a tentative move towards a specialised operation for this purpose at No. 10.

The private secretaries were at the centre of the system and began to form into an institution. They had, according to

---

99   For 1929 see: Cockett, *Twilight of Truth*, p. 4. For 1931 see: C. Seymour-Ure, *Prime Ministers and the Media: Issues of Power and Control* (Oxford: Blackwell, 2003), pp. 127–8.

witnesses from the 1920s and 30s, access to Cabinet papers, responsibility for managing the Prime Minister's time, and organised engagements and the diary. Though important to the daily life of the premier, private secretaries did not generally have much direct impact on policy. They used a filing system first introduced by John T. Davies for Lloyd George, and a book of precedents and guidance, again possibly dating to the Lloyd George period, updated thereafter (Asquith apparently left nothing behind). Though some formality was developing, common sense and on-the-job learning were important. Private secretaries built up an institutional memory, transmitting accounts of their jobs orally to their successors.

Although administrative aides other than career officials might have been to some extent marginalised within No. 10 and distanced from the levers of the Whitehall machine, they were not completely eradicated, as the practices of MacDonald demonstrate. Showing his need for assistants with a close personal link to him, he made aides of his children, particularly Ishbel and Malcolm, repeating the practice of Law and Gladstone before him. Furthermore, during both his premierships of 1924 and 1929–35 he included other non-Whitehall members in his team. Rose Rosenberg dealt with his parliamentary party and the press, took some dictation and handled constituency business. According to our oral sources Rosenberg sat in a room on the St James's Park side of the Cabinet room. Her pay came from Treasury funds. She caused some suspicion in No. 10 because she insisted on having her own Labour shorthand typist. Other staff in the building thought she accepted too many gifts, among them shoes. Based in a room next to Rosenberg, Herbert Usher, a former journalist and unsuccessful Labour parliamentary candidate, performed a role harder to define, handling party business as Fry did for Law and Baldwin. Usher later became a career official, possibly at the instigation of Macdonald in recognition of his support. The private secretaries passed Rosenberg and Usher the work they felt was less appropriate for career officials to handle. Both aides demonstrated that their individual loyalty to MacDonald superseded their party attachments by continuing to work for him when he broke with Labour to become Prime Minister in the National government in 1931.

MacDonald obtained further support from beyond career Whitehall. In 1930 in the face of surging unemployment he set up the Economic Advisory Council (EAC). The economist Hubert Henderson was assistant secretary from 1930 to 1934, and then joint secretary to the EAC. Among other roles he became in all but name an aide to MacDonald. He is regarded as the first economic adviser to a Prime Minister working within government yet separately from the Treasury.[100] The EAC as a whole was a support body for the premier who acted as its chair. Formed out of the already-existing Committee of Civil Research, it included ministers and an array of prominent outsiders, among whom were the economist John Maynard Keynes and the trade unionist Ernest Bevin. It was not sufficiently incorporated into the machinery of government to achieve an impact on the course of policy. The full EAC ceased to meet after January 1932, with only sub-committees taking place. It was officially abolished in 1939. In January 1930 Oswald Mosley, the Chancellor of the Duchy of Lancaster, had proposed a version of this body more ambitious than was ultimately established.[101] He had a brief from MacDonald to deal with unemployment. Mosley outlined an interventionist economic programme, which a new entity he termed the 'Prime Minister's department' would drive through

---

100 D. Marquand, *Ramsay MacDonald* (London: Jonathan Cape, 1977), p. 524.
101 The National Archive, Public Record Office (TNA/PRO) CAB 24/209.

the Whitehall machine. It would comprise a team of expert economists – presumably recruited from outside the career civil service
– and an 'Executive Organisation' made up of ministers and
officials. The head of the civil service would be closely involved.
Mosley's plan never materialised.

Horace Wilson (1882–1972)

During this phase of permanent civil service ascendancy, which
ran from about 1919 to 1940, one career official, Horace Wilson,
stands out for the influence he achieved as an assistant to successive prime ministers. Wilson closely supported both Baldwin
and Chamberlain. Though he was a regular civil servant, the
post from which he assisted both prime ministers was tailored
for him. While some other assistants have had a broader overall
influence for longer, the extent to which Wilson came to be relied
on as a staff member, in particular by Chamberlain, is probably
unsurpassed by any type of aide across all time periods. With this
importance came an equally exceptional infamy.

Wilson's mother ran a boarding house and his father dealt in
furniture. He gained an economics degree as an evening student
at the London School of Economics before progressing in the
civil service through the War Office, Board of Trade and Ministry
of Labour. Wilson advised Baldwin during the General Strike of
1926. In 1930 Wilson became Chief Industrial Adviser to HM
Government, and was an adviser to Baldwin and Chamberlain at
the 1932 Ottawa Imperial Economic Conference. Upon becoming
Prime Minister for the third time in 1935 Baldwin made Wilson
his most important personal aide at No. 10 – where he had an
office – in practice supplanting the Principal Private Secretary. In
one account his status was akin to that of the head of a Whitehall
department, a permanent secretary to the premier, though no
such title formally existed. Our interviews presented conflicting

attitudes towards Wilson among prime-ministerial staff. One view was that he was reluctant to take on a role at Downing Street, sensing he would become a scapegoat, but that Warren Fisher, head of the civil service, pressed the move upon him. Another interpretation was that he was ambitious and coveted the position, his friendship with Fisher helping him achieve it. Baldwin probably felt that having an aide with high rank at No. 10 would give him more influence. Wilson was not engaged with detailed day-to-day office business but concerned with overall strategic direction. Though he retained the 'Industrial Adviser' title, his interests ranged more widely.

Wilson was a significant figure during the crisis of 1936 brought about by the determination of King Edward VIII to marry the divorcée Wallis Simpson, culminating in his abdication at the end of the year. Baldwin was in poor physical condition at this time and dependent upon his aide. Wilson played a part in the tapping of Edward's telephone conversations and acted as liaison between the government and the Palace. His files on the abdication[102] include a note of his personal assessment of Simpson (or, as she eventually became, the Duchess of Windsor). It demonstrates the contempt held for her at the highest levels in Britain and that objections to her extended beyond her personal qualities and included her political allegiances. Wilson held that she never displayed any genuine feelings for Edward. Rather her intention was to further her own ends. A number of close observers, Wilson claimed, remarked on her ability to manipulate the King. Some felt her motive was personal greed. He noted the view that she had political contacts in Germany. Wilson suggested this claim gave added force to allegations she had pressed the King to become more forceful in his approach. People who knew Simpson

102   TNA PRO CAB 127/157.

described her as ambitious and intent upon becoming influential, intervening in politics and having an impact upon public life. Wilson closed by making his position even more clear, describing Simpson as 'selfish, self-seeking, hard, calculating, ambitious, scheming, dangerous'.

Given this assessment of Simpson, Wilson was not satisfied the issue had been fully resolved even when Edward abdicated. On 10 December 1936, the day Edward signed the Instrument of Abdication, with Baldwin unavailable Wilson wrote to Chamberlain, then Chancellor of the Exchequer, about Simpson's future plans.[103] Wilson believed that Simpson intended, supported by substantial public subsidy, to set up her own 'Court' and create difficulties for Edward's brother George VI, the new King. He felt it should not be taken for granted that she had completely relinquished the hope of becoming Queen. Simpson, Wilson went on, was known to possess endless ambition, had contacts with the Nazis and had 'definite ideas as to dictatorship'. In this note he pressed the idea of making public financial provision contingent upon the couple remaining out of the country for a substantial period of time. He supplied relevant figures. Wilson became interested in various other possible solutions to the perceived problem and in December 1936 explored with Simpson's solicitor whether she might be paid to vanish from the scene. This particular plan did not materialise.

Following the retirement of Baldwin in May 1937 the new premier, Chamberlain, retained Wilson who took on an even broader role. Wilson portrayed Chamberlain as a decisive leader eager to proceed once he had formed an opinion. Within this approach Wilson's role seems to have been to help Chamerlain think through his ideas and implement his will. Wilson's description

---

103   Ibid., PREM 1/453, Horace Wilson to Neville Chamberlain, 10 December 1936.

of the second premier he supported suggests personal closeness between the two of them. Chamberlain was, according to Wilson, an introverted character who could overcome his reticence with people only after a long time; once he had conquered this timidity he placed complete faith in the individual concerned. Wilson was a recipient of this special trust. A letter from Chamberlain to Hitler of 26 September 1938 stated that in a final bid to avert war he was despatching Wilson to the Führer with a message. He insisted Wilson had his 'full confidence, and you can take anything he says as coming from me'.

This note was produced near the culmination of the effort which dominated Chamberlain's premiership and Wilson's service for him: the failed pursuit of the appeasement of Hitler.[104] In a private account written in October 1941 Wilson explained the former Prime Minister's rationale. He had dual motives. First he sought to determine whether a positive form of appeasement, actively seeking to pacify Hitler, in place of the earlier more negative approach, could preserve peace. Second he wanted to gain time to prepare for war if it came. Wilson accompanied Chamberlain on three missions to Germany and went once on his own. Wilson's activities could involve bypassing officials in the Foreign Office, among whom there was opposition to appeasement. He acted as a direct channel of communication with German sources on behalf of Chamberlain. Working in conjunction with Joseph Ball and George Steward, Wilson played a public-relations role in support of the policy, including briefing the press, in particular *The Times*.

Part of Wilson's task seems to have been not only to convince the public about the viability of appeasement but people within government, perhaps even including Chamberlain and himself.

---

104 See: G. Peden, 'Sir Horace Wilson and Appeasement', *The Historical Journal*, 53, 4 (2010), pp. 984–1014.

Wilson's account of the appeasement policy includes a description of his first meeting with Hitler on 15 September 1938. Wilson recounts how, looking at the Führer, he found Hitler's eyes as unpleasant as Wilson had the feeling of his hand. Wilson decided Hitler had a 'cruel mouth' and would not want to be at his mercy if ever he held something against him. Yet Hitler was the man with whom it was hoped some kind of viable deal could be struck. On 16 September 1938, on return from the meeting with Hitler, Wilson produced an account of the visit for circulation to the Cabinet. In it Wilson described how Herbert von Dirksen, the German ambassador in London, had told him that Hitler had formed a favourable impression of the Prime Minister and that Hitler – who was of the opinion it was the kind of move he would make himself – was impressed by Chamberlain's decision to travel to Germany. Wilson reported that other officials had made similar claims. However, Joachim von Ribbentrop, Hitler's foreign minister and a former ambassador in London, did not echo these views about the opinions of Hitler and his discussion with Chamberlain. Wilson judged this opinion was typical of von Ribbentrop; he stated he had stressed to Sir Nevile Henderson, the British ambassador to Germany, the need urgently to establish contact with Hermann Göring – whom von Dirksen had described as having a restraining effect on Hitler. While Ribbentrop's attitude was dismissed as being a product of his flawed personality, the flattery of others was taken at face value.[105]

When appeasement failed to halt Nazi aggression and became subject increasingly to public attacks, Wilson had to shoulder some of the blame. The 1940 book attributed to 'Cato' named Wilson – alongside Baldwin and Chamberlain – as one of the

---

105   Ibid., CAB 127/158.

fifteen *Guilty Men* responsible for this approach to the Nazis.[106]
The book argued that Wilson dominated Chamberlain and that
eventually the premier consulted his aide over all major government decisions, with Wilson becoming for more than two years
the second most important British public figure. In a recent article
G. C. Peden concludes that such interpretations of Wilson are
excessive, but that he was important, facilitating Chamberlain's
heightened engagement in foreign policy and often actively pushing the case for appeasement.[107] The identification of Wilson with
the Prime Minister and appeasement, which took place publicly
in the press as well as Parliament, was a problem for a career
official. Though Wilson had become Permanent Secretary to the
Treasury and head of the civil service at the beginning of 1939,
the changeover to the Churchill premiership in May 1940 saw
Wilson isolated. His forced retirement came in 1942. Wilson
spent the last three decades of his life barely visible in public.[108]

The 'Secret Circle' of Winston Churchill

Winston Churchill's claim to greatness lies in the wartime leadership he provided as British premier from 1940 to 1945. The
impact he achieved in this role is central to his reputation. He was
able to make such a personal imprint by the way he assembled,
structured and deployed his support group. Clear parallels exist
between the use of aides under Churchill and by Lloyd George
during the previous world war: the establishment by both of a
smaller, more streamlined War Cabinet; the expansion in the
overall size of the prime-ministerial team; a shared proclivity for
staff who did not originate in Whitehall (though the bias towards

---

106 'Cato', *Guilty Men* (London: Victor Gollancz, 1940). Cato was in fact
three journalists from the left of the political spectrum: Michael Foot,
Peter Howard and Frank Owen.
107 Peden, 'Sir Horace Wilson and Appeasement'.
108 See generally: R. Lowe, 'Wilson, Sir Horace John', *ODNB*.

outsiders was greater under Lloyd George); and the creation of specifically prime-ministerial bodies to assist intervention in the business of the departments. Although some have attempted to distinguish Churchill and Lloyd George's methods,[109] the similarities are plain.[110]

Individuals drawn from outside the career civil service were an important component of the Churchill entourage, particularly because he liked, if possible, to have familiar faces around him. Members of this inner group included the *Daily Express* owner Lord Beaverbrook, the businessman Oliver Lyttelton, and Duncan Sandys, Churchill's son-in-law, all of whom eventually took up ministerial posts. When moving from the post of First Lord of the Admiralty to No. 10 Churchill took with him his Parliamentary Private Secretary, Brendan Bracken. Rumoured to be the illegitimate offspring of Churchill, Bracken had provided support to Churchill since the 1920s. Acting as a general counsellor to the premier, he took a particular interest in patronage. He assisted Churchill in the courting of the key aide to the US President Franklin Roosevelt, Harry Hopkins, who visited Britain early in 1941. Later that year Bracken was appointed Minister of Information, though he did not cease to provide assistance to the Prime Minister.

Two further longstanding friends and allies of Churchill, Frederick Lindemann and Desmond Morton, became prime-ministerial assistants at the outset of the Churchill premiership. Morton, following distinguished military service, took on an

---

109 One Churchill staff member, Desmond Morton, stressed that the Garden Suburb was concerned with 'politics' in a way the Churchill staff was not. R. Thompson, *Churchill and Morton: The Quest for Insight in the Correspondence of Major Sir Desmond Morton and the Author* (London: Hodder and Stoughton, 1976), p. 57.

110 See e.g.: I. Jacob in J. Wheeler-Bennett (ed.), *Action This Day: Working with Churchill* (London: Macmillan, 1968), p. 163.

intelligence role in the Foreign Office. During the 1930s, suppos-edly with the permission of successive prime ministers, he supplied Churchill, who was out of office and lived nearby, with confidential information to help him in his campaign for rear-mament. Morton probably stretched the limits of whatever brief he had to help Churchill. As premier Churchill used Morton as an assistant. In her work on Morton and Churchill, Gill Bennett notes that the exact influence of the aide is difficult to ascertain.[111] Possibly Morton talked himself up as being more important than he was. As a courtier he came into conflict with another member of the group around Churchill, Sandys. Morton's most significant role arose from the responsibility he was given for passing to Churchill the intelligence acquired through the breaking of the Enigma code, information among the most restricted in Whitehall. Morton took a concerned interest in possible security leaks. He acted as Churchill's liaison with General de Gaulle and other governments in exile, a role the Foreign Office resented. Morton's importance seems to have declined over the course of the war, as intelligence-briefing mechanisms for the Prime Minister became more systematised. Churchill may have lost some confidence in his aide, and had less need for him as more formal intelligence briefing arrangements developed.

Churchill deployed other outsiders. Various new Whitehall departments and administrative structures appeared. An accom-panying influx of staff from beyond career Whitehall occurred, drawn from academia and business, in possession of skills lack-ing within the permanent civil service. Churchill established two bodies with a connection to the premiership, which employed experts as temporary civil servants. The Economic Section of the War Cabinet appeared officially in 1941. Composed of

---

111   G. Bennett, *Churchill's Man of Mystery: Desmond Morton and the World of Intelligence* (London and New York: Routledge, 2007), p. 225.

between ten and twenty professional economists, it was formally attached to the Lord President of the Council, a minister given an economic coordination role during wartime. In practice its staff provided support to Churchill. Outsiders were recruited to another body, the Statistical Section, which had a specifically prime-ministerial remit.

Churchill's habit of relying on personal allies and placing outsiders in official posts had implications for the career civil service. Its ascendancy since the 1920s as the dominant provider of support to prime ministers was partially reversed. Furthermore, Churchill refused to deal with Horace Wilson, by this time the Permanent Secretary to the Treasury and head of the civil service. But it would have been impossible for Churchill to have functioned completely without support from senior permanent officials, and he came to rely on some heavily.

Edward Bridges provided Churchill with a vital link to the bureaucracy. Churchill had a reputation for being uninterested in the finer details of how decisions were put into action, but he needed people who could ensure they were. The son of the Poet Laureate Robert, Bridges had been Cabinet Secretary since 1938. He established a good working relationship with Churchill. In an account Churchill's private secretary, John Colville, gave us, Churchill tended to use Bridges in place of his Principal Private Secretary (and relied similarly on Hastings Ismay for military issues). Bridges helped Churchill with such tasks as determining how his Minister of Defence role would function in practice and also provided the Prime Minister with the precise details of what equipment, resources and other assistance to request from President Roosevelt before the US entered the war. Churchill received critical help from Bridges in the organisation of the network of Cabinet committees. He stressed to Bridges that the number of committees should be limited to those essential, to ensure ministers were not wasting their time. Bridges attended key Allied conferences. He was so useful to the Prime Minister that Churchill was not willing to let him depart from the post of Cabinet Secretary. In 1945, rather than leave the Cabinet Office to take on the role of Permanent Secretary to the Treasury and head of the civil service, Bridges had to combine these new functions with his existing office. It was an extraordinary concentration of administrative responsibility, which required the establishment of special support mechanisms for Bridges.

Further down the permanent civil service hierarchy but nonetheless important to Churchill were the private secretaries.[112] Much of the stress created by the war and Churchill's leadership style fell upon this group, which included Colville. From the Foreign Office, he moved to No. 10 in 1939 when Chamberlain was Prime Minister. Colville told us that before joining No. 10 he had wanted to sign up for the Grenadier Guards. The Foreign Office Permanent Secretary, Alexander Cadogan, fearing others would soon follow, said he could not leave and impressed on him that he would serve his country better by staying. According to Colville, the Foreign Office then put in a claim for having a private secretary, both to keep Colville happy and to provide it with a voice at No. 10. He joined a team which totalled four private secretaries, who used to have a daily afternoon cup of tea, joined by the Parliamentary Private Secretary. It was a time of tension between the Prime Minister and the Foreign Office, which Chamberlain marginalised in his personal pursuit of appeasement. Colville felt he was unusual among Foreign Office staff, particularly the younger contingent, in supporting the Munich agreement.

Initially Colville was unenthusiastic about Churchill when he succeeded Chamberlain. He recounted how hostility existed

---

112   See e.g.: J. Colville, *The Churchillians* (London: Weidenfeld and Nicholson, 1981), pp.52–65.

in No. 10 to the new Prime Minister because some felt he had intrigued against their previous chief, and even regarded Churchill as frightening. But Colville soon became a Churchill admirer and got on well with him, becoming part of his social circle in a way the other private secretaries did not. In Colville's account the term 'Private Office' was first applied under Churchill in 1940, a term imported from the Admiralty (our other interviews suggested some earlier use of the phrase may have taken place at certain points from Lloyd George onwards, but it is difficult to be certain). Colville left Downing Street to join the Royal Air Force in 1941 but rejoined the No. 10 staff in 1943. When Operation Overlord, the Allied assault on Western Europe, began in 1944, Colville left his post again to serve with his squadron for three months from May to August. He stayed on to serve Attlee for a time after the 1945 general election. When Churchill returned to office in 1951 he recruited Colville as his Joint Principal Private Secretary, a demonstration of the confidence he had won from the Prime Minister.

Anthony Bevir was another private secretary already in post whom Churchill retained when he became premier in 1940. Bevir was not suitable for regular attendance on Churchill. He was keen on drink, for which he had acquired a taste after being shell-shocked and gassed during the First World War. An eye had to be kept on him at parties, presumably in case his alcohol-fuelled behaviour got out of hand. Whatever his personal weaknesses he took on a task he made his own. In another instance of functional specialisation within the Private Office, he focused on church appointments and other patronage, excluding honours. Bevir retained these functions to the end of his long tenure, which lasted until 1956. Because of his ecclesiastical role he acquired the nick-name 'heaven's talent scout'. He also took on the role of office manager, yet another task the other private secretaries felt was a chore distancing them from more important matters. Eventually Bevir was made a Knight Commander of the Royal Victorian Order – 'KCVO' – a personal honour from the monarch. The night before the announcement, a worse-for-wear Bevir lost his set of No. 10 keys in a taxi. Replacing all the locks cost thousands of pounds. This event led to the joke that KCVO stood for 'keys can vanish overnight'.

Eric Seal moved to No. 10 with Churchill and became the Principal Private Secretary, replacing Arthur Rucker who accompanied Chamberlain to the post of Lord President of the Council. Seal lasted less than a year in a role. Some at No. 10 did not hold him in high regard, seeing him as an unsystematic bumbler out of his depth. He did not gel with Churchill, in one account pressing views on the Prime Minister about how to conduct the war. Churchill moved Seal on with a fake promotion. The successor as Principal Private Secretary in 1941 was John Martin, who had joined No. 10 from the Colonial Office the previous year. Martin told us he had the impression Bracken had played a part in picking him out for Churchill. He knew Bevir beforehand as well. When Martin went to see Churchill, the Prime Minister asked him no questions, but looked him up and down. Finally Churchill said Martin would join the team. As Principal Private Secretary Martin endeavoured to introduce a more structured approach, with a clearer division of functions, a rota and a work schedule. A rota of some kind was still in place at least thirty years later. In 1945 Leslie Rowan succeeded Martin. Rowan had first come to No. 10 from the Treasury in 1941. John Peck was another who came from the Admiralty in 1940. Peck acted as a link between No. 10 and the Admiralty and War Office. He took on some press-liaison duties from Steward, who was probably isolated under Churchill and quietly retired in 1944. As a journalist, Churchill felt equipped to deal with the media himself, and Colville and Bracken provided further support in managing the media for the Prime Minister.

Another Churchill administrative innovation led to the appearance of an important aide drawn from inside the official machine, though his origins were in the military rather than civil side. When he became Prime Minister, Churchill combined with the premiership a new post of Minister of Defence that gave him senior responsibility for the conduct of the war. Rather than creating a new super-ministry Churchill worked through the existing military departments, making the Chiefs of Staff Committee responsible directly to him. Here Hastings Ismay was a crucial aide. After a long period of army service he had joined the staff of the Committee of Imperial Defence in 1925, of which he eventually became secretary in 1938. Ismay became an aide to Churchill shortly before he became premier, assisting Churchill as chairman of the Chiefs of Staff Committee. When Churchill became Prime Minister and Minister of Defence, Ismay became his Chief Staff Officer. He was a channel of communication and smoother of relations between the Prime Minister (or Minister of Defence as he strictly was in this role) and the Chiefs of Staff. In particular Ismay helped ensure the War Cabinet generally and Churchill individually worked well with the man who was head of the army and chair of the Chiefs of Staff Committee, Alan Brooke.

Within the group of permanent officials and outsiders surrounding Churchill the boundary between professional and personal life was unclear. For him work did not end and he expected his staff to take a similar attitude and be available for him at all times. The Prime Minister might work from the bath or his bed. Though he could at times appear inconsiderate towards his staff, he was not always so. Churchill labelled his inner team the 'secret circle',[113]

---

113   For this phrase see e.g.: Wheeler-Bennett (ed.), *Action This Day*, p. 9. This book is a collection of memoirs of Churchill by his aides.

whose members could be treated almost as part of his family. Their purpose was to ensure the will of the Prime Minister came to bear on the conduct of the war and that bureaucratic obstacles did not hamper him. First-hand accounts of Churchill's leadership suggest he maintained a considerable degree of individual control over his enhanced prime-ministerial team. Although he was willing to listen to the views of others, both ministers and aides, Churchill had strong views which he was not afraid to assert. The main exception was with his military advisers whom he was reluctant to overrule, perhaps fortunately given his reputation as an amateur dabbler in military strategy. Churchill seems to have ensured the premiership remained his personal vehicle, partly through his habit of minimising the number of issues he was considering at any given time to keep him focused. His habit of dictating minutes – often bluntly expressed – sent out in his own name, rather than using private secretaries as a medium of communication, both helped enforce and demonstrate his individual will. The words in his speeches were his own.

Frederick Lindemann (1886–1957)

As Prime Minister Churchill was determined to have a substantial overview of how the war effort was progressing. An important part of the picture he needed was data on physical resources such as armaments-production figures. Churchill created a body, attached personally to him, to ensure he received the necessary information. It was a means by which he could prise open the official machine, with which he was often impatient. The Statistical Section was both a descendant of the Garden Suburb and a precursor to later bodies such as the Policy Unit. At its head he placed his good friend, Frederick Lindemann, a physicist nicknamed the 'Prof.', who became involved in some of the most controversial decisions of the war.

In some ways Lindemann resembled Lord Acton. Both men were intellectuals of mixed national backgrounds who found their way into the confidence of prime ministers. Lindemann, from a wealthy family, had been Professor of Experimental Philosophy at Oxford since 1919. As head of the Clarendon Laboratory he established and managed an effective team, as he would do later in Whitehall. Members of his Clarendon group included Reginald Victor Jones, who during the war provided Churchill with vital breakthroughs in the field of air defence. Lindemann had a gift that would benefit Churchill for interpreting and explaining complex issues. He also had quirky and reactionary political beliefs. Colville wrote that he was 'basically anti-Semitic' (though he assisted many Jewish refugees from Nazi Germany), found blacks 'inferior and repulsive' and loathed Germans.[114] He was an early identifier of the threat posed by the Nazi regime and worked with Churchill, in particular lobbying for the introduction of better air defences. Lindemann was an academic with an interest in seeing his ideas applied in practice by government and was willing to take steps to bring about this outcome. The official files reveal his longstanding practice to promote his ideas about military strategy and technological innovation, sometimes drawing on his personal connection with Churchill to do so.[115]

Following the outbreak of war in 1939 Churchill re-entered government as First Lord of the Admiralty and recruited his friend and ally to help him. Lindemann provided scientific advice to Churchill and headed a newly established body, known as the Statistical Branch or 'S-Branch', responsible for providing statistical briefings to the First Lord. When Churchill became premier in May 1940 Lindemann and the new body, now called the Prime Minister's Statistical Section, accompanied him. Lindemann soon

114 Colville, *The Churchillians*, pp. 32–3.
115 See e.g.: TNA/PRO AIR 2/301, 5/425; MUN 8/1; T 172/1583.

became a Peer and Paymaster General, though continuing in the same role for Churchill. He had direct physical access to the Prime Minister during the Second World War, seeing him virtually every day, spending weekends at Chequers and accompanying him to major international conferences. People who enjoy privileged positions within the circles surrounding prime ministers can come into conflict with other members of those entourages. Over time strong personal animosities developed between him and other Churchill acolytes, namely Sandys and Beaverbrook. Sandys disagreed with Lindemann over the threat from German rockets and their warheads, while Beaverbrook found Lindemann interfering in his ministerial brief.

A note from Lindemann to Churchill dated 27 August 1941 gives a revealing glimpse of the aide at work in an important area. Lindemann (by this time Lord Cherwell) wrote to the Prime Minister with momentous news.[116] He had frequently discussed with Churchill a 'super-explosive' which utilised energy in the nucleus of the atom. It was approximately a million times greater, proportionate to weight, than the energy of normal explosives. Scientists in Britain and the US – and, Lindemann supposed, Germany – had carried out considerable work. Useable bombs might be ready within two years. Though there were various complications, it was plausible that a single plane could carry an intricate bomb, weighing about a ton, which would have an explosive force equivalent to about 2,000 tons of TNT. Lindemann then considered the policy options for the Prime Minister. The manufacturing process involved extracting the rarer of the two components of natural uranium. Lindemann noted there was ample uranium available in Canada and the Congo. While the Germans had access to

---

116 Ibid., CAB 126/329, Lord Cherwell to Winston Churchill, 27 August 1941.

less, ominously Lindemann feared the supply in Czechoslovakia was enough. This threat cemented the urgent need to proceed with preparation for production as quickly as possible. Cherwell recommended that plans should begin now with a final decision made six months later, when a clearer idea of the plausibility of the project would be possible.

Lindemann was concerned not only about the Germans. Although British and American scientists had worked closely together on the project, Lindemann strongly believed the plant should be constructed in 'England' (as he put it) or if necessary in Canada. He conceded there were reasons not to do so, including the danger of bombing and limitations on the availability of labour. But Lindemann asserted the chances of preserving secrecy were greater if the US were not directly involved in production. Even more important was that the owner of such a plant could 'dictate terms to the rest of the world'. However much trust allies might merit, Lindemann felt, it was not advisable to yield such power to them. He recommended not pressing the Americans to take on the task. Rather he advised continuing to share information and start production without raising the issue of who should be responsible for it. Lindemann concluded that though success was far from guaranteed it was essential to proceed. He warned it would be unacceptable to allow Germany to gain the lead, enabling it either to win the war or to reverse the outcome after losing.

This submission shows how Lindemann provided more than mere technical information to the Prime Minister. He discussed the policy implications and gave strong views on courses of action to be followed, on scientific policy and wider concerns, such as the geopolitics of the Second World War. Lindemann was important to Churchill, who trusted him sufficiently to engage his aide on his behalf in such sensitive and weighty matters. Yet he was capable of drawing perverse conclusions, which in this case Churchill seems to have disregarded. The strong encouragement that Lindemann gave to Churchill to proceed was significant, though the idea Britain could have been able to do so without the Americans simply by not raising the subject does not seem plausible.

The Statistical Section had a total staff of around twenty, with about six economists, a scientific officer, a civil servant trained in economics, about six 'computers', two or three typists and a team of 'chartists' tasked with drawing charts and diagrams. Initially based in Richmond Terrace, at the end of 1940 the body moved to Great George Street, directly above Churchill's war room. The overall function of the section was to advise Churchill, using statistics, on the availability and allocation of resources as part of the war effort, later on taking an interest in projected post-war topics. A particular focus of the section was on the efficient use of shipping and manpower. The public presentation of figures and their implications for national morale was a constant concern of Lindemann. The section pursued inquiries made by the Prime Minister, and sometimes by Lindemann himself. Staff members attended both ministerial and official committees on behalf of the section. It was in contact with the outside world, communicating with the scientific community and fielding their suggestions. Donald MacDougall, an economist and deputy to Lindemann, made substantial contributions, particularly through his innovative presentation of statistical information in pictorial form and recommendations on space-saving in the transport of trucks.

The main method by which the section communicated with the Prime Minister was through minutes from Lindemann to Churchill. Over the course of the war the aide sent about 2,000, a rate of approximately one a day. Churchill insisted they be short.[117] They could lead to direct interventions by the Prime Minister. On 25 September 1940 Churchill sent a note to the Minister of Supply expressing pronounced unease at comments the Statistical Section had made on the most recent figures on Small Arms Ammunition. Churchill called for 'a most tremendous effort' to increase production in a range of areas. He closed by remarking: 'I am well aware of your difficulties. Will you let me know if there is any way in which I can help you to overcome them?'[118]

Given the possibility of this sort of intervention, the section was not always popular within the departments it was monitoring. It was suspected of presenting information in an unhelpful or misleading way. Departments complained about not having sufficient time to comment on submissions from the section to the Prime Minister, and sometimes contested the data supplied. The attitude of Lindemann compounded this institutional defensiveness. He was disposed to regard all outside his team (other than Churchill) with suspicion, and could be indelicate in his personal approach. Colville believed Lindemann, although useful to Churchill, sometimes tried to interfere in policy without a clear mandate from the Prime Minister.

A serious struggle took place over the ability of the section to obtain access to information from the departments. On 24 September 1940 Lindemann wrote to Bridges complaining of delays and obstructions, and suggested the need for an instruction to the statistical departments of the Service and Supply ministries that the section had the right to see any of their

---

117 Earl of Birkenhead, *The Prof in Two Worlds: The Official Life of Professor F.A. Lindemann, Viscount Cherwell* (London: Collins, 1961). See also: R. Harrod, *The Prof: A Personal Memoir of Lord Cherwell* (London: Macmillan, 1959).

118 TNA/PRO CAB 21/1366 Churchill to Minister of Supply, 25 September 1940.

material. On 27 September 1940 Bridges received a letter from the economist Roy Harrod, a section staff member (and subsequent biographer of Lindemann) describing how since 22 July he had been trying to obtain figures for gains and losses of operational aircraft from the Air Ministry. The Battle of Britain, which ran from early July to the end of October, was taking place and this information was critical. The ministry had informed him it was not willing to provide the figures in their existing form because it intended to recalculate the data, a task that would take a significant amount of time. Showing his exasperation Harrod went on: 'However tasty the meal that they are preparing, we are hungry now and will gladly take what they can bring straight from the larder, provided only that they can bring it at once.' Prompted by these disputes, on 7 October 1940 Bridges – fulfilling his role as Churchill's administrative fixer – proposed trying to produce a paper, agreed with the departments involved, setting out the position of the section. The consequent note, circulated to various ministries in October 1940, stressed the need to ensure that Churchill obtained the statistical information he wanted in the way he wanted it.[119]

When the war ended Lindemann resumed his academic functions at Oxford, while continuing as a Conservative politician. In 1951, when the Conservatives returned to power under Churchill, he became once more Paymaster General, now as a Cabinet member, accompanied again by MacDougall, with the section re-established. In 1953, under university pressure to end his absence from Oxford, Lindemann resigned. Lindemann was happy to leave, and had sought to leave sooner but the Prime Minister had begged him to stay. Before his final exit Lindemann had defeated his rival, Sandys, in securing the establishment of

---

119 TNA/PRO CAB 21/1366.

the Atomic Energy Authority as an independent public body removed from the control of the civil service.

Thomas Wilson, a member of the Statistical Section, subsequently produced a detailed assessment of the impact of Lindemann, particularly during the war.[120] Wilson described how in 1940 Lindemann provided the government with access to important information about the way the Germans were guiding bombers to particular targets. Lindemann cast doubt on the idea that the enemy might develop a giant rocket and in this instance was proved wrong when the V-2 was built, but he correctly predicted that a pilotless plane, which appeared in the form of the V-1, was a possible threat. Lindemann was a supporter of the strategic air offensive against German cities. Many have condemned this approach for the death and devastation it caused, and for bringing about neither the damage to German defence production nor the disappearance of morale that was intended. Critics have drawn further attention to the loss of life and resources the policy entailed for Britain and the Commonwealth. Wilson challenged the view that the strategy was futile, arguing it achieved more and absorbed less than had been alleged. The scientist and novelist C. P. Snow later drew on the bombing of civilian targets as part of his criticism of the Lindemann–Churchill relationship as a whole. Snow argued Lindeman possessed 'more direct power than any scientist in history'. Lindemann, Snow held, used his closeness to Churchill to isolate or destroy those who opposed him. Consequently he was able to force through with relatively little resistance the policy of an offensive on cities. Describing the relationship between the two men as 'court politics', Snow concluded no one scientist should be given the decision-making power that had been granted to Lindemann.[121]

---

120   T. Wilson, *Churchill and the Prof* (London: Cassell, 1995).
121   C. Snow, *Science and Government* (London: Oxford University Press, 1961), pp. 63–66.

Developments and precedents

During 1916–45 one cannot underestimate the impact of Lloyd George. In an immediate and straightforward sense his innovations enabled him to obtain support from the team he wanted, helping him dominate government from the centre and achieve the outcomes he sought. The longer-term consequences were more complicated. His use of aides undermined his own position over the course of his premiership. The Garden Suburb effectively ended long before Lloyd George left office, however, it proved to be a precursor and in some cases an explicit model for later bodies such as Churchill's Statistical Section and, as we will see in the next chapter, Harold Wilson's Policy Unit. The Cabinet Office, which Lloyd George instigated, was not attached directly to No. 10 and came in part to entrench collective rather than prime-ministerial government, though it could serve the individual purposes of premiers as well, as under Lloyd George. Changes that Lloyd George instigated helped create a more cohesive career civil service. Prime ministers became increasingly dependent on a permanent bureaucracy and its staff – the opposite of what Lloyd George sought and achieved for himself.

During this period the office of Prime Minister was in its second historical phase.[122] Focused on a coordinating role it was generally non-departmental in nature and not disposed towards a direct policy role. Ramsay MacDonald briefly (in 1924) combined the premiership with the role of Foreign Secretary and Churchill created the role of Minister of Defence for himself. Otherwise the office of Prime Minister did not take on a specific portfolio or staff on a departmental scale. There was some testing of the limits of this second-phase premiership. The Lloyd George innovations, in particular the Garden Suburb, and those of Churchill,

122   For the phases see A. Blick and G. Jones, *Premiership*, pp. 134–155.

especially the Statistical Section, represented in part an augmentation of the office within its existing cross-governmental form, though taking on more active policy-involvement at the same time. No specific department of the Prime Minister appeared, aside arguably for the briefest of moments in 1917. Some favoured the idea, such as Adams and initially at least the Haldane committee. Any enhancements to the size or remit of the prime-ministerial staff meant a challenge to others in Whitehall, including departments and their ministerial heads and especially the traditional central department, the Treasury. Such innovations met with institutional resistance, as well as criticism in Parliament and the media. These negative reactions would have been greater with any attempt to establish a full prime-ministerial department.

Less rapid and, on the surface, less dramatic than the Lloyd George or Churchill reconfigurations, was the rise of the permanent civil service as the primary source of assistance for the Prime Minister. The attractions of civil servants were clear. They could provide valuable impartial advice, the stability of continuity and the capacity to operate the official machine upon which premiers and governments as a whole were dependent. The history of this period shows that prime ministers needed other types of aides as well, and that the apparent institutional dynamic of career Whitehall to expand its prominence within prime-ministerial support structures raised problems. Even before the fuller development of the permanent civil service the heavy reliance of Lloyd George on outsiders suggested that career officials might not provide certain qualities, including a direct personal link to a particular Prime Minister, that premiers regarded as essential. If regular civil servants became attached in this way, problems could follow. When Horace Wilson developed a close association with an individual Prime Minister, Neville Chamberlain, and a certain policy he pursued – appeasement – insurmountable difficulties faced the official when there was a change of incumbent at No. 10. The use Conservative premiers made of aides such as Davidson and Ball also showed that the need for staff with close links to the party was likely to continue. The principle of generalism within the civil service meant that specific policy expertise was not necessarily available. The only way to rectify this deficiency was through recruiting specialists from beyond Whitehall.

An important contribution to the rise of the career civil service at No. 10 itself came when Ramsay MacDonald kept on Ronald Waterhouse in 1924. It might seem surprising that the first Prime Minister of a party representing previously marginalised groups, and in theory at least committed to a new social order, should make no impact on the development of aides to the premier greater than helping ensure more permanence in its staffing and the firming-up of the position of the existing bureaucracy. But this outcome was in keeping with the moderate approach of the MacDonald Labour governments. Over time increased interest developed within the Labour Party in the idea of refashioning the staff of the Prime Minister, and the civil service as a whole. Negative interpretations of these early periods of office provided inspiration. In future decades Labour prime ministers would more than compensate for the absence of administrative overhauls in the 1920s and 1930s.

CHAPTER FIVE

NATIONAL DECLINE AND ADMINISTRATIVE REFORM, 1945-1997

In this post-war period and beyond prime ministers struggled to establish a team to help them reverse the fortunes of a declining imperial power. It began with the permanent civil service re-establishing a position of preponderance within the prime-ministerial staff. The challenge which Winston Churchill posed through his use of outsiders during the Second World War subsided. Most of the officials serving the premiership were attached neither to particular prime ministers nor to their parties. They could remain in post when the incumbent changed. It became possible for officials to spend substantial portions of their entire working life serving different premiers in various capacities. Yet there were always gaps the permanent civil service could not entirely fill and important roles it was not fully suited to perform.

From the late 1950s a crisis of national self-confidence led to questions about the organisation and values of the regular civil service. Critics proposed different bureaucratic models and in the following decade party-political staff and experts drawn from outside Whitehall began to develop into an established feature of the administrative system. This process of change generated controversy. The incomers were not entirely welcome in Whitehall and their relationship with representatives of the established machine was sometimes uneasy. This power struggle could not be fought to a definite conclusion and the two groups had to cooperate. Between them they comprised an enhanced support team for the premiership, helping successive prime ministers engage with the problems of a diminishing world power. The premiership continued to develop as an institution. Yet throughout the period some advocated more radical changes than ultimately came about.

Reassertion of career civil service predominance

Following his arrival at No. 10 Churchill's practices challenged the position of the permanent civil service established during the 1920s and 1930s. However, over the course of his premiership Churchill came to rely more and more on regular officials and less on the circle of outsiders whom he had brought with him to the premiership. Then in July 1945, after Victory in Europe but before Victory in Japan, a general election produced an outcome which surprised many. The Labour Party won its first-ever Commons majority – of 145 seats – and its leader Clement Attlee replaced Churchill as Prime Minister. Labour had a radical programme. It promised schemes for universal welfare, including healthcare free at point of delivery, and the nationalisation of key utilities and industries. The Labour government delivered these changes during its period of office, which ran until 1951. By this time it had achieved substantial changes in British politics and society. But while a determination not to return to the social inequality and hardship of the 1930s characterised the overall approach of the government, there was a partial relapse to this earlier decade in administrative methods, including the support provided to the Prime Minister.

The only previous Labour premier, Ramsay MacDonald, had

not taken major steps to fashion a distinctive staff. His most significant impact was enhancing the role of the existing permanent civil service as the main provider of support at No. 10. The advent of Labour as a party of government in the 1920s and 1930s did not make a mark on the prime-ministerial team reflective of the arrival of a new force at the highest level in British politics. But in 1945, unlike on these earlier occasions, Labour had taken office on an ambitious programme of change, aimed at establishing an enhanced social role for government as a regular feature of peacetime and not just as an expedient of war. Attlee could have decided that to implement and maintain this approach he needed a prime-ministerial staff personally committed to the programme, in possession of relevant expertise and perhaps larger in size than the one he ultimately deployed.

However, the new premier made little effort in this direction: Attlee established no equivalent of Churchill's Statistical Section; he did not import as many outsiders into No. 10 as had Churchill; nor did he display an urge to speed up the turnover of career officials in the Private Office (a term in use by this time but probably not habitually). During the war Attlee had promoted the idea of expanding the remit of the Prime Minister, through taking on from the Treasury responsibility for management of the civil service, with a powerful senior official overseeing this function on behalf of the premier. However, Attlee let the idea drop. This lack of action was part of an overall approach to the civil service which Labour followed from 1945 to 1951. He and his ministers were generally comfortable with the administration. Many of them – Attlee included – had recent and extensive experience at high levels in government, having served in the Churchill coalition. The official machine had achieved in wartime the social intervention Labour now contemplated continuing in modified form during peacetime. Some of the key policies the party implemented from 1945 emerged from Whitehall during the coalition period. But curiously Labour seems to have concluded that the permanent civil service, rather than the combination of career officials and a substantial body of temporary outsiders which had operated during the conflict, was generally sufficient for its purposes. After the war, many of the non-career officials returned to previous activities in academia and business. At the same time the Treasury, which had lost influence during the conflict because of the reduced emphasis on financial control, reasserted its status as the dominant office of government.

The personal political style of Attlee was distinctive. Unlike incoming premiers such as Lloyd George and, in future, Blair, Attlee did not have a ready-assembled or substantial entourage of colourful characters to bring with him to No. 10. He was and remains legendary for his uncharismatic, undynamic leadership. He managed a Cabinet of egos, such as Herbert Morrison, Ernest Bevin, Stafford Cripps and Hugh Dalton. But while he was ambitious, the quietly ruthless Attlee did not share their desire for public applause. He lacked the craving to make the direct personal impact of someone like Churchill, preferring to operate within the collective institution of Cabinet and its committees. Consequently Attlee felt he did not require the larger, more customised team that had served his immediate predecessor at No. 10. As an adept bureaucratic manipulator he had less need for aides charged with second-guessing or short-circuiting administrative systems, which he could work for himself. The change-over to Attlee was a jolt for the No. 10 staff. John Colville told us of the contrast with Churchill – stiff not soft collars, lamentable food, a formal rather than a free-and-easy atmosphere.

A key figure in No. 10 under Attlee was Leslie Rowan, the Principal Private Secretary inherited from Churchill. When Attlee became Prime Minister, one of his first tasks was to attend the

Potsdam Conference. Joseph Stalin – not noted for his devotion to continuity of personnel – expressed surprise that the new British premier had brought with him Rowan, the same aide who had supported Churchill.[123] Starting his career in the Colonial Office, Rowan subsequently joined the Treasury. He became a private secretary to Churchill as premier in 1941 and Principal Private Secretary in 1945. He had grown personally close to Churchill and his family, but made a successful transition to supporting Attlee. Rowan was a private secretary's private secretary and was praised fulsomely by colleagues in our interviews. Colville described him as the 'perfect' civil servant: able and possessing personal integrity, push, drive and initiative. Others noted Rowan's grasp of the detail of the work and of how different issues were interconnected. A private secretary Paul Beards used the phrase 'Chief of Staff' in describing his principal. Rowan worked from the small office next to the Cabinet room, on the Whitehall side, at No. 10. He was discreet in his dealings with the premiers he served. He did not seek directly to impose his views upon them; rather he would guide them towards certain conclusions through questions and suggestions. By this means he was able to have policy influence.

When there is a change of Prime Minister it is essential for permanent civil servants to adapt to the needs of the new incumbent, regardless of their particular personal style and party. Rowan displayed this flexible quality. Under Churchill, with his irregular practices and in the ongoing crises of war, work tended to be unstructured. With Attlee and his more formal approach

---

123   Our interviews have enabled us to expand on or modify the account in: D. Jay, *Change and Fortune: A Political Record* (London: Hutchinson, 1980), p. 128. Variants on this story include a stress on the whole Churchill team being kept on, or that Stalin was primarily puzzled by the idea of an unpredictable election outcome, and that President Truman was perplexed by the continuity of staffing because of the US spoils system.

it was different. At first he may have found the new Prime Minister suspicious of him and a little prescriptive, but trust built up. Rowan took the opportunity to bring about an influential reorganisation of the Private Office. He arranged a clearer division of responsibilities between the junior private secretaries: one handling foreign affairs, two domestic issues, and another parliamentary and other matters. Rowan established a system for ensuring all staff members had access to current papers, called the 'dip', which survived until the early twenty-first century when electronic communications rendered it obsolete. He updated a document that had come to be known as the 'Bible', a compilation of precedents providing guidance to the office on how to handle various possible circumstances. Some of its contents were superficially esoteric, covering such issues as Trinity House and royal proclamations. Nonetheless, they could suddenly become important, and such an authoritative document was invaluable. A further administrative rationalisation pursued by Rowan was the introduction of colour-coded files for different categories of business. He also developed the way in which No. 10 interacted with other parts of government, forging close links with the Cabinet Office.

Rowan stayed on until 1947 when he was succeeded by Lawrence Helsby, a promoted junior private secretary. Within No. 10, beneath the level of the Private Office, was the secretarial staff – all women – of the Garden Room, so-called because it was next to the Downing Street garden at the rear of the building. Seemingly dating back to the Lloyd George period, they provided the collective memory and knowledge of established practice which enabled No. 10 to function. Though the Private Office under Rowan and then Helsby was the centre of No. 10, a partisan component of the prime-ministerial team persisted. Attlee received help in handling relations with the Parliamentary

Labour Party from his successive parliamentary private secretaries, Geoffrey de Freitas and Arthur Moyle.[124] In 1945 Attlee made two notable administrative appointments with clear partisan connections: Francis Williams and Douglas Jay. Beards suggested to us that Attlee was motivated by a desire for a party-political kind of briefing that the Cabinet Office was not suited to provide, and that the Prime Minister sensed that he needed economic expertise that No. 10 lacked to enable him to assess departmental proposals, produced by ministers who had fuller support staff than he did.

Williams was a media aide to Attlee from 1945 to 1949. The son of a farmer, Williams became editor of the Labour journal, the *Daily Herald*, in 1936. During the Second World War he took up a post in the Ministry of Information. His Labour connections, media background and experience within government made him a good choice as a press-handler for Attlee. When Attlee became Prime Minister he asked Williams to join him. Attlee was no self-publicist, nor was he interested in his public image. He told Williams he was 'allergic to the press'. But he wanted advice on the likely public reception of policies and to ensure journalists had the information they required. After some discussion about his job-title Williams became Adviser on Public Relations to the Prime Minister. Williams recalls being nonplussed by questions raised in Parliament about the propriety of his appointment. In his view he had come to an already-established role. Working from an office at the front of No. 10 he spoke to Attlee – with whom he had a close working relationship – each morning in the Cabinet room, which the Prime Minister used as his office. The aide saw all the Cabinet minutes and papers and all the significant Foreign Office telegrams. He did not attend Cabinet but could go

---

124   D. Kavanagh and A. Seldon, *The Powers Behind the Prime Minister: The Hidden Influence of Number Ten* (London: HarperCollins, 2000), p. 55.

to Cabinet committees if he thought it useful to do so. Attlee delegated to Williams significant discretion as to how precisely he should act. Williams got on well with Violet, the wife of the premier, and was able to make her laugh. He was well-placed to handle internal government relations since most members of the Cabinet were old friends. Williams insists that, though some saw him as a substantial behind-the-scenes influence on Attlee, the Prime Minister was his own master.[125]

Douglas Jay, like Williams, had experience as a journalist and a wartime civil servant. When appointed as an assistant to Attlee in 1945, he met some bureaucratic obstruction over the details of his position, but downplayed these difficulties and insisted that behaving reasonably with civil servants, rather than assuming they were engaged in conspiracies against him, was the best way to proceed. Jay told us how he and Williams used to go from their offices at the front of the building to join the private secretaries who had tea and cake every afternoon at 4.30. He stressed the importance of this event as a means of talking and exchanging views. After initial resistance Jay obtained access to Cabinet economic papers and joined Cabinet committees on subjects such as coal and food. Attlee would not let him go to the Lord President's Committee on the grounds it was too political. Jay observed that – in contrast to popular perceptions of a dominant office – the premiership could often be impotent and subject to external circumstances. Jay focused on economics and the press. He produced briefs on Cabinet papers, responded to requests from Attlee, sought prime-ministerial approval for his own initiatives, and wrote speeches for the premier. Attlee's notes to Jay were short, and in conversation Jay was unable to extract more than a few words from the Prime Minister. Jay foresaw and

---

125   F. Williams, *Nothing So Strange* (London: Cassell, 1970), p. 215.

attempted – unsuccessfully – to avert one of the disasters of the Attlee premiership, the fuel crisis of early 1947. He sought to alert Attlee to a problem which he saw coming, but got nowhere. In 1946 Jay had left to become an MP because he felt that the dual role of partisan and official was inappropriate.[126] After being elected to Parliament that year he served as a junior Treasury minister under Attlee; and as President of the Board of Trade in the Harold Wilson Cabinet (1964–7).

Post-war orthodoxy

Attlee lost office at the 1951 general election, when Churchill returned to No. 10 for his second and final spell as Prime Minister, which lasted until 1955. By this time a group of interlinked orthodoxies had emerged about the way ministers in general and premiers in particular were to be supported. The first principle of the administrative system was that the Treasury lay at the apex of the civil service. It wielded influence in two key ways, both of which ultimately were associated with its responsibility for resources. First the Treasury, where the head of the civil service was usually based, had an organisational role managing the Whitehall machine. Second through the exercise of financial control the Treasury played an important part in the overall policy direction of government. The Treasury was a key player in decisions about what was to be done and how. Its staff, who came from the best-rated recruits to the home civil service, were of the highest calibre in Whitehall. Since the mid-nineteenth century the Treasury had moved outside the direct remit of prime ministers (though premiers had ultimate responsibility for management of the civil service), representing a reduction in the direct influence of the premiership over government.

---

126   Jay, *Change and Fortune.*

The second orthodoxy concerned the premiership not being a departmental entity, and within conventional understandings there was no pressing reason it should be. Prime ministers had few specific executive responsibilities and exercised leadership to a significant extent through their position as chair of the Cabinet. To help them perform this role on behalf of the collective prime ministers obtained support from the Cabinet Office. For their other tasks, such as disbursing patronage, parliamentary business, handling the press and policy issues requiring their attention, they used the relatively small Downing Street team. A more substantial prime-ministerial staff might pose a controversial challenge to the position of the departments and the collective system of government.

A third orthodoxy concerned the composition of the prime-ministerial aides. The accepted view was that at the core of this team was a group of career officials comprising the private secretaries in the Private Office, headed by the Principal Private Secretary. They managed most relations with the outside world (though a function for dealing with journalists distinct from the Private Office had appeared) and official communications with other parts of Whitehall. Those prime-ministerial assistants who were not permanent civil servants generally occupied the roles of Parliamentary Private Secretary, the whips, sometimes the Press Secretary, and more informal assistants such as individuals whose counsel prime ministers valued. The daily administrative operations of the premiership at No. 10 were to a large extent the work of career staff. Prime ministers were reliant too on the permanent civil servants of the Cabinet Office and Whitehall as a whole.

The institution that provided such crucial assistance to the premier had a distinctive set of values. For career civil servants it was vital to be able to provide loyal support to any given minister, while preserving their ability to serve any future potential holder of the ministerial office. These civil servants generally avoided discernible personal and party-political attachments, or associations with particular policies. Their continuing employment at Whitehall was not dependent upon the fortunes of individual politicians. Allegiance was to the civil service. Officials tended collectively to develop particular policy preferences which they pressed on the politicians they supported.

Alongside this doctrine of impartiality, a philosophy of generalism pervaded Whitehall. The civil service recruitment-process sought individuals in possession of general intelligence, which they supposed could apply to any administrative task. Accordingly these staff moved around a variety of different roles within the civil service. Specific skills, knowledge or experience relevant to particular duties were less valued. F. A. Bishop, Principal Private Secretary to Anthony Eden and Harold Macmillan, conveyed to us how important was the idea of the non-expert all-rounder in Whitehall. When interviewed for the position of secretary, which he took on in 1953, to a mixed committee of ministers and officials on economics, Bishop stressed 'I'm not an economist'. The reply from the high-level Whitehall panel which included Norman Brook, the Cabinet Secretary, was 'just the chap we want'. Within a couple of years Bishop had a job part of which involved providing policy briefs on economics to a Prime Minister, Eden, who was similarly lacking in expertise in this area.

An important test for these various understandings came when Churchill returned to office in 1951, this time without the same dynamic approach of 1940. For the first six months of his second premiership, as in his first, he held the additional portfolio of Minister of Defence; he also experimented with the creation of an inner group of ministerial 'overlords'. But circumstances did not require the centralised leadership of May 1940, and he was not in a position to provide it as, being in his late seventies, his drive was less forceful. This time around, more than helping impose his will Churchill's aides were propping him up (his doctor, Lord Moran, became an important personal influence). When a stroke rendered Churchill inactive in mid-1953, staff members including his joint principal private secretaries, his Parliamentary Private Secretary (PPS) and Norman Brook combined to ensure the government continued functioning without the public becoming aware of Churchill's illness. In a dramatic demonstration of how the premiership is very much a group effort they took decisions on behalf of Churchill which he could not personally confirm. Churchill's main concern about aides at this point seems to have been to ensure he was surrounded by people he was familiar and comfortable with. For instance his son-in-law, Christopher Soames, became his PPS, at first informally and then officially from 1953.[127]

Though Churchill's requirement for people he already knew and approved of might have been modest, it tested the official orthodoxies. Initially Churchill was suspicious of the whole team of private secretaries he inherited from Attlee. Accounts given to us suggest the Prime Minister felt they were 'steeped in socialism' or that he told Brook they were 'drenched in socialism'. A complete displacement would have been a drastic break with prevailing conduct and ultimately Churchill did not attempt it. When he sought to remove the incumbent Principal Private Secretary, David Pitblado, Churchill met with resistance from senior officials. Removing Pitblado would have been unfair to him personally and would also set a bad precedent. First Churchill tried to obtain Rowan for the post. But he was now too senior. Churchill then proposed Colville, his former wartime private secretary and friend. Colville told us he was not comfortable with the idea of

---

127   Kavanagh and Seldon, *The Powers Behind the Prime Minister*, pp. 56–8.

ousting Pitblado, and as a foreign-affairs specialist did not feel confident on home policy. But Churchill wanted Colville. Edward Bridges, head of the civil service and Permanent Secretary to the Treasury, found a way through with the idea Colville and Pitblado be made Joint Principal Private Secretaries. This arrangement proved acceptable and the two worked together harmoniously. In practice Colville was probably more important than his nominal equal. When Eden became premier in 1955 Colville confirmed his personal link to the outgoing premier by leaving No. 10 (and the civil service altogether). Pitblado verified his impartiality by remaining as sole Principal Private Secretary. The Private Office system had proved flexible enough to accommodate Churchill while at the same time preserving continuity.

Norman Brook (1902–1967)

Churchill caused further disruption by seeking to force an official, Norman Brook, to remain in his existing post. In 1951 Norman Brook was about to hand over to Thomas Padmore as Cabinet Secretary. Churchill knew Brook from the wartime period and managed to keep him on, to Padmore's cost. Yet while there was some interference in his career from Churchill, and it was possible to question whether Brook was always completely impartial, Brook exemplified the strength of the career civil service at this time and how important a permanent official could be as an aide to successive prime ministers.

Brook provided confirmation of the preponderance of Oxbridge graduates within the civil service, but did not come from an especially privileged social background. His father had a number of jobs, including tax assessor, school inspector and schoolmaster. Brook secured a scholarship to read Classics at Wadham College, Oxford. He entered the civil service in 1925. Brook became Cabinet Secretary at the beginning of 1947, going on to support four prime ministers from this position until his retirement in 1962. From 1956 Brook took on the additional roles of Joint Permanent Secretary to the Treasury and head of the home civil service. He went on to the chairmanship of the BBC.

By the time Churchill insisted on keeping him as Cabinet Secretary Brook had already provided valuable support to Attlee. There was always a danger of treading on others' toes. But Brook once commented after a specific enquiry from Attlee that he supposed the Prime Minister was entitled to ask him anything. Brook's tasks for Attlee included advising on the emerging issue of atomic weaponry, a new concern for the Cabinet Secretary alongside the other sensitive business they had to deal with. Brook's engagement in this subject, including the development and maintenance of a British deterrent, and incorporating the new destructive force into war planning, continued. Under Churchill, Brook was the most important prime-ministerial aide. In combination with his broader bureaucratic functions he assumed tasks that the No. 10 Private Office might otherwise have taken on. His role was similar to that performed by Bridges for Churchill during the war. Brook advised on political relationships, defence, constitutional matters and more minor issues. He accompanied Churchill on foreign trips and provided him with advice on ministerial appointments. Over time the premier consulted his Cabinet Secretary on civil service personnel decisions, including choosing the premier's private secretaries, though they were more properly the business of Bridges as head of the civil service.

Brook was the central official figure during the policy disaster that defined the premiership of Anthony Eden (1955–7). In July 1956, the Egyptian government announced the nationalisation of the Suez Canal. Eden participated in a response agreed with France and Israel in October the truth of which he concealed from the public, the US and to some extent his own Cabinet.

Israel attacked, followed by a joint operation by Britain and France to occupy the area on the pretext of keeping the peace. The operation began late in October 1956, but Britain declared a ceasefire early the following month because of opposition from the US, on which Britain was financially dependent. Eden, whose physical and mental health were deteriorating, left office in January 1957. Brook had been secretary to what was in practice the 'inner Cabinet' Eden used to conduct his Suez policy, the Egypt Committee; Brook was also chair of the Egypt (Official) Committee and the Defence (Transition) Committee of Whitehall permanent secretaries. He was one of the few officials who possessed full knowledge of the scheme Eden devised. Brook was unhappy about the policy but oversaw its implementation, and provided advice to Eden on how to manage the difficult politics of Suez within government. During the Suez crisis Eden had little contact with Bridges, nearing the end of his term as Permanent Secretary to the Treasury and head of the civil service. According to the historian D. R. Thorpe, Bridges later claimed privately that had he still been Cabinet Secretary at this time 'then Suez would never had happened'.[128]

Prime ministers came and went, but Brook continued, now under Macmillan (1957–63). Brook was a member of the group that accompanied Macmillan abroad, and advised him on policy and personnel decisions. Late in 1957, Macmillan commissioned Brook to produce an official review of the role of Britain in the world and the resources it possessed to exercise it, which ended up promoting the idea that Britain should continue to operate as a global player.[129] Brook's involvement in security issues

---

128 D. Thorpe, *Eden: The Life and Times of Anthony Eden, First Earl of Avon, 1897–1977* (London: Chatto and Windus, 2003), p. 495 n.

129 P. Hennessy, *Having It So Good: Britain in the Fifties* (London: Allen Lane, 2006), pp. 472; 477–87.

persisted. He had some, limited, advanced knowledge in 1961 of the 1963 Profumo scandal. The Security Service prompted him to warn Profumo, the Secretary of State for War, about his association with Stephen Ward because Ward knew Yevgeni Ivanov, the Soviet naval attaché. Brook did not know at the time that Ivanov and Profumo were both having an affair with the same woman, Christine Keeler. He did not bring this issue (or rather the extent of his knowledge of it) to the attention of Macmillan. In some of his advice to Conservative prime ministers, however, Brook lost his impartiality. He even offered views on how the Conservatives should conduct the 1955 general election campaign, seeking to involve the retired Churchill. This kind of attachment is a problem when displayed by a permanent civil servant in such a senior position.

Brook had the skills of a courtier and made himself useful to prime ministers. He combined this ability with the advantages of an embedded bureaucrat, adept at manipulating the administrative system. As Cabinet Secretary he was responsible for the network of Cabinet and official committees that underpinned collective government. The Cabinet Office had a vital source of authority in framing Cabinet discussions through briefing the Prime Minister (or whoever took the chair of a given Cabinet committee). Two functions were key: distilling the contributions of the departments (over which they might even consult Brook in advance) and making a fresh input. Though Brook could come across as slightly dry, his prose flowed and his submissions made an impact. The private secretaries at No. 10 were reluctant to add substantive comments to them since they had already passed through the Whitehall system. By contrast, prime-ministerial staff were less likely to be deferential towards suggestions from the departments. In this sense Brook had a direct line to the Prime Minister as chair of Cabinet, not mediated or filtered by others.

In 1956 Brook added to his Cabinet Secretary portfolio the posts of head of the home civil service and Joint Permanent Secretary to the Treasury. He was 'in effect, permanent secretary to the prime minister – the PM's chief adviser across the full range of prime-ministerial functions'.[130] Staff at No. 10 viewed him as a quasi-permanent secretary for No. 10, albeit at arm's length, long before 1956. Such a role did not exist formally – and then only briefly – for another half-century, taken on by Jeremy Heywood for Gordon Brown in 2008, continuing under David Cameron until the end of 2011. Philip de Zulueta, a private secretary under Eden, Macmillan and (in the post-Brook era) Home, described to us how Brook was always 'there behind the scenes' providing support to Private Office staff. They would go to him for advice. He told them he would always back them, provided they did not 'get across' the permanent secretaries of their home departments. Bishop told us that Brook advised him on how to 'steer policy' and to give advice to the Prime Minister. Brook was a frequent presence in the No. 10 building and Zulueta described him as the Prime Minister's 'Chief of Staff'. This position entailed tensions, Zulueta implied, because Brook had to support the Cabinet as a whole, rather than assisting one particular member of it.

Brook's overall role was immensely demanding, even for an official of his abilities. The workload he undertook over the years ground down his health and perhaps shortened his life. But he bought exceptional achievement at this price. The compound of proximity to a run of prime ministers and his centrality in the civil service network, sustained for a period of well over a decade, made him probably the most important prime-ministerial aide there has been. Bridges comes close, but late on in his career Brook began to eclipse him. Earlier comparisons are difficult:

---

130 K. Theakston, *Leadership in Whitehall* (Basingstoke: Macmillan, 1999), p. 102.

perhaps John Scrope as Secretary to the Treasury for Walpole and Pelham can be considered a potential rival. The careers of others who sought to balance politics and administration, and their rival sources of authority, in the way Bridges did – Horace Wilson in the 1930s and William Armstrong in the 1970s – demonstrated how difficult and hazardous a task it was.

Challenges to the Whitehall orthodoxy

It had just about proved possible to keep Churchill happy about his desired appointments without compromising the career civil service. But there remained hints of a need for different arrangements altogether. In 1951 another aide Churchill acquired from his previous stint at No. 10 was Lord Cherwell (Frederick Lindemann). As before, Cherwell supported Churchill from the post of Paymaster General. Cherwell recreated the Statistical Section which he had headed during the war, though in a smaller form than before. Once again Donald MacDougall was his deputy. Cherwell in this later period seems to have been somewhere between a straightforward prime-ministerial aide and a minister in his own right, providing briefings to Churchill and following his own initiatives.[131] Cherwell was one of the 'overlords' intended to be responsible for policy coordination within Churchill's failed scheme to re-establish a system akin to the War Cabinet he had used previously. The staff under Cherwell and MacDougall included three economists and two career officials with economics training. Both Cherwell and MacDougall took flats in No. 11 Downing Street.[132] They made their most significant contribution in helping to block a proposal emanating from

---

131 A. Seldon, *Churchill's Indian Summer* (London: Hodder and Stoughton: 1981), pp. 171–3.

132 D. MacDougall, *Don and Mandarin: Memoirs of an Economist* (London: John Murray, 1987), pp. 82–3.

the Treasury in the spring of 1952. Known as 'Robot' it involved substantially increased flexibility for the sterling exchange rate. Until the early 1970s the defence of sterling within the Bretton Woods system, intended to provide currency stability, often dominated economic policy. Had the government adopted Robot, Britain and the world, for better or worse, might have followed a different path.

As Prime Minister, Macmillan tended to draw on extra-Whitehall assistance, including from his friend the economist Roy Harrod, though the full extent of his influence is difficult to assess. More challenging to usual practice was Macmillan's incorporation of an outsider into the Private Office who sat alongside the private secretaries. John Wyndham was born to a military and landowning family. As a wartime temporary civil servant he became private secretary to Macmillan, who was then a junior minister at the Ministry of Supply. They developed a close relationship, with Wyndham supporting Macmillan through numerous subsequent government appointments, but not becoming a career official. Macmillan became Prime Minister in January 1957 and on 27 May wrote to Wyndham asking if he would be 'willing to rejoin the old firm'. Wyndham stayed at No. 10 until the end of the Macmillan premiership in 1963. He worked unpaid.

The Principal Private Secretary at the time, F. A. Bishop, recalled Macmillan asking him 'I wonder if you object to letting John Wyndham join the team?' Bishop was worried about the idea of someone who was not a permanent civil servant coming into the Private Office and seeing all that went on, but Macmillan was determined to obtain the help of Wyndham, a friend he felt to be reliable. Prime ministers can, if they force the issue, have the last say. Ultimately the arrangement proved harmonious. Bishop found Wyndham congenial and said there was never a cross word between them. Staff from the time told us they felt his past as a civil servant meant he was not really an outsider. Tasks Wyndham performed for Macmillan in this role included providing political intelligence of various sorts, handling relations with government ministers, helping with practical arrangements, and providing personal support, including improving the mood of the Private Office through humour. He assisted with non-parliamentary speeches, collecting material from the departments, and played a part in handling relations with the Conservative Party. Bishop played down Wyndham's importance, and said he had no impact on policy. Wyndham recorded that a 'private secretary should be totally frank with his master, but he should never try to become an éminence grise'.[133] Here he captured the nature of his relationship with Macmillan, supporting but not overbearing him.

Macmillan obtained political assistance from two employees of Conservative Party Central Office, George Christ and Eldon Griffiths. Late on in his tenure he added to them two further aides, Nigel Lawson and John MacGregor, both of whom later became Conservative Cabinet members. They were based at the Conservative Research Department and not on the public payroll, but were available to support the Prime Minister. Both were journalists recruited primarily to help with party speeches. When he became Prime Minister in 1963, Alec Douglas-Home retained all four of these party-political aides. An early task was the fighting of a by-election, since Home had renounced his peerage to make himself acceptable as a premier and he needed a seat in the Commons. This task was difficult for career officials to engage in. Lawson and MacGregor were central to the successful campaign. Lawson later coached Home for television appearances in the lead-up to the general election of October

---

133 Lord Egremont, *Wyndham and Children First* (London: Macmillan, 1968), pp. 161; 191.

1964.[134] During the campaign Lawson and MacGregor moved into Downing Street.

When prime ministers sought to impose their own choices of private secretary or boost the outside support available to them, they probed the limits of the existing model and explored other possible options, without fully committing to them. A change of national mood then created circumstances conducive to more decisive change. Retrospectively, it seems the trigger for this change of tone was the Suez crisis of 1956. The affair exposed Britain as no longer an independent global power; its political institutions, associated with a failed and duplicitous policy, did not emerge favourably. William Clark resigned from his post as Press Secretary to Eden because of his opposition to the Suez operation. On 4 November, having already decided he wanted to go, Clark complained in his diary of 'the deception, the hypocrisy'. He believed Eden was mad. Clark wanted to become a journalist, his previous occupation, so he could help bring down the government to which he was attached and keep 'cowards and crooks' away from power forever. 'God, how power corrupts,' he wrote.[135]

Suez induced an atmosphere in which various British social institutions, previously largely immune to serious criticism, suddenly appeared vulnerable. Though such discussion did not start immediately, it began within a few years. A number of general tendencies and events spurred this anguished self-reflection. Britain had not joined the European Economic Community (EEC), which became operative in 1956. Instead Britain initiated another economic bloc, the European Free Trade Association, in 1960. But, judging this latter experiment not to be

---

134 D. Thorpe, *Alec Douglas-Home* (London: Politico's, 2007).
135 W. Clark, *From Three Worlds* (London: Sidgwick and Jackson, 1986), diary entry for 4 November 1956, p. 209.

a success, Britain then applied for membership of the EEC, only for France to veto this bid in 1963. Data showed British economic growth rates to be relatively low in international comparison. With these perceived problems and failures in mind, observers blamed assorted manifestations of the so-called 'Establishment'. The supposed culprits included the education system, the City of London, Parliament – and the civil service.

Numerous analysts cast doubt on various assumptions underpinning the way permanent officials operated. Some argued that career-long employment produced an institution out of touch with the outside world. Accounts portrayed the Treasury, with responsibility for bureaucratic management and sweeping policy influence, as bloated and excessively powerful. The Treasury was depicted as wedded to failing, laissez-faire economic policies. Doubts surrounded the ability of a politically impartial civil service effectively to provide for all the needs of elected politicians. Critics argued the philosophy of generalism denied governments the technical expertise they required. Against this background one of the great reformers of the institution of the premiership, Harold Wilson, took office as Labour Prime Minister in 1964.

Harold Wilson and the Kitchen Cabinet, 1964–70

Harold Wilson's historical reputation is tainted both by supposed shortcomings in his personal style and by policy failures. He often emerges from accounts as a short-termist lacking in principle, favouring gimmickry over more substantial action. A central policy of his 1964 government was planned economic growth. He failed in this objective, partly because of his insistence on defending sterling at its fixed exchange rate of $2.80. Ultimately his governments conceded defeat here too and devalued to $2.40 in November 1967.

Yet there are some lasting aspects of his legacy; for example in his approach to the office of Prime Minister, Wilson was a significant innovator. He introduced new models for its institutional structure and the staff employed within it. Though his changes were subject to criticism from contemporaries, his successors at No. 10 have largely worked within the patterns he created.

Labour came to power in 1964, offering a change of policy direction after thirteen years of Conservative government. It sought to reverse perceived British decline. In particular the party proposed overhauling the supposedly stagnating British economy through the introduction of a National Plan. Integral to this approach were alterations to the structure and staffing of Whitehall. For the first time, and forty years after Ramsay Macdonald became the inaugural Labour Prime Minister, a Labour government took office with specific plans to make a substantial impact upon the machinery of government. Wilson established a Department of Economic Affairs, intended as a counterweight to the Treasury and other departments. To help staff these new creations, and in some longer-established parts of government, including the office of the Prime Minister, a number of temporary aides entered Whitehall from beyond the career civil service. Some of these individuals made up the first wave of 'special advisers' in British government – temporary civil servants assisting particular ministers on whose patronage they were employed, not bound by the usual Whitehall impartiality rules and able to some extent to pursue the objectives of the party of government.[136]

One reason for this influx was the lack of expertise among permanent officials. In particular a perception existed that economists within Whitehall – who made up the largest portion of the outsiders recruited from 1964 onwards – numbered too few. In 1966

---

136 A. Blick, *People Who Live in the Dark: The History of the Special Adviser in British Politics* (London: Politico's/Methuen, 2004). For Wilson's overall approach see: G. Jones and J. Burnham 'Innovators at 10 Downing Street'.

Wilson commissioned Lord Fulton to chair a committee of inquiry into the civil service. The report produced in 1968 was critical of generalism and recommended a change of approach. Alongside the desire for more specialised knowledge within Whitehall, another motive for the recruitment of outsiders was the desire to ensure that institutional inertia among the already-existing staff did not hamper the introduction of the Labour programme. A further influence was the observation of foreign methods. Features of the British civil service such as the emphases placed on generalism, continuity and political impartiality were internationally exceptional. Increased domestic criticism of British performance made such qualities the subject of controversy. A number of observers drew attention to examples from abroad of officials being trained experts, of greater interchange between the administration and the outside world, and of staff being more closely attached to individual politicians and their programmes. Partly because of its association with the successful use of indicative economic planning, the French administrative model was fashionable. French ministers obtained support from *cabinets* comprising both career staff they personally selected and outsiders with technical expertise. These teams differed from the Whitehall Private Office because of the greater extent to which the minister handpicked their membership: they were more clearly a personalised group.

Wilson made extensive use of outsiders in his prime-ministerial team for a variety of reasons. Wilson had caricatured his immediate predecessor, Home, as an ineffectual aristocratic anachronism, with whom Wilson contrasted himself as a purposeful moderniser. Wilson imported the aides he thought he would need to give his leadership the thrust he desired. He would need help to take an active role in government policy instead of being a dispassionate chairman. Wilson was a trained economist and saw value in staff drawn from this same background. He had worked in the

Economic Section of the War Cabinet during the Second World War, participating in an earlier use of outsiders at the centre of government, which had included in it the attachment of a group of temporary officials working directly for the premiership in Churchill's Statistical Section.

Wilson was of a conspiratorial – even paranoid – disposition. Given this mindset he suspected career civil servants might seek to frustrate him in part because his policies threatened the position of the Treasury. Aides drawn from beyond Whitehall could help him circumvent such resistance. These recruits were suited to assisting in a further struggle. Since the 1950s a fissure had opened in the Labour Party between the leftist followers of Aneurin Bevan and the more centrist devotees of Hugh Gaitskell. Wilson came from the 'Bevanite' group (though he was not as doctrinaire as many within it), but numerous senior figures within his party and government were 'Gaitskellites', or, at least, not Bevanites. Aides loyal to him and his particular orientation within Labour could be valuable in such circumstances. At the same time Wilson should not be seen purely as a schemer trying to outwit the permanent civil service and the right of his party. In some senses he was an admirer of the Whitehall machine. He did not attempt more radical approaches to his staff, such as formally introducing a full *cabinet* system, much less a shift to the spoils system as deployed in the US, involving mass clear-outs of officials with changes of political leadership. Equally he understood the value in a leader rising above faction and he often sought to conciliate within his party. He advanced the careers of the young Gaitskellites Denis Healey, Roy Jenkins and Tony Crosland, though partly as a means of playing them off against each other and reducing potential threats to his leadership.

Wilson was a politician who placed a premium on communicating with the public and consequently had a keen interest in the media. To ensure it was handled as he wanted he employed an outsider, Trevor Lloyd-Hughes, previously political correspondent for the *Liverpool Daily Post*, as his Press Secretary in 1964. Lloyd-Hughes advanced the development of No. 10's press operation into an established team. Though he came from beyond Whitehall, Lloyd-Hughes was not a partisan appointment and he was studiously impartial when speaking to the lobby journalists. Wilson sought Gerald Kaufman, later a Labour MP, to provide supplementary briefing of a more party-political nature. In 1969 Joe Haines, a Labour-supporting journalist, succeeded Lloyd-Hughes, and gained the new label 'Chief Press Secretary', a title which future holders of the post retained.

That Wilson came to power with a sizeable entourage, all eager for jobs, had a major impact on his personnel recruitment policy. This loose grouping of allies, which had grown out of the Bevanite faction, came to be labelled his 'Kitchen Cabinet' and continued to meet in various guises once Labour came to power. Some of its members became ministers. Richard Crossman and Barbara Castle, both MPs and old Wilson collaborators, served in the Cabinet throughout 1964–70. Wilson deployed others as prime-ministerial aides. Most senior in this group were Marcia Williams, who held the title of Personal and Political Secretary; Thomas Balogh, initially described as Economic Adviser to the Cabinet; and George Wigg MP, holding the sinecure office of Paymaster General. All three were loyal to him and came from his group within the Labour Party. Wigg took a particular interest in security, supplementing the role played more regularly by the Principal Private Secretary and Cabinet Secretary on behalf of prime ministers, and other issues of a personally or politically sensitive nature. He earned the nickname the 'Spymaster-General' because of his obsession with the intelligence and security agencies.

Wilson's approach to staff was a challenge to prevailing arrangements. During the 1950s, outsiders had worked in administrative roles within the prime-ministerial team, even, in the case of John Wyndham, within the Private Office. The idea of appointing a press officer who came from beyond the machine (Clark for Eden) or who had clear party orientation (Williams for Attlee) was reasonably acceptable. But Wilson incorporated aides from outside Whitehall in a more deliberate fashion. The number of imported aides was greater than at any point since the Second World War. Both Williams and Balogh had their own distinct bodies and teams of staff, rather than having to operate in and around existing structures. The introduction of these outsiders forced consideration in Whitehall of issues such as where they should be housed, security clearance, access to papers and meetings, and job-titles and terms and conditions of employment. Consequently, even if they were to some extent constrained by the official machine, their presence became more established and legitimised, though the process of formalising arrangements developed only slowly over the decades that followed.

Derek Mitchell, the Principal Private Secretary when Wilson took office, found the experience testing. His time at No. 10 had begun unusually early in the year during the Home premiership. Mitchell told us that his predecessor as Principal Private Secretary, Tim Bligh, had built up close personal relationships with both Macmillan and Home and had become somewhat detached from the civil service. Senior Conservatives, Mitchell felt, regarded Bligh as impossible to replace. He had brought about what Mitchell regarded as a problematic blending of the party-political and the official, for instance in his desire to move Lawson from the Conservative Research Department to Downing Street. Laurence Helsby, a private secretary to Attlee, and from 1963 to 1968 head of the home civil service and

Joint Permanent Secretary to the Treasury, told us he thought
Bligh went beyond what was proper. When Mitchell arrived, Bligh
refused to leave. The two sat together in the Private Office for
a number of months, with Mitchell hoping Bligh might take a
day off sick and provide a chance to oust him. Probably because
of the unusual position he was in, Mitchell said he struggled to
form a relationship with Home. A Labour victory in the forthcoming general election seemed likely, but Mitchell believed that
Bligh hoped Wilson would decide to keep him on. Although Bligh
officially left a month before the poll, he showed up at No. 10
on election night to support Home and his family; then he was
finally gone.

Mitchell had sympathy for the incoming Labour government.
He said the civil service as a whole looked forward to a change,
but he struggled to cope with the abrasive personalities of the
'Kitchen Cabinet', their demands and the proprietary issues their
presence in the prime-ministerial team raised. Tensions existed
not only between the external appointments and the regular
staff, but between members of the Wilson entourage: especially
Wigg and Williams, who were both prickly personalities, jeal-
ously guarding their access to the Prime Minister. In 1966 Wilson
replaced Mitchell (who left by mutual consent) with Michael
Halls, against advice from the permanent civil service.

Halls had been Wilson's junior private secretary when he was
President of the Board of Trade under Attlee. In this sense Wilson
was further imposing his mark on his team, making a personal
selection of the career official to head his Private Office. Perhaps
he was moving informally towards a *cabinet* system at No. 10.
Halls was fiercely loyal to Wilson. Marcia Williams regarded him
as an ally. Balogh too felt he was helpful in providing access to
papers, whereas Mitchell had been obstructive. Though good at
managing the office he was reluctant to delegate. Halls died in

1970 while still in post. The pressure of the job had fallen heavily upon him, perhaps justifying civil service doubts about his suitability. But health difficulties were not unique to Halls among prime-ministerial aides over the years. Helsby reeled off for us a list of principal private secretaries who had suffered serious illness and even premature death in the second half of the twentieth century. Eric Seal, Helsby recounted, was 'ground down' by working for Churchill during the war. Supporting the same Prime Minister, John Martin had a 'nervous and physical breakdown'. Rowan, who assisted Churchill and Attlee, suffered duodenal ulcers, was in 'poor shape' and was having an operation when Helsby took over from him in 1947. Helsby himself complained he 'got chicken pox and mumps' and was 'under strain'. As well as Halls, both Rowan and Tim Bligh, who worked for Macmillan and Home, 'died early'. In seeking a replacement for Halls, Wilson overrode the Whitehall view once again, obtaining Alexander ('Sandy') Isserlis. Both Halls and Isserlis were not former Treasury officials: Wilson was wary of the Treasury. Wilson took this assertive approach on a further occasion when he returned as Prime Minister, insisting on Kenneth Stowe when Robert Armstrong left as Principal Private Secretary in 1975.

Though Wilson challenged the position of the career civil service, it remained a significant source of support to him. His style as a leader – partly conscious, partly the product of indecision – was to create competing poles of influence so he was never dependent on just one. A manifestation of this approach was that in taking policy advice he liked to consider views from different sources, such as permanent officials and party-political advisers, and then arrive at his own decision. Completely neutering the regular civil service was not part of his agenda. Nor would it have been a practical objective, except through a far larger operation than the incorporation of outsiders to No. 10 and other parts of government that took place in 1964. Wilson needed career officials to make the bureaucratic machine work for him. They included the Cabinet Secretary, Burke Trend, a man who over time became increasingly important to Wilson. After some effort the Cabinet Secretary eventually succeeded in ousting Balogh from the prime-ministerial staff on grounds of his inappropriate handling of official papers, and Wigg left in 1967. Williams stayed on throughout the 1964–70 Wilson premiership (and afterwards) but the overall influence of the Kitchen Cabinet faded over time. The Wilson experiment, however, had a lasting impact. His first premiership marked a tangible shift in the nature of prime-ministerial support staff. It suggested there was a firm place for outsiders in peacetime, making the premiership more customised to suit the needs of particular prime ministers, enhancing both its party-political dimension and its capacity to engage in policy.

Marcia Williams (1932–)

Marcia Williams is a controversial figure who, nevertheless, made a major contribution to the career of the Prime Minister she served – though she hampered it as well. Aside from her particular significance to Wilson, her impact on the development of the office of Prime Minister is substantial. She began working as a secretary for Wilson in 1956 and their association would last for decades in and out of government. She ran his office in the Commons as Leader of the Opposition from 1963. At No. 10 she put in place the Political Office, which became responsible for handling the relationship between prime ministers and their parties, both within and beyond Parliament.

Williams was at the centre of the team that travelled with Wilson during the 1964 general election campaign, which ended in a narrow Commons majority of five for Labour. She subsequently noted that when Wilson and his entourage arrived at

No. 10 that year only a small number of staff was waiting for them; there was no round of applause. Williams contrasted this entrance with those of both Wilson and Edward Heath after they had won clearer poll victories in 1966 and 1970 respectively. On these occasions larger groups attended, clapping enthusiastically. She judged members of the existing personnel were unwilling to show enthusiasm for a less secure government. The version of the handover Derek Mitchell put to us stressed that while staff were personally upset at the thought of Home and his wife having to leave, they were ready to get on with their job.

Strained relations with the permanent civil service defined Williams's time as a prime-ministerial aide. She described how she had held talks with Bligh before the 1964 general election about the plans Wilson had for his staffing arrangements if Labour took office. Bligh, in her account, put forward a view on behalf of the official machine that she and members of her office could not be housed at No. 10. Despite the objections, Wilson took Williams and her team with him into Downing Street. She had already earmarked for her use – with the approval of Wilson – the Cabinet waiting room at the other end of the Cabinet room. Wilson instructed Mitchell it would be her office. It became a centre for ministers – particularly those who were allies of Wilson – to gather and talk to the Prime Minister after Cabinet. She later had a further space partitioned for her at the House of Commons. As Wilson took to working not in the Cabinet room but in the study upstairs Williams often attended him there.

The permanent civil service objected to the job title Williams would have preferred, 'private secretary', presumably because applying it to her would have been a threat to those in the Private Office who already held this title. Consequently Wilson and Mitchell agreed on the description 'Personal and Political

Secretary to the Prime Minister'. Williams found Mitchell concerned to preserve the distinction between outside staff and career officials. The consequence in her view was that the personal appointments brought in by Wilson felt alienated and they began to behave in a hostile fashion. Williams took exception to the exclusive social background of the women who worked in the Garden Rooms. Mitchell, for his part, related how he had a long emotional talk with her about roles at the beginning. She told him she believed the existing No. 10 staff were disloyal and needed a purge, introducing Labour supporters. Her attitude continued and he was unable to establish a strong working relationship with her.

At the core of the dispute between Williams and Mitchell, as proxy for Whitehall, was the prospect of an entity composed of outsiders appearing in the prime-ministerial staff, taking on functions previously performed by career officials, in particular the Private Office. The handling of correspondence was a key battleground. Initially, according to Williams, Mitchell wanted her and her staff to deal only with letters from Labour Party branches and Wilson's constituents. But she eventually ensured she obtained responsibility for all correspondence with the Parliamentary Labour Party, all Labour Party members and all Labour-affiliated trade unions. From the point of view of the Private Office, the idea of no longer handling letters from Labour MPs was the most objectionable. After thirteen years of Conservative government the other types of correspondence were less familiar and therefore would not be missed. Williams became responsible as well for the political, constituency, personal and private engagements of the Prime Minister. Dealing with Whitehall was not the only challenge Williams faced. She recorded the Labour Party machine was not prepared for government and it took time to establish a proper communications network linking No. 10, party headquarters at Transport House and the Parliamentary Labour Party.[137]

Williams's battles led to the establishment at No. 10 of the Political Office. During her period it employed between eight and twenty-four staff. When she and Wilson returned to No. 10 for his 1974–6 premiership the intervening Conservative government had retained it, though in substantially scaled-down form. Yet there were flaws in Williams and her relationship with Wilson that detracted from her achievements. Williams possessed an explosive personality that added to the tension in her relations with career civil servants and others. Members of the Wilson inner circle observed his emotional dependence on Williams. It may be that these negative tendencies became more pronounced as time progressed. Two accounts in particular, from Joe Haines and Bernard Donoughue, senior policy adviser to Wilson from 1974–6, portray her playing psychological games with him and ruthlessly attacking any rivals within his entourage, while he nervously humoured her. The consequence was his distraction from other more important issues. Mitchell described how the division Wilson introduced in No. 10, with Williams responsible for 'political' matters and Mitchell for 'official' matters, meant the Prime Minister constantly had to deal with even trivial disputes. Whether the hold Williams had over Wilson was derived from any specific knowledge she had about his past is not clear. Insinuations were made over the years about the true nature of their relationship but nothing definitive has been placed in the public domain. Even her detractors agree she possessed significant valuable qualities as an aide, including her political awareness.[138] A more neutral

---

137 M. Williams, *Inside Number 10* (London: Weidenfeld and Nicolson, 1972).

138 B. Donoughue, *The Heat of the Kitchen* (London: Politico's, 2004), pp. 223–69; J. Haines, *The Politics of Power* (London: Jonathan Cape, 1977); J. Haines, *Glimmers of Twilight: Harold Wilson in Decline* (London: Politico's, 2003).

observer, Michael Palliser, a foreign affairs private secretary to Wilson, described to us her constructive input to speeches. Kenneth Stowe, Wilson's final Principal Private Secretary from 1975, noted Williams could have a good point about something but make it in a tactless way. It is probably the case that while she may have used her sex to her benefit at times, it was not an automatic advantage. Williams could not have achieved what she did as a female while being weak; yet, because she was a woman, her aggressive behaviour was more likely to meet with condemnation.

Thomas Balogh (1905–85)

The Budapest-born Balogh was both problematic and important. In the history of aides to the Prime Minister he played multiple roles: as a theorist and advocate of particular ways of supporting the premier; a practitioner; and a precursor of future structural developments in the office. During his training as an economist he worked under the President of the German Reichsbank, Hjalmar Schacht, who later became Economics Minister to Adolf Hitler from 1934 to 1937. Balogh's subsequent proposals to Wilson partly drew on his positive assessment of the policies Schacht devised for Hitler, including the construction of a central European trading bloc. In 1930 Balogh moved to Britain, becoming a protégé of J. M. Keynes, with whom he would later have an irreparable split. In 1939 he was appointed a Fellow of Balliol College, Oxford, where he became a friend of Wilson. Balogh was active in Labour circles. Traditionally the party had fewer resources for research staff than the Conservatives, and such academics as Balogh who were willing to provide their services for free were valuable. But, as Balogh did, they could have strong agendas of their own.

Balogh was the sternest member of the school of criticism of the permanent civil service that had developed since the late 1950s. He attacked career officials for their lack of expertise and identified a tendency for them to impose their own economically liberal preferences on politicians. Balogh advocated direct intervention in the economy and felt the Treasury-dominated civil service was not suited to this task. In promoting these views Balogh was influential in the establishment in 1964 of the Department of Economic Affairs. He had a further impact on Whitehall that may not have appeared as important at the time but proved more enduring. One of his proposed solutions to the supposed weaknesses of the administrative machine was the introduction of expert economists from outside, loyal to the particular party of government and the ministers they served. Such aides would enter and leave office with the politician to whom they were attached. They became known as special advisers.

Balogh's appointment in 1964 attracted public interest, partly because another Hungarian economist, Nicholas Kaldor, an old friend and rival of Balogh, was appointed as a special adviser at the Treasury at the same time. Some portrayals of Balogh depicted him as a sinister figure. Initially he was given a room in the Cabinet Office building in 70 Whitehall, adjoining No. 10, and at first he was described publicly as employed within the Cabinet Office, with the title Adviser on Economic Affairs, though internal documentation described him as Special Adviser to the Prime Minister. After the 1966 general election he moved to an office inside No. 10. Balogh produced a vast quantity of written submissions to Wilson and had frequent personal meetings with him. He used his contact with the premier not only to seek to influence policy but to expand his remit and that of his team of assistants. Balogh was notoriously obstreperous and consequently Wilson could find him tiresome and at times avoided him. The aide's relations with ministers and officials were often tense. Balogh entered into disputes with permanent civil servants over what his salary should be, his access to official papers and his rights to attend official committees. He told us that these struggles gave him a heart attack. Balogh's view that permanent officials were conspiring against him had some degree of truth – or perhaps it was self-fulfilling. The Treasury set up a committee, probably early in 1965, to make contingency plans for the devaluation of sterling, which eventually happened in November 1967. The existence of this body was kept secret from him, despite his position as economic adviser to the Prime Minister.

Balogh was assertive in his attempts to shape many features of policy, using his connection with Wilson and other contacts. He seems to have influenced Wilson's decision not to devalue sterling at the outset of his premiership in October 1964. By the end of this year Balogh had reversed his position. He apparently thought that sterling should float rather than move to a new fixed rate. But he could not persuade Wilson. The Prime Minister banned discussion of this issue within Whitehall. Balogh opposed plans for British membership of the EEC. A policy success attributed to Balogh was the revision of the pricing arrangements for North Sea gas. Alongside policy advice, Balogh provided counsel to Wilson on party-political issues including ministerial appointments. He maintained contact with journalists, acquiring the reputation of being a source of leaks.

Balogh headed a small prime-ministerial team but felt Wilson was reluctant to publicise this body. All but one of its members were economists: of the two initial staff members, Michael Stewart (deputy to Balogh) and John Allen, the latter was a political aide. Allen, who was close to Marcia Williams, left his post in 1965. Within months of his arrival in May 1966, aide Richard Pryke resigned because of his objections to the course of economic policy. Replacements for both joined the team and its overall size grew to three and then four in 1966. Then later on it shrank in size and importance. Following the forced exit of Balogh in 1968,

Andrew Graham, a Balliol colleague of Balogh's, who had joined his staff in October 1966, succeeded him as its head. The general purpose of the group was to oversee the whole of government economic policy on behalf of Wilson and deal with specific issues as they arose. Particular team members did not specialise and might take on work falling within any area.

By 1967, like Lindemann before and others in similar positions after him, Balogh was experiencing growing pressure from Balliol to return to academic work. He was also involved in a dispute with Trend. A particular concern for Burke Trend was that Balogh might insert himself between the Cabinet Office and Wilson as chair of Cabinet, providing an independent commentary on Cabinet Office briefs, which the Cabinet Office regarded as the final word from Whitehall. Trend used Balogh's eccentric behaviour against him. The Cabinet Secretary alleged to Wilson that Balogh had a habit of surreptitiously viewing confidential papers not intended for his eyes. The claim had at least some basis in truth. It seems the private secretaries in the Private Office knew not to leave papers out on their desks when they went to lunch because Balogh was likely to snoop. Eventually Wilson eased Balogh out of his role in the middle of 1968 and made him a Peer. Despite officially leaving the Prime Minister's inner sanctum, Balogh carried on counselling the Prime Minister informally and was still a frequent presence in No. 10. In 1974 when Wilson became Prime Minister again, he appointed Balogh a Minister of State at the Department of Energy.

The balance shifts: Heath and after

The changes Wilson introduced from 1964 suggested a definite shift in the make-up of the prime-ministerial staff. A period from the 1920s, with an interruption during the Second World War, had seen the career civil service as the dominant provider of support to the Prime Minister. Now this stage was ending. From 1970 onwards the Wilson experiment took hold. The component of aides to the premier drawn from outside Whitehall both expanded and gained a firmer footing. Partisan appointments made wholly on the patronage of a given Prime Minister no longer needed to be as vague or marginal as previously. The way in which the premiership and government as a whole operated became different.

The Conservative successor to Wilson, Edward Heath, sought to avoid the fraught atmosphere at No. 10 associated with the staff Wilson had imported. But, as with the change from David Lloyd George to Andrew Bonar Law and Stanley Baldwin in the early 1920s, the Heath alterations involved a shift of tone as much as or even more than substantive modification. Greater harmony within the prime-ministerial team under Heath was largely attributable to easier personal relations between the members concerned. More of a shared social background existed. The media did not show the same interest in outside aides to Heath as they had in appointments under Wilson. But, while the personnel were different and controversy was less, key features of the Wilson team persisted.[139]

The Political Office, always staffed by partisan recruits who were by convention paid from outside rather than official funds, survived the changeover to Heath. His Political Secretary was Douglas Hurd. The son of a Conservative MP, Hurd attended Eton College, where he knew Heath's Principal Private Secretary Robert Armstrong, and Trinity College, Cambridge. Hurd later became an MP himself and eventually Foreign Secretary. He began his career as a Foreign Office official, then joined the Conservative Research Department. As Leader of the Opposition, Heath

---

139 See: Kavanagh and Seldon, *The Powers Behind the Prime Minister*, pp. 72–102.

obtained Hurd's services as an adviser on foreign policy. Heath then brought Hurd to No. 10 following the 1970 general election. The clearest guidance Heath seems to have given Hurd about his role was to avoid the tension of the Marcia Williams period. Yet, sitting in the office she had obtained next to the Cabinet room, Hurd was clearly enjoying the benefits of her traumatic breakthrough.

After arriving at No. 10 Hurd handed back some responsibilities that Williams had assumed. The Private Office would now have primary responsibility for the Prime Minister's diary, dealing with letters from MPs, working on official speeches and selecting guests to invite to official receptions. Hurd's slimmed down Political Office would liaise with the Conservative Party and handle the party-political activities of the premier, such as attendance at party conferences. Hurd noted that clear distinctions of this sort were not always possible. For arrangements to be workable, different types of staff had to work happily together, which they did. Hurd obtained access to the official information he needed. He was able to see the Prime Minister at virtually any moment. Heath sometimes visited him in his office in the late evening. Hurd did not attend Cabinet nor its sub-committees, but he sometimes went to more informal meetings of ministers. Hurd monitored developments from a party political angle for the premier. Though he enjoyed smooth relations with permanent civil servants, he felt that the Prime Minister did not receive sufficient political advice and that civil service counsel was dominant. Hurd found Heath's lack of interest in his speeches a flaw. In 1973 Hurd left to concentrate on the parliamentary seat he was fighting. His replacement was William Waldegrave, another future Conservative MP and minister. In the years that followed, the Political Secretary and Political Office became a fixed part of the premiership, providing the link between prime ministers and the parties they led.

Heath received support from special advisers, though fewer than had assisted Wilson. The Wilson-era experiment of using these aides across government as well as at No. 10 continued. Though it later became clearly established that aides appointed in this way were paid from public funds, some at this time were supported from external party-political sources. Under Heath the first in a series of failed attempts by partisan members of the prime-ministerial staff to galvanise special advisers throughout Whitehall into a cohesive force took place. Michael Wolff had a presentational role, including helping with speech-writing and preparing the Prime Minister for press conferences. Another special adviser supporting Heath, whose activities have not attained the recognition they merit, was Brian Reading. An economist, Reading previously worked in the Conservative Research Department and as a personal counsellor to Heath when in opposition. When Heath came to power in 1970 he appointed Reading as a special adviser, officially based in the Cabinet Office but in practice working directly to the Prime Minister. Late in 1971 Reading moved formally to the Central Policy Review Staff (CPRS), though his link to Heath continued. Primarily Reading advised on economic policy. Echoing Balogh in some ways he sought to challenge the Treasury. From mid-1971 Reading was a strong advocate of the Heath 'U-turn', which entailed abandoning the initial Conservative commitment to government disengagement from the economy in favour of active reflation. Alongside his policy interventions Reading took an interest in communication and sought to obtain for the office of the Prime Minister an overview of government announcements, anticipating the idea of the Strategic Communications Unit introduced under Tony Blair at the end of the century.

Heath established a new body that also included outsiders in it. Heath, like Wilson, pursued a programme of economic reform that he intended to achieve partly through administrative innovation. Perversely perhaps, in pursuit of his goal of less government he created an official institution. When established in 1971 the CPRS was formally a creature of the Cabinet as a whole, but, given the Prime Minister was chair of the Cabinet, the linkage between him and the CPRS was close. The effectiveness of the latter was dependent upon the continued confidence of the former. The CPRS was a body of about sixteen that mixed seconded career officials with temporary outside appointments. Lord Rothschild, a research scientist, banker and former bomb-disposal expert, was the first head. It reviewed national economic performance, studied long-term issues falling within the remit of more than one Whitehall department, and produced briefs either for Cabinet or the Prime Minister on particular ministerial policy proposals. The CPRS survived the transition to Labour in 1974. Margaret Thatcher initially retained it in 1979, but wound it up in 1983.

Though he used external advisers, Heath revealed a stronger affinity for certain career officials. Both of his chief press secretaries, Donald Maitland (1970–73) and Robin Haydon (1973–74), came from the Foreign Office and his Principal Private Secretary, Robert Armstrong, was a crucial figure in his team. In the early 1970s William Armstrong, head of the home civil service, became one of the most prominent prime-ministerial assistants of all, though with unfortunate consequences. In 1968 he had become the first holder of the post of head of the home civil service to be based in the newly formed freestanding civil service department. In this office Armstrong initially concentrated on implementing the spirit if not the recommendations of the Fulton Report on the civil service. But under Edward Heath, who succeeded Harold Wilson at No. 10 in 1970, Armstrong took on different functions and became a key prime-ministerial assistant. He was one of a small number of people in politics who succeeded in developing a close relationship with Heath, and became for a time the most important of the Prime Minister's advisers.

Armstrong was central to the defining policy shift of the Heath government. A surge in unemployment led Heath by late 1971 to lose confidence in his efforts at economic disengagement. Armstrong played into Heath's thinking by advocating increased public spending to assist selected companies. Heath, who did not wholly trust the Treasury, chose to construct his own team to bring about this change of direction. Heath placed Armstrong at the head of a secret committee based in the Cabinet Office. Working with the CPRS and officials from different departments, reporting directly to the Prime Minister, it devised various spending proposals.

Heath became increasingly dependent upon Armstrong for economic and other advice. He came to be labelled informally and critically the 'Deputy Prime Minister'. Observers speculated that Heath intended to create a department of the Prime Minister with Armstrong at its head. Armstrong was central to the development of the statutory incomes policy introduced late in 1972 and developed an increasing personal commitment to the new policy agenda of the Prime Minister which spilled over into public association with Heath and his agenda. When the second stage of the incomes policy was launched, he appeared on the stage at the Lancaster House press conference sitting next to the Prime Minister. The loss of impartiality was compounded when Armstrong took on a belligerent and public role on behalf of the government during the civil service strike of 1973. But the reflation and pay-restraint programmes Armstrong oversaw did not work. Unemployment and inflation rose. His counsel became increasingly partisan and unbalanced. He offered Heath advice on election-timing and developed conspiracy theories about left-wing plots which he believed the government needed to crush. Early in February 1974 Armstrong, in poor physical health, suffered a mental breakdown. He returned to work in March 1974 but had already determined to take early retirement. Had he not done so, there may have been problems in someone so closely identified with the previous Prime Minister and his policies serving under his successor.[140]

The Policy Unit: 1974–79

When he returned to No. 10 in 1974 Wilson expanded the major contribution he had already made to the development of the prime-ministerial team. The partisan aides who accompanied him from opposition included Marcia Williams and Joe Haines, who had become his Chief Press Secretary at Downing Street in 1969 and continued in this role after the 1970 poll defeat. A third key outsider supporting Wilson during his second premiership was Bernard Donoughue. A political scientist from the London School of Economics and Political Science, Donoughue became part of the Wilson team during the February 1974 general election campaign, despite coming from the Gaitskellite wing of the Labour Party. The body which as senior policy adviser Donoughue created, the Policy Unit, represented a further Wilson innovation in the office of Prime Minister. Wilson justified the introduction of the Policy Unit as following the recommendations of the Fulton Report of 1968. It was another manifestation of Wilson's desire to create competing power bases and to receive advice from different sources. He intended it as a counterweight to the permanent civil service, in particular the Treasury. A further consideration for Wilson in establishing the Policy Unit was that of divisions in his own party. While in the 1960s Wilson

140   K. Theakston, *Leadership in Whitehall*, pp. 192–201.

was more concerned about the Labour right, now the radical left was a problem for him, in particular the Cabinet minister Tony Benn, who advocated heavily interventionist government economic policies. In such circumstances it was important for the Prime Minister to have a source of support distinct from Labour ministers and the party.

The Balogh team of the 1960s provided the immediate precedent for the Policy Unit, but the latter body was larger, had a more defined role and was based fully at No. 10. On the advice of Joe Haines, Donoughue resisted being based in the Cabinet Office, even though it meant being given a lower equivalent rank to career officials than he would otherwise have received. During this period the unit comprised around seven to ten advisers, many of them academic experts, with each given particular policy areas to oversee on behalf of the Prime Minister. They were all drawn from outside Whitehall, but knew how it worked: they were employed as special advisers. The Policy Unit represented an expansion at the prime-ministerial centre, supporting a more active policy role by the premier, using aides who were not permanent civil servants and not subject to full Whitehall constraints. Once again Wilson was challenging more conventional approaches to the premiership and the civil service.

Facing this threat, and probably motivated as well by a genuine desire to make a success of the new arrangement, a senior figure within the Whitehall machine moved to codify the position. In April 1974, the Cabinet Secretary, John Hunt, produced a note, agreed by Donoughue and the Principal Private Secretary Robert Armstrong, on the role of the Policy Unit. During the tough negotiations involved in the drafting of this document, Donoughue had insisted on changes which enhanced the access of his unit to committees and papers. He was content with the portions of the text seeming to impose constraints on his team, since he did not want its members to overreach themselves in their engagements across government and cause problems for Wilson. As Donoughue saw it, the 'concordat', as it came to be known internally, helped change special advisers at No. 10 from buccaneers to a more normal part of the environment.

The paper was circulated in the Cabinet Office (to a limited number of staff) but not more widely and it was never published. It afforded Policy Unit members more privileges than special advisers elsewhere in Whitehall. In particular staff at the No. 10 team could occasionally attend official committees of the Cabinet. The note stipulated clear limitations upon Policy Unit aides. It emphasised they were employed as civil servants paid from public, rather than party, funds. They did not have an all-embracing policy scope: they would be focused on the short term and on specified domestic issues, largely excluding international affairs and defence. Donoughue would devise a work programme or list of topics for his staff to follow which he would discuss periodically with Hunt. Alongside a delineation of the areas in which the Policy Unit could operate the note sought to prevent the new body from encroaching upon the Private Office as the conduit for official communications with the departments. Any direct contact with permanent civil servants in other parts of Whitehall required authorisation from within No. 10 and the minister involved. It could be only for the purpose of acquiring information – not for passing on ideas, comments or decisions. Policy Unit staff who attended Cabinet official committees would not show the Prime Minister their papers nor report back to him on the views expressed by individual officials, except following consultation with Hunt.

The firmest insistences came at the end of the paper. The first involved the 'steering brief' produced by the Cabinet Secretary and the Cabinet Office. It was sent to the Prime Minister to facilitate his chairing of Cabinet and Cabinet committees. Authorship of this document was crucial because it provided the opportunity to frame and guide Cabinet deliberations. While members of the Cabinet secretariat involved in its production could have informal discussions with Policy Unit staff, Cabinet Office responsibility for the brief remained as it was before the existence of the Policy Unit. The Policy Unit would not receive a copy, though the Prime Minister could request a view on it from members of this team if he wished. Second the Policy Unit should never be used as a means of communication between the Prime Minister and the No. 10 Private Office, nor between the Prime Minister and the Cabinet Office. In a later letter of September 1974 Armstrong described a further safeguard on the position of the Private Office. Donoughue did not involve himself in management, appointments, staff or intelligence, which remained within the purview of Armstrong as Principal Private Secretary.[141]

Despite these restrictions the Policy Unit became a genuine force in Whitehall. At its head Donoughue was an effective operator. He often attended Cabinet (and describes on one occasion sending in his place his deputy, Andrew Graham, a veteran of the Balogh team of the 1960s).[142] For Donoughue, it was crucial to have good relations with the Private Office. At the same time the unit had to be distinct from the career civil service. Donoughue did not want any career officials in his team – a practice that would change under subsequent heads of the unit. Emphasising that they were not part of the permanent machine, staff made submissions on green paper which Wilson could easily pick out from other papers. These approaches helped the Policy Unit make a difference to what the government did, particularly in the domestic field, such as the economy, finance and health. It also

141   See: TNA/PRO PREM 15/104.
142   Donoughue, *The Heat of the Kitchen*, p. 162.

counselled Wilson on renegotiation of the terms of membership of the European Economic Community in 1974–5. Furthermore, the Policy Unit helped Wilson steer his government in particular ideological directions. A specific member of the staff took on the task of monitoring Tony Benn. When Benn was Secretary of State for Industry his department produced in 1975 an interventionist white paper which the Policy Unit rewrote for Wilson to make it more acceptable to him. Benn believed that Donoughue was briefing the press against him.

When James Callaghan became Prime Minister in 1976 he retained Donoughue and the Policy Unit – a testament to the political skill of the former and the perceived value of the latter. Callaghan found the staff useful in enabling him to play a more active part in policy formation. He was a less chaotic premier to work for than Wilson. In late 1976, in the midst of a sterling crisis, the Cabinet agreed to a £3.5 billion reduction in the Public Sector Borrowing Requirement up to 1979 so it could obtain support from the International Monetary Fund. The issue had threatened to split the government and Labour Party. But Callaghan, supported by the Policy Unit, skilfully achieved consensus through collective discussions. In some of his work for Callaghan, including contributing to the Prime Minister's call for a 'great debate' on education, Donoughue extended beyond the short-term role envisaged for him in the initial agreement with Hunt. Donoughue suggested to Callaghan that the forthcoming general election be held late in 1978. Had Callaghan followed this advice the poll would have taken place before the industrial action known as the 'winter of discontent' of 1978–9. The chances of a Labour victory would probably have been greater.

Margaret Thatcher and her aides

Prime Minister Margaret Thatcher (1979–90) set out to alter

radically the nature of government and society in Britain. Over the course of her premiership she began the process of moving nationalised industries and utilities into private owner-ship, established new legal restrictions on trade unions, broke with established ideas about economic management and imple-mented various free-market policies, like full convertibility for sterling and competition within the public sector. In pursuing these various goals she faced resistance from many sections of society, including in her own party and Cabinet. She overcame objections using an assertive leadership style, often seeking to limit full collective discussion. Prime-ministerial aides were crucial to the development of the Thatcher programme and her attempts to impose her views on government. Yet there were tensions in the pursuit of smaller government and less bureaucracy which relied on centralised Whitehall structures to achieve them; her use of staff played a significant role in her demise as premier.

During her premiership Thatcher made full use of Wilson's innovations in the deployment of outsiders. But initially she was not convinced about the value of the Policy Unit. Its maintenance could conflict with an agenda of more efficient government. The employment of party-political aides was arguably an inappropri-ate use of public resources. Thatcher felt Heath had placed an excessive emphasis on the use of the machinery of government. She maintained the unit, but with only three staff. Thatcher did not fully trust the permanent civil service, which she felt was as a public sector institution inherently averse to implementing her agenda. Given this attitude the unit could be useful, and she later incorporated some career officials into it. At first the slimmed-down Policy Unit focused on only a few core concerns. When Thatcher abolished the CPRS in 1983 the unit grew and later had between seven and nine members, who were able to achieve wider coverage of the business of government, with each aide tackling a specific area. The Policy Unit began communicating with departments in ways that the concordat established by Hunt and Donoughue in 1974 prohibited. Contacts became habitual and involved Policy Unit staff passing on ideas, messages and views, not simply obtaining information. In such circumstances the distinction between a suggestion and an instruction could blur. Such activity by implication undermined the position of the Private Office.

The first head of the Thatcher Policy Unit was John Hoskyns. He was associated with the Centre for Policy Studies (CPS), a free-market think tank. In opposition, Hoskyns and others from the CPS had influenced Thatcher's thinking and helped her to develop ideas independently from the Conservative Party. He was a self-made businessman rather than one who had taken on an existing concern. Hoskyns saw himself as promoting the value of such supposed wealth-creators, who he felt were socially undervalued in Britain. Ferdinand Mount, a journalist, succeeded Hoskyns in 1982. His tasks for Thatcher included writing the 1983 Conservative general election manifesto, which included key commitments of the Thatcher period, including legislation to regulate trade unions. John Redwood joined the Policy Unit in 1983 and became head in 1984. A key interest for him while at No. 10 was implementing the privatisation programme. Brian Griffiths, an LSE economist, served from 1985 to the end of the Thatcher premiership. His particular concerns included education. He was determined that he and his staff should spend time outside Whitehall absorbing external influences.

Ian Gow, Thatcher's Parliamentary Private Secretary until 1983, was an important aide and helped connect the Prime Minister with her MPs. He was often regarded as her best PPS, winning the confidence of her backbenchers while conveying her wishes skilfully to them. Tragically, he provided her with some controversial advice on Northern Ireland, supporting the Unionist cause. He was killed in 1990 by the Irish Republican Army. While Gow was renowned as the most effective PPS to Thatcher, Peter Morrison was so incompetent in the post as to be blamed for her losing the premiership in the coup that brought her down in 1990.

Thatcher took with her to No. 10 as Political Secretary Richard Ryder, who had served her in an equivalent role in opposition. He was said to be so discreet that he wore his wrist-watch face down to avoid showing anyone the time. He left in 1981 and became an MP in 1983. Probably the most important of Thatcher's political secretaries was Stephen Sherbourne, previously of the CRD and a departmental special adviser.

Another more nebulous outside appointment was David Wolfson, of Great Universal Stores. He took the title Chief of Staff but his role was not as prominent as this label suggests. According to one of our interviews, Thatcher arrived at No. 10 saying she wanted Wolfson to be her equivalent to Hastings Ismay for Churchill. A long-serving staff member who had been at No. 10 in Churchill's time pointed out that Ismay had not been 'Chief of Staff' but 'staff officer to the Chiefs of Staff'. Wolfson sat in a room beyond the two private secretaries' rooms in the direction of the Cabinet Office known as the 'Wiggery' for its previous occupant George Wigg. The functions Wolfson performed included ensuring the smooth operation of No. 10 and providing personal support to Thatcher. He was one of the few people around Thatcher who felt able to talk to her abruptly when required. Thatcher brought with her from opposition a personal assistant, Caroline Stephens, who married Ryder. She kept Thatcher's diary. Career officials were keen to bring this function under their control. Stephens worked alongside Cynthia Crawford, an aide who could help Thatcher with personal matters, such as her styling.

In 1979 Thatcher appointed Derek Rayner of Marks & Spencer to advise her on reducing administrative waste in government. Though he was based in the Cabinet Office, Thatcher saw him very much as part of her team. Working one day a week without payment he set up an Efficiency Unit comprising staff transferred from different parts of Whitehall. In spring 1980 he set out through his unit to reduce paperwork in the short term; to improve the performance of specific governmental functions in the medium term; and to bring about cultural changes in the long term. The Efficiency Unit operated through a programme of scrutinising departmental functions. Support from the Prime Minister and the full engagement of the particular department involved were vital. The size of the unit was deliberately kept small – by the mid-1980s it had a staff of about eight to ten. While there is scope for debate about how successful the unit was in achieving financial savings, it had a wider impact on overall attitudes and perceptions within Whitehall. Under Robin Ibbs, successor to Rayner from 1983 to 1987, the unit produced the *Next Steps* report. When implemented it led to substantial reform of the civil service, with the creation of arms-length executive agencies carrying out much of the work of implementing government policies.[143]

From time to time in the Thatcher period a miscellaneous collection of advisers and would-be advisers flitted through No. 10, usually from the extreme right wing of the Conservative party, concerned to ensure the Prime Minister kept to the true faith of Conservative ideology. Some of them enjoyed their reputation as exerting influence behind the scenes. Thatcher used them intermittently, to act as links to their supporters, or perhaps for murky

---

143 C. Haddon, *Reforming the Civil Service: The Efficiency Unit in the early 1980s and the 1987 Next Steps Report* (London: Institute of Government, 2012).

tasks inappropriate for civil servants, like keeping a watch on potentially disruptive elements in trade unions. Names like David Hart and Alfred Sherman cropped up in the press as slipping in and out of 10 Downing Street. Perhaps for old times' sake and their past loyalty Thatcher did not want to tell them to leave, but they never exerted as much influence as her less covert advisers and aides.

While Thatcher had an ambivalent attitude towards the permanent civil service, she was willing to enlist career staff in her cause. The Efficiency Unit, though headed by an outsider, was staffed by career officials. Under Hoskyns a permanent civil servant joined the Policy Unit; the presence of regular officials within that body, though in a minority, became standard practice. This inclusion might be seen as compromising the distinctiveness of the Policy Unit, or civil service impartiality, or both. Thatcher's suspicion of the Foreign Office spurred her reliance on some of its own staff. Working as her foreign-affairs private secretary, Charles Powell, who came from the Foreign Office, acquired the reputation within his home department of having grown too close to Thatcher; he never returned to the Foreign Office, leaving Whitehall altogether after serving Thatcher's successor, John Major, for a time. In 1982 Thatcher appointed a foreign policy adviser, Anthony Parsons, a retired diplomat. In 1984 Percy Cradock, the former ambassador to China, succeeded him. From 1985 Cradock combined his role as aide to Thatcher with being chair of the Joint Intelligence Committee in the Cabinet Office. Cradock stayed on for a time under John Major, until 1992.

The most visible of Thatcher's No. 10 team was another regular official, her Chief Press Secretary Bernard Ingham. Before arriving at No. 10 he had been a journalist and Labour supporter. Ingham had ample relevant experience, including dealing with five No. 10 press secretaries during his time as a departmental head of information. Ingham saw his job at No. 10 as a spokesman for the premier and, if needed, the government as a whole; advising the Prime Minister and the government on presentation; and coordinating government communications at official level.[144] In 1989 Thatcher added to Ingham's portfolio the role of head of the Government Information Service, previously held by the head of the Central Office of Information. No Prime Minister's Press Secretary had held this post before or since, though Ingham downplayed the significance of this unique coupling. Such was the closeness of Ingham to Thatcher that critics treated him as embodying many of the supposedly undesirable features of her premiership. Ingham subsequently recorded various charges levied against him, including his association with an inappropriately personal prime-ministerial system; presenting a presidential image; participating in the leak at the centre of the Westland scandal; favouring particular newspapers over others; being a 'Deputy Prime Minister'; denigrating ministers; introducing a tabloid dimension to government information; and facilitating a centralised form of government.[145]

Increasingly, as her premiership progressed, Thatcher alienated Cabinet colleagues through her leadership style. Her use of aides to watch over and even counteract her colleagues was a source of resentment. An important illustration of this tendency was Alan Walters. A special adviser, he was an economist who had been involved in promoting the doctrine of monetarism to Thatcher when in opposition. He was too senior to be included in the Policy Unit but worked alongside it. Walters had two stints at No. 10, 1981–84 and 1989, with an interlude in academia in the US. He played a part in devising the 1981 Budget, which controversially increased taxes to reduce the Public Sector Borrowing

144 B. Ingham, *Kill The Messenger … Again* (London: Politico's, 2003), p. 177.
145 B. Ingham, *The Wages of Spin* (London: John Murray, 2003), pp. 100–107.

Requirement during an economic downturn. In 1989 Walters provoked – or provided an excuse for – the resignation of the Chancellor of the Exchequer, Nigel Lawson (once a prime-ministerial aide to Macmillan and Home). Lawson was unhappy about the public exposure of differences between him and Walters, in his view encouraged by Walters. In October 1989 Lawson told Thatcher that either he or Walters must leave. Thatcher refused to countenance losing Walters, and Lawson resigned; Walters left soon afterwards. When John Major became premier in 1990 he cultivated a more inclusive approach to the role, less interventionist and more collegial. But his No. 10 staff – including the first head of his Policy Unit, the economics journalist, Sarah Hogg – remained available to facilitate prime-ministerial interventions when required.

The persistence of career Whitehall: Robert Armstrong (1927–) and Robin Butler (1938–)

The landscape of the prime-ministerial support staff had changed. By the 1980s outsiders were entrenched. But ample scope still existed for permanent officials to occupy key roles. To some extent the model of a permanent civil service was self-sustaining. Who better to assist in handling the personnel and procedures of the Whitehall machine than aides drawn from within it? Their familiarity with the bureaucracy, built up over long periods of employment, made them invaluable. Two career officials in particular during this period spent much of their time in Whitehall as prime-ministerial aides, both supporting a series of premiers in different capacities.

Another Etonian prime-ministerial aide, Robert Armstrong had up to 1970 spent most of his civil service career in the Treasury, with a spell in the Cabinet Office. He told us how in April of that year he heard on a car radio that Michael Halls,

Principal Private Secretary to Wilson, had died. Armstrong had a hunch that he was headed for No. 10. Initially Wilson insisted on having Sandy Isserlis rather than Armstrong. The agreed arrangement seems to have been that if Heath became Prime Minister he would have the option of revisiting the appointment. When he became premier, Heath duly replaced Isserlis with Armstrong, who stayed on until 1975. William Armstrong, the head of the home civil service, hoped Robert Armstrong would form a bond with Heath, who was notoriously awkward in his social interactions, through their shared love of music. When studying at Balliol College, Oxford, Heath was an active musician and became friends with Armstrong's father, Thomas, an organist and conductor of the Oxford Bach Choir. William Armstrong's plan proved to be a success; aide and Prime Minister became close. When the head of the home civil service tried to move the Principal Private Secretary on after two-and-a-half years (to a promotion in the Treasury), Heath insisted on keeping him.

In July 1970 William Armstrong told Robert Armstrong that Heath wanted him, and did not need to interview him. Robert Armstrong turned up on his first Monday for a handover with Isserlis. At six in the evening Heath came out of the Cabinet room, said there was lots of hard work to be done, and went back in again. Armstrong found the 'Bible' of office procedure was out of date and later produced a renewed account. As Principal Private Secretary he had a general responsibility for management of the office, with the appointments secretary handling day-to-day operations. Armstrong took a close interest in private-secretary appointments and over time built up a team he had chosen. Other areas of responsibility included honours, relations with the Palace and security issues. Armstrong commented on policy proposals from the departments, often in a forthright fashion. He exercised more forbearance with Cabinet Office briefs. Heath used Armstrong as an intermediary within government, speaking to others on his behalf and reporting their views back to him. Armstrong had frequent contact with the inner group of ministers Heath trusted most. These functions emerged, Armstrong felt, because of Heath's reserved, distant manner. Institutionally Armstrong had close dealings with the Cabinet Office. The Principal Private Secretary assisted Heath as the premier took a prominent personal role in negotiations for British membership of the EEC, apparently causing some unease in the Foreign Office. The No. 10 Private Office dealt directly with French President Pompidou's team. Armstrong was available to help at any time with whatever was of foremost importance to Heath. Though they had ongoing contact, it was not even necessary always. The aide felt he knew his chief's mind without having to talk to him.

This connection carried dangers. William Armstrong told Robert Armstrong he had been put forward as Principal Private Secretary because he was judged able to stand up to the pressures. William Armstrong cautioned that in himself he was nothing. He was only of use if he genuinely reflected the premier and acted as a channel of communication. Robert Armstrong knew that to believe he had power in his own right was a corrupting view, but one that was hard to resist. An earlier Principal Private Secretary, Tim Bligh, had succumbed.

When the Conservatives lost their majority in the February 1974 general election Heath attempted – unsuccessfully – to form a coalition with the Liberal Party. He met the Liberal leader Jeremy Thorpe at No. 10 with Armstrong present.[146] Despite his strong link with Heath the new Prime Minister Wilson was keen to retain the services of the incumbent. Unlike during his first premiership, and in contrast to Heath, Wilson was a less

---

146 J. Campbell, *Edward Heath: A Biography* (London: Jonathan Cape, 1993).

interventionist Prime Minister this time around, seeing himself now as more in the Attlee mould. Wilson chose not to live at No. 10 in his second term so he was not as readily accessible to staff. Though Marcia Williams may have initially been hostile to Armstrong, he eventually proved effective at handling her, reducing her level of influence but not incurring her hatred. He and Bernard Donoughue, who set up the Policy Unit for Wilson at this point, forged a mutually supportive relationship. After ending his spell at No. 10 Armstrong moved to the Home Office, becoming Permanent Secretary in 1977. In this role he built on his acquaintance with the intelligence world which he had already developed during his time as Principal Private Secretary to the Prime Minister: a connection which was a staple component of his next post.

Robert Armstrong served as Cabinet Secretary from 1979 to 1988 (going on to combine the role with that of head of the home civil service). In this time he supported only one premier: Thatcher. He did not establish as firm a personal connection with her as he had with Heath. Some within her circle may not fully have trusted him, but Armstrong gained the respect of Thatcher, who needed him for his ability to operate the machine and admired his work in helping her pursue her streamlined style of government. Armstrong played an important role in the negotiation of the Anglo-Irish Agreement of 1985, an historic point in the development of the Northern Ireland peace process. As joint head of the home civil service from 1981 (with the Permanent Secretary to the Treasury) and then sole head from 1983 he found Thatcher taking a greater interest in Whitehall promotions than had previous prime ministers. Her attitude prompted criticism on the grounds it entailed politicisation.

Armstrong obtained a higher degree of public exposure than many earlier senior civil servants, though he did not want it. First the Westland affair of 1985–6 brought him into the open. This scandal centred on a conflict between the Secretary of State for Defence, Michael Heseltine, and Thatcher, over the future owner-ship of a British helicopter manufacturer. Armstrong was drawn into an appearance before the Commons Defence Committee, with the task of explaining that No. 10 was not the source behind a leak of law officers' advice which took place during the dispute. Armstrong's reluctant celebrity status was enhanced further by the *Spycatcher* case in 1986. The government wanted to prevent the appearance of a book by a former Security Service agent, Peter Wright, which contained embarrassing allegations about the conduct of domestic intelligence operatives. Armstrong was despatched to Australia to argue the British official case. He was subsequently subject to nine days of strenuous cross-questioning. During his appearances he used the phrase 'being economical with the truth'. The subtlety of his words – which were quoted from an earlier prime-ministerial aide, Edmund Burke – was lost on the media, which derided him.[147]

Few aides have served as many different prime ministers as Robin Butler, who supported three Conservative and two Labour premiers over a period of a quarter of a century. In 1972 Butler was working at the CPRS when Robert Armstrong, who knew him from the Treasury, recruited him to No. 10 in the face of some institutional resistance. Between 1972 and 1975 Butler was a private secretary first to Heath then Wilson. He was Principal Private Secretary to Margaret Thatcher from 1982 to 1985. Butler was present with Thatcher at the Grand Hotel in Brighton during the 1984 Conservative Party conference when an IRA bomb attack took place.[148] Butler looked after the official papers in the

---

147   Theakston, *Leadership in Whitehall*, pp. 202–26.
148   J. Campbell, *Margaret Thatcher*, vol. 2, *The Iron Lady* (London: Jonathan Cape, 2003), p. 430.

aftermath. He was unfortunate enough to be present for another terrorist incident, at a meeting chaired by Major in the Cabinet room in February 1991, when the IRA launched a mortar attack on Downing Street.

After serving as Second Permanent Secretary to the Treasury (1985–7), Butler succeeded Robert Armstrong as Cabinet Secretary and head of the home civil service. In his time in the post (1988–98) he served Thatcher, Major and Tony Blair. When Major replaced Thatcher as Prime Minister late in 1990 Butler was waiting to greet him when he entered No. 10 and he figures prominently in accounts of the Major premiership (1990–97). They knew each other from their earlier shared time at the Treasury. The Prime Minister found Butler helpful, easy to work with and effective. They came from different social backgrounds but had a common interest in cricket. Major describes how Butler 'knew the Whitehall machine and all its ways'.[149]

Butler advised Major on ministerial appointments including the construction of his first Cabinet in 1992 and subsequent reshuffles. Butler was important to the implementation of the Citizen's Charter, a programme intended to secure rising standards in public services. After its initial launch in spring 1991, Major felt the departmental response to his initiative was unenthusiastic and disappointing. He found the significant administrative strength of the Cabinet Office a useful supplement to the relatively small No. 10 machine. Butler helped Major establish an official committee based in the Cabinet Office, working with the Policy Unit and the Treasury, to implement the Charter. He also played an important part in the attempts to achieve a peace settlement for Northern Ireland and in 1993 made on behalf of the government a covert trip to Ireland to receive a sensitive document from Albert

149   J. Major, *The Autobiography* (London: HarperCollins, 2000), p. 101.

Reynolds, the Irish Taoiseach. Later in the same year he made a further secret journey to Ireland to convey a message from Major.

During the Major premiership various scandals prompted increased media, and hence public, concern about the integrity of public-office holders including ministers and MPs. Butler counselled Major on issues of propriety. He helped investigate allegations of misconduct by members of the government, such as Jonathan Aitken, when Minister for Defence Procurement. Butler advised on the establishment of inquiries into the role of the government in supplying arms to Iraq and on the setting up of the Committee on Standards in Public Life. He advised Major in 1994 on how to approach parliamentary opposition to the European Finance Bill, which came from within the Conservative Party. In 1995, when Major's leadership was under heavy fire, the senior Cabinet minister Michael Heseltine was given the portfolio of Deputy Prime Minister, partly as a means of guaranteeing his loyalty. Since this is a vague role Heseltine was concerned to define the details of his new office; Butler helped establish them.[150]

After Labour's victory in the May 1997 general election Tony Blair entered the Cabinet room at No. 10 for the first time in his life. Butler was waiting for him as he had been for Major. The aide showed the new premier which chair at the Cabinet table belonged to the Prime Minister. Butler explained that the civil service had been studying the Labour manifesto and asked Blair what he wanted him to do next. Butler served for the first eight months of the Blair premiership. Blair found him a loyal aide who did his utmost to implement decisions whether or not he agreed with them. Butler continued providing ongoing support to the premier. For instance in the summer of 1997 he participated in discussions about how to handle the exposure of the

---

150 Major, *The Autobiography*; A. Seldon with L. Baston, *Major: A Political Life* (London: Phoenix, 1997).

extra-marital relationship of the Foreign Secretary, Robin Cook. But Butler objected to the style of decision-making under Blair and his extensive use of special advisers.[151] Later after retirement he gave public expression to such concerns, through his chairmanship of the official review of intelligence leading up to the Iraq War and other interventions.

Rise of the premiership but not a department

The firmer incorporation of outsiders into the prime-ministerial team from the 1960s onwards was part of a wider process. The premiership was becoming larger. It developed increasingly discernible specialised functions. It was a more entrenched institution, a definite entity in its own right. By the time of the Heath premiership the total number of staff in the Prime Minister's Office was in the low sixties. Between 1974 and 1989 it varied from the mid-sixties to the low seventies. Then in the Major era by 1995 it had risen to eighty-one. Support staff, such as cleaners, who had previously been registered as Cabinet Office staff, began to be counted in No. 10's figures. In 1995 the grand total calculated on this basis was 107. These figures include many staff who were not senior aides to the Prime Minister and small changes in methods of calculation, such as reclassification of Cabinet Office personnel, could produce relatively large increases. But overall growth – even when produced by alterations of methodology rather than reflecting new employees – was a manifestation of the ongoing development of the premiership as an institution. At the top level, though the numbers involved were fewer, there was expansion, with teams including the Policy Unit introduced. Further assistants, such as members of the Central Policy Review Staff, could to some

---

151   T. Blair, *A Journey* (London: Arrow, 2011).

extent support prime ministers without formal inclusion in their staff – and were consequently not included in figures.

This trend of expansion connected with the increased subdivision of functions. Various tasks were separated from the Private Office and shifted to new, purpose-designed entities within the prime-ministerial remit, including staff with more specialised roles than the multi-tasking private secretaries. Some of them, unlike the generalists of the career civil service, possessed policy expertise. The staff of the premier could now facilitate activity, such as detailed engagement in departmental business, to an extent that would have been difficult previously. Though this division of labour was dramatic, it should not be mistaken for a complete separation of tasks between individuals and different parts of the team, which is never possible. For instance, a Press Secretary provided advice on policy or appointments because of the need to consider how to present such issues and the likely public response to them. In so doing they could eventually extend far beyond their immediate brief, which a premier who valued their opinion might wish them to do so. Sometimes, as with William Clark for Eden, they might overplay their hand, proffering unsolicited and unwelcome views. But a media aide such as Joe Haines for Wilson could become a trusted counsellor on various issues. Yet, just as press secretaries were not clearly constrained, the Press Office never wholly monopolised contact with the media. Other parts of the prime-ministerial team were likely to take part in briefing journalists. A member of Callaghan's party-political staff said in 1977 that No. 10 consisted of four 'interlocking rings' – the Political Office, Private Office, Policy Unit and Press Office, each of which was involved in the work of the others.

Signs appeared that the premiership was becoming a more developed institution. During the Macmillan period the practice of the Prime Minister's personal staff attending Cabinet began.

At this early point it was just one private secretary, the principal (perhaps with a further private secretary).[152] Over time the prime-ministerial retinue at Cabinet would increase. The first head of the Policy Unit, Bernard Donoughue, was able to go to Cabinet frequently. The Prime Minister's Office first appeared as an entity in its own right in the *Civil Service Yearbook* for 1977. Its anachronistic inclusion as part of the Treasury – traceable to a time when the title First Lord of the Treasury was a genuine job description – now ceased. This change was the work of a member of Callaghan's Private Office who told us he was perplexed when he could not find his own office in the departmental directory called the 'white book'.

The premiership was more sophisticated, numerically larger and more entrenched. Yet at various points some proposed that developments should go further still, perhaps establishing an entity that would resemble or explicitly be a department of the Prime Minister. Often those who advocated such changes were themselves serving, past or future aides to the premier. In this sense a job creation scheme was contemplated. General encouragement for enhancement of the premiership, whether through deploying more aides or other changes, came from a number of members of the Kitchen Cabinet associated with Harold Wilson. Ironically they included Richard Crossman, who publicly was a leading exponent of the then-fashionable view that the Prime Minister was becoming increasingly powerful at the expense of other constitutional institutions, which begged the question why more assistants were required. When Wilson was Leader of the Opposition (1963–4), Thomas Balogh promoted the idea that with Labour in office there should be a substantial enhancement of the prime-ministerial team, including attaching to it machinery

---

152   J. Lee, G. Jones and J. Burnham, *At the Centre of Whitehall* (Basingstoke: Macmillan, 1998), p. 67.

for economic coordination, and ministers of state with responsibility for home, foreign and information policy. As a special adviser to Wilson when premier, Balogh promoted alterations to the machinery of government to strengthen the role of the premier in economic policy, expanding Balogh's own team. But Wilson was wary of excessive growth in the number of aides. Visiting the White House of Lyndon Johnson in the 1960s he observed a President constantly surrounded by members of his vast entourage, harassing him for approval for plans which their chief, Wilson suspected, might end up signing without adequate consideration. In enlarging the premiership prime ministers could lose personal control over the office of which they were head.

The CPRS, which Heath introduced, was formally attached to the Cabinet as a whole. David Howell and Mark Schreiber first developed the concept of the CPRS during the Conservative policy review which took place when the party was in opposition during the 1960s. Initially they labelled it the 'Crown Consultancy'. They intended it to be part of an administrative grouping known as the 'Central Capability' which would drive greater coordination from the core of government. Howell and Schreiber both envisaged the 'Crown Consultancy' as directly supporting the premier. Howell was influenced by the support-mechanisms established by Lloyd George and Churchill during the First and Second World Wars. He specifically desired the establishment of a prime-ministerial department, emulating systems surrounding the US President and the West German Chancellor. Such ideas met resistance from career Whitehall. The Cabinet Secretary, Burke Trend, successfully advocated the attachment of the CPRS to the collective Cabinet rather than the individual Prime Minister.

Though observation of the US President in the 1960s encouraged Wilson to be sceptical about larger teams of aides, he introduced the Policy Unit following his return to No. 10 in February 1974, and subsequently seemed on the surface to contemplate further centralisation. Shortly after the October 1974 general election, Wilson asked the Cabinet Secretary, John Hunt, to consider the possibility of incorporating the Policy Unit into the Cabinet Office, reporting to Hunt. Later in the month Hunt wrote a letter on this subject to the No. 10 Principal Private Secretary, Robert Armstrong. Hunt felt that existing arrangements were generally functioning satisfactorily. If there were scope for improvement, it was in a more complete implementation of the concordat already agreed with Bernard Donoughue, head of the Policy Unit. The possible purposes of the arrangement Wilson had proposed, as Hunt saw it, would be to incorporate a more political dimension into Cabinet Office briefs or to provide Donoughue with a part in the setting of priorities or chasing implementation. Hunt judged that, while he had a good relationship with him, 'I do not think things would be helped by having Dr Donoughue at my elbow'.

The Cabinet Secretary believed this plan could lead to an unhelpful blurring of the roles of special advisers and permanent officials across Whitehall, posing a possible threat to the value of the former and the impartiality of the latter. While the Cabinet Office had a special relationship with the Prime Minister, at the same time it supported all ministers as a group. Shifting the Policy Unit to the Cabinet Office might create problems for this collective role, unless the intention was fully to establish a 'Prime Minister's department' with responsibility for the Cabinet secretariat. If Donoughue retained direct contact with Wilson – which presumably he would – this arrangement would create confusion. Hunt stated his conviction that Donoughue and the Policy Unit should not play a part in establishing the overall priorities and strategy of government (which was the role of the CPRS), nor in progress-chasing (which fell to the Cabinet secretariat). Hunt decided the options were on the one hand to retain existing arrangements, or on the other hand to abolish or reduce the size of the Policy Unit, possibly moving some staff into the CPRS. He preferred the first. His view prevailed.[153] The diary kept by Donoughue gives another perspective on this episode. He describes Marcia Williams as wishing to devalue the Policy Unit and move it out of the way of No. 10 – and persuading Wilson to go along with this idea. Donoughue gained the support of Robert Armstrong in opposing it, and they then managed to enlist Hunt in their cause.[154]

The idea of setting up a Prime Minister's department would not go away. After succeeding Wilson as Prime Minister, Callaghan considered this possibility and asked Donoughue, head of the Policy Unit Callaghan had inherited from Wilson, to look into it and advise on what to do. Donoughue was against, as was the Principal Private Secretary at the time, Kenneth Stowe, who feared a department would be less flexible than existing arrangements. He was reluctant to become the manager of a larger hierarchy. Donoughue's successor, John Hoskyns, the first senior policy adviser and head of the Policy Unit under Thatcher, came to a different view. In 1982 when Hoskyns informed Thatcher of his intention to stand down she tried to dissuade him. His terms for staying were that he should be made the formal head of a small Prime Minister's department. Hoskyns would have the rank of permanent secretary and report directly to Thatcher. He would combine responsibility for the Conservative Research Department with control over the CPRS. It seems Thatcher consulted Robert Armstrong who felt the idea of Hoskyns including the CPRS within his remit was unacceptable. Thatcher did not accept the ultimatum from her aide and Hoskyns left.

---

153 See: TNA/PRO PREM 15/104.
154 B. Donoughue, *Downing Street Diary: With Harold Wilson in No. 10* (London: Jonathan Cape, 2005).

Even Major, less prone to interventionism as a leader, considered strengthening the centre in response to the deep disunity that developed in his government. He subsequently asserted that in the hypothetical circumstances of his winning the 1997 general election he would have expanded the size of his Policy Unit through seconding career officials and appointing more outsiders. Major would have increased the staff of the Cabinet Office as well. The purpose of both changes would have been to provide more direct advice to the Prime Minister, distinct from what came from the departments. Major said he would have simultaneously reduced substantially the number of departmental special advisers, tilting the relative balance of such assistance in his direction. He did not favour the full creation of a prime-ministerial department. Though Major did not achieve the opportunity to put such ideas into practice, the Labour leader from 1994, Tony Blair, observed the difficulties his Conservative counterpart had experienced and drew similar conclusions about what to do in office.

Another Prime Minister who considered but ultimately rejected the idea of a prime-ministerial department was Macmillan. Though he did not establish such a body, he implemented changes in the physical geography of the centre of Whitehall that helped bring a large-scale staff increasingly within the ambit of the premiership. Early in his premiership Macmillan authorised an architectural overhaul of the dilapidated Downing Street buildings and the adjoining 70 Whitehall complex. One consequence of this project – which required him to decamp for a time from No. 10 to nearby Admiralty House – was there was more space for aides at No. 10 and at the rebuilt No. 12, the base for the whips. Even more important from a constitutional perspective was that Macmillan opted to make 70 Whitehall, previously a Treasury building, the headquarters of the Cabinet Office. Consequently from 1963 the Cabinet Office occupied premises adjoining No. 10 with access between the two through an internal connecting door. Prime ministers had always had a close relationship with the Cabinet Office. Now utilising it for their specific purposes became practically easier. Over the decades that followed premiers used the Cabinet Office as a physical space in which to house their staff for whom room was not available in No. 10, and drew upon the support of staff located in the Cabinet Office.

The early 1980s saw further key developments. From 1968, following the Fulton Report on the civil service, responsibility for the management of Whitehall fell to a separate civil service department, whose permanent secretary was the head of the home civil service, previously a Treasury position. But in 1981 Thatcher abolished the civil service department. For a time the Treasury Permanent Secretary and Cabinet Secretary split the headship of the home civil service between them. Then in 1983 the civil service department functions moved into the Cabinet Office, and the Cabinet Secretary became the sole head of the home civil service. The outcome was centralisation. Responsibility for managing the civil service and the Cabinet rested in a single institution with one official at its summit, in close organisational and physical proximity to the premiership.

The balance of power and the institution

With hindsight, the post-Second World War period of permanent civil service pre-eminence was fleeting and never absolute. The person who did most to personify the position of the civil service at this time was Norman Brook. Even while he exercised his enormous personal sway in Whitehall, there were exceptions to and strains upon the orthodoxy. From 1964, prime ministers sought to inject a more party-political dimension to their teams and used changes in their staff to claw back some of the functions their predecessors had ceded from the mid-nineteenth century. They acquired new aides who could support them in their dual role as party politicians and administrators. At the same time they expanded their capacity to engage in policy. Once prime ministers were in direct control of the Treasury, but now it was a rival to No. 10. Enhancing their staff gave premiers a more substantial and autonomous role in economic decision-making, as well as in other domestic fields and foreign affairs.

There was a struggle between the career civil service and outsiders. Limitations applied to the conduct of both sides. The wave of imports from 1964 onwards created discomfort among regular Whitehall officials. The strict constitutional position was that civil servants derived their legitimacy from ministers. If prime ministers – who from 1968 held the post of Minister for the civil service – wanted to make partisan appointments, then it was difficult for career staff directly to oppose them. But permanent civil servants could press for constraints on the activities of irregulars and create difficulties over matters such as room allocation, the niceties of job titles, access to certain documents and through less than enthusiastic day-to-day cooperation. Outsiders could draw upon their personal attachment to the Prime Minister and any valuable skills they possessed in combating such tactics, but over time they might exhaust such resources and assist their own marginalisation. A constant battle against the permanent bureaucracy, with its numerical superiority and organisational might, could not be won.

Over time the presence of outsiders within the premiership became firmly institutionalised. On the one hand, this development was a partial defeat for career Whitehall since it represented a definite shift away from their pre-eminence within the prime-ministerial staff. On the other hand the temporary imports were now contained to a significant extent within organisational structures which career Whitehall had played a significant part in delineating. In this sense the struggle was without a conclusion. Alongside conflict was a need for cooperation: tension co-existed with mutual dependence.

The sometimes painful experiences in incorporating outsiders were part of a broader process. The premiership, which originated as an unofficial role whose very existence was denied by those who performed it, was continuing to evolve as an institution. This entrenchment of the office of Prime Minister partly involved it developing subdivisions. Such differentiations included those between types of staff, such as special advisers and career officials; and between different functional bodies within it, such as the Policy Unit, Private Office, Political Office and Press Office. A number of prime ministers contemplated going further, possibly establishing a fully fledged department to encompass and support them all. The next premiership, which began in May 1997, would see expansion on a scale never before considered, even by Lloyd George.

CHAPTER SIX

NEW LABOUR, 1997-2010

In May 1997 the eighteen-year occupation of government by the Conservative Party came to an end. During this period, both Margaret Thatcher and John Major had made full use of the expanded staff introduced by the Labour Prime Minister, Harold Wilson. But they were not innovators in the same way that Wilson was. Now Labour had returned to power. Just as the desire to modernise Britain lay behind Wilson's overhaul of the prime-ministerial support staff, so it did for Blair. Like Wilson in his early years Blair wanted to be a dynamic leader, dominating his government. He not only replicated many features of Wilson's approach; he magnified them. A large entourage of allies surrounded Blair at No. 10. He set out to change the way the system worked and during his premiership Blair sought new means to achieve his goals. He established mechanisms of labyrinthine complexity, and on a vast scale. But he was always restrained in what he could do by his powerful rival and Chancellor of the Exchequer, Gordon Brown. When Brown succeeded Blair as Prime Minister in 2007, one of his ways of marking himself as different from Blair was through a distinctive use of aides. However, through deliberately taking a separate path he may have deprived himself of the kind of assistance his natural inclinations as a leader required. Inadvertently he created the opportunity for the civil service to reassert some of the authority it had once possessed, but lost.

Aides to Tony Blair

As a politician Tony Blair always sought to lead from the front, and was open about his desire to do so. As Prime Minister he preferred dealing with ministers one-on-one and working in more informal small groups, rather than the official, collective procedures of Cabinet government. Aides were integral to this style. He used them more extensively and in greater numbers than any previous Prime Minister. His staff attained great public prominence and became subject to substantial criticism. Observers denigrated them for hyperbolic, misleading presentational methods – 'spin'; accused them of rupturing the British constitution and of pursuing bad policies.[155] The police even investigated them. Vilification became intense.

Blair chose aides partly because they possessed characteristics he did not and because he wanted them to perform tasks he did not want to himself. He had a tendency to avoid personal conflict. For instance, Alastair Campbell, his media aide, did not share such coyness and was robust in his dealings with others. An advantage to Blair of this approach was that the aides, rather than himself, would be blamed by people inside government for difficult decisions.

Blair conveyed the impression that his relationship with the Labour Party was partly that of an onlooker, rather than being fully absorbed within it. He saw this distance as a strength. Seeking to avoid such divisions as had weakened the party in the 1970s and 1980s, he tried not to mediate between different groups within it, but to take it along a specific path he had chosen. For this objective he needed a team he could personally rely on. In opposition

---

155 See, for instance: F. Beckett and David Hencke, *The Blairs and Their Court* (London: Aurum, 2004); N. Jones, *Sultans of Spin: The Media and the New Labour Government* (London: Orion, 1999); P. Oborne and S. Walters, *Alastair Campbell* (London: Aurum, 2004).

his aides had helped him dominate and reform his party and plan a centralised premiership. Once in office he could rely on them to help him dominate and reform government. Another motive for Blair was to provide an antidote to the perceived weakness of John Major in his tenure as Prime Minister. Blair drew some favourable conclusions about Margaret Thatcher's less collegiate style. As he came close to assuming power, Blair made clear the prominent role No. 10 would play in the coming Labour government. He and his advisers were determined to force through key objectives untrammelled by ministers or the constraints of the administrative machine.

Aides were important to one of the most distinctive features of Blair's approach. When the Cabinet system that Lloyd George formalised in 1916 is considered as a whole, Blair's premiership stands out in contrast for the extent to which – assisted by an unprecedented number of aides – he minimised the roles of Cabinet and its committees, and emphasised informal discussions and direct dealings with individual ministers and their officials. Although critics of Blair and those around him saw them as 'control freaks', Blair was open about seeing this approach as the right one. It was simply good management: a problem should be dealt with early, directly between No. 10 and the department concerned rather than through collective discussion. Cabinet, Blair and his aides recognised, remained a latent force, which was why they put so much effort into handling it. Aides helped Blair stage-manage Cabinet meetings to ensure problems did not arise. However, in to some extent suppressing Cabinet, he found he had to obtain the valuable qualities it possessed elsewhere. He used assistants to perform tasks that might more normally be carried out by Cabinet. Blair partially substituted its policy development, coordination and implementation roles with units answering to him. Some of Blair's staff fulfilled a function traditionally associated with the ministerial collective, talking through the different possible perspectives on particular proposals. Aides voiced disagreement both with each other and sometimes Blair at the regular meetings he held with them.

Some concluded that Blair's staff brandished power on their own behalf or manipulated the Prime Minister. Peter Mandelson, a ministerial aide to Blair early on in his premiership and an informal counsellor thereafter, was even labelled the 'Prince of Darkness'. A biography of Alastair Campbell portrays Blair as dependent upon Campbell.[156] But the more satisfactory thesis is that proposed by Francis Beckett and David Hencke in their book *The Blairs and Their Court*. These authors suggest the Prime Minister never yielded command of a team he deployed for his own ends.[157] While Blair delegated much, it was as part of a conscious approach. He thought about how his staff should operate in a general sense, though leaving the details to others; it was a kind of organised chaos. In a diary entry for 7 April 2002 Campbell noted that what both he and Jonathan Powell, Blair's Chief of Staff, did was determined mainly by what Blair wanted, as well as their personalities, rather than any kind of formal job description. As a consequence 'gaps' and incoherence could develop.[158] Blair describes how he required his inner team – his 'close political family' – to put their work ahead of all else, but to enjoy themselves when appropriate; not to recriminate with each other; to protect, respect and preferably like one another; and to maintain unity.[159]

Blair did not solicit a single recommendation from his senior aides. Often they disagreed with each other over such issues as

156 Oborne and Walters, *Alastair Campbell*, p. 158.
157 Beckett and Hencke, *The Blairs and Their Court*, p. 262.
158 A. Campbell, *The Blair Years: Extracts from the Alastair Campbell Diaries* (London: Arrow, 2008).
159 T. Blair, *A Journey*.

introducing more choice into public services, the level of public expenditure and the prospect of British membership of the European single currency. Blair received a variety of opinions, then took a decision of his own. Personal rivalry within the Blair circle could be intense, as between Campbell and Mandelson (though their relationship was more complex than being one of straightforward conflict). Mary Ann Sieghart noted in *The Times* on 26 January 2001 that the 'passionate and volatile' relationships within the Blair circle were similar to those of a girl's boarding school, or of a 'tempestuous girl band'. Powell noted how Blair could play his different aides off against each other. From Blair's point of view this friction reduced the chances of challenges to his decisions or authority by members of his staff. His involvement of assistants in his decision-making was similar to that of premiers such as Harold Wilson who took sometimes contradictory advice from different sources before reaching a conclusion. It may be too that, again like Wilson, he thrived on having 'creative tension' fizzing around him.

Blair's staff helped him wield significant influence across government, covering internal and foreign policy, and shorter- and longer-term issues. Parliamentary committees, recognising the significance of Blair aides, sought to take evidence from them and complained of obstacles raised to these staff appearing before them. The paradox was that, while aides could help Blair to achieve what he wanted, their ability to do so depended on how great was his political stock at any given time. While the Prime Minister's authority, particularly from the outset of his premiership to around 2003, was high, it had limits. Blair's colleague and rival, Gordon Brown, was a strong counterweight. He had his own historically large team of party-political staff. Brown wielded considerable influence across a wide span of domestic policy and acquired a crucial role in the decision-taking process about possible British membership of the European single currency. Blair's economic adviser, Derek Scott, found the Prime Minister under-engaged in economic policy and Scott struggled to obtain important information from the Treasury.[160] Andrew Adonis, a policy aide to Blair, describes the debilitating experience of negotiating each step with the Treasury, which slowed down the achievement of objectives.[161]

Despite the constraints upon Blair and his staff, various negative accounts appeared describing his aides as the dominant force within Whitehall, even comparing them to a quasi-presidency. The way Blair handled the decision to participate in the US-led invasion of Iraq of 2003 became a lightning rod for criticism of his leadership. The then Secretary of State for International Development, Clare Short, argued he had bypassed Cabinet, relying on an inner team of aides, and in the process neglected proper constitutional procedure. The Blair team, intended to further his purposes, had become a means for opponents to attack the Prime Minister and diminish his standing. Powell has argued that such criticisms depended on an idealised and unrealistic account of methods which had prevailed before the Blair premiership; if pure Cabinet government had ever existed, it had disappeared long before 1997.[162]

The potential for Blair's staff to become a focus of controversy manifested itself in another way late in his term of office. During 2006–7 the Metropolitan Police conducted an investigation into possible offences under the Honours (Prevention of Abuses) Act 1925 and the Political Parties, Elections and Referendums

---

160 D. Scott, *Off Whitehall: A View From Downing Street by Tony Blair's Adviser* (London: I. B. Tauris, 2004).
161 A. Adonis, *Education, Education, Education: Reforming England's Schools* (London: Biteback, 2012).
162 J. Powell, *The New Machiavelli: How to Wield Power in the Modern World* (London: Vintage, 2011).

Act 2000, and into whether actions intended and tending to pervert the course of justice had taken place. The initial trigger for this process was a complaint that various people had made large financial loans to the Labour Party with the expectation of receiving peerages. Eventually the investigation widened its scope to take in all three main parties in Britain. Of the four individuals arrested, two were aides to Blair: Lord (Michael) Levy, a fundraiser and envoy for the Prime Minister focusing on the Middle East, and Ruth Turner, the Prime Minister's Director of Government Relations. Blair himself became the first serving Prime Minister interviewed in the course of a criminal investigation. Ultimately the Crown Prosecution Service decided in 2007 it would not bring charges against anyone. As with the pursuit of Robert Walpole and his aides in 1742, finding hard evidence to support suspicions about activities within the ambit of a Prime Minister had proved impossible.

Opposition and power

Many of Blair's key prime-ministerial assistants were in post supporting him as Leader of the Opposition before May 1997, including Campbell and Powell. Peter Mandelson, an MP, was the most important among Blair's counsellors in this early stage. Another political strategist with a particular interest in public opinion and focus groups was Philip Gould. Anji Hunter, whom Blair had known since he was sixteen and regarded as his best friend, had assisted him for many years as a gatekeeper and personal adviser. Sally Morgan handled relations with the party. David Miliband was head of policy and James Purnell was an important policy adviser. Michael Levy (from September 1997 Lord Levy) helped with fundraising.

Because of his supposed pronounced habit of finding places for allies, the phrase 'Tony's cronies' entered into popular use. In

1997 Blair had a winning team around him. He wanted to keep it together and ensure they implemented the plans they had already laid. The permanent civil service was unfamiliar to Labour, which had spent eighteen years out of government, with its leaders hearing reports about the supposed 'politicisation' of Whitehall under the Conservatives. Some members of Blair's team could provide experience of government. Powell had previously been a member of the Diplomatic Service (and Charles, his elder brother, had been one of Thatcher's most influential aides when serving as her foreign affairs private secretary). Derek Scott, an economic counsellor to Blair since 1994, had been a special adviser during the last Labour term of office of 1974–9; so too had Roger Liddle who joined the No. 10 Policy Unit in 1997.

Aides were central to Blair's overhaul of the Labour Party and helped to transform it into New Labour and pursue its new orientation in government. Such methods worked, but were bound to cause resentment among those who felt excluded. Blair drew a distinction within his partisan aides between those who were supporters of Labour but not fully embedded within the party and those who were more a part of it. Blair placed Powell and Hunter in the first category and Campbell and Morgan, as well as his Parliamentary Private Secretary, Bruce Grocott, in the latter. Aides who had a closer understanding of Labour were of particular value to attempts to alter it. In opposition, with the support of his staff Blair bypassed shadow ministers to carry out interventions in policy. Working closely with his personal team throughout he successfully changed Clause IV of the party constitution, deleting the reference to collective ownership of the means of production, distribution and exchange, as part of a wider rebranding of Labour as 'New Labour'.[163]

---

163 A. Seldon, *Blair* (London: Free Press, 2004), p. 221–2.

Handling the media was a prominent and controversial function of the Blair staff during the opposition period. Many Blair
aides saw communications as a key component of overall strategy, rather than as a means of selling a decision to the public
once made. Labour had lost four general elections in a row since
1979. Blair's fundamental initial task was persuading sceptical
voters that the party had genuinely changed. The press had given
Labour a difficult time in the 1980s and early 1990s. Blair feared
this experience could be repeated, as might the damage the media
had caused to Major as premier during his 1992–7 term of office
(after the more favourable treatment Major received in 1990–
92). Other longer-term trends provided a reason to give close
attention to communications. The media were less deferential
and not as prone to giving politicians the benefit of the doubt as
in the 1950s.

Technological and business developments were important.
Broadcast outlets had proliferated, with rolling news stations
stimulating the need for information, and in turn a requirement
for aides who could provide it. During the Blair premiership
another front opened up with the rise of the internet. Though
this development has yet to run its full course, its impact was
without question great, including for No. 10, most obviously in
its establishment of a 'Web Team' at the turn of the century. The
Blair approach to presentation included enthusiastically seeking
to win over newspapers and reporters that had not previously (or
not for some time) supported Labour, and creating, through the
use of new technologies, procedures for rapidly responding to
breaking stories.

The growth in the staff size Blair triggered at No. 10 came in
the Policy Unit (which rose from nine on 1 April 1997 to sixteen
a year later) and with the creation of a new body, the Strategic
Communications Unit, which employed eight staff by 1 April

1998. Official figures for the total number employed at No. 10 are
not always directly comparable and are sometimes contradictory.
It seems Blair inherited from Major a number in the low-to-mid
100s, if the method of counting applied later is used. It then rose
to and remained at a peak of around 190 by the early twenty-
first century. These figures take in all staff paid from public funds
working at No. 10 – from messengers to policy advisers. Much of
the increase in senior staff (which in turn necessitated a growth in
the support capacity for them) came about because of the greater
number of special advisers Blair imported. While there was
a general rule that Cabinet members could employ up to only
two such party-political aides, there was no limit for the Prime
Minister. The number of special advisers employed in No. 10 in
1996–7 was eight, rising to the mid-to-high twenties thereafter.
Blair made additions to the permanent civil servants on his staff
too, particularly with his additions to his team of foreign affairs
private secretaries.

Though moving towards 200 in total, the No. 10 staff remained
small compared with that of other departments. As of 2001 the
Treasury employed 830, the Department of Trade and Industry
4,960, and the Department of Health 3,440. In international
perspective No. 10 was small. Blair pointed out to the House of
Commons Liaison Committee in July 2002 that he had a similar
number of staff at Downing Street to the Irish Taoiseach, and
less than both the French Prime Minister and President, and the
German Chancellor. He insisted he was not establishing a Prime
Minister's department. One constraint was space. Some discussion took place of moving elsewhere. Powell was interested in
going to the Queen Elizabeth II Conference Centre and turning
Downing Street into a museum. The idea came to nothing. Blair
made increasing use of Cabinet Office buildings for his staff, in
premises such as 70 Whitehall and Admiralty Arch. At times more

of his aides were based outside No. 10 than inside it, though it remained the focal point for his team. A problem associated with such a large body of assistants was confusion within Whitehall about who spoke for Blair. Not all his aides could possibly know his mind.

In office the emphasis on presentation and media management continued. While the Press Office concentrated more on day-to-day briefing the new Strategic Communications Unit, set up in 1998 (SCU), took a longer-term approach. It helped Blair consider what messages he wanted to get across over coming months, and how he would do so. The reach of the SCU extended across government. It coordinated a 'grid' of announcements and events using the 'Agenda' computer system. Departments had to produce a communications strategy for examination by the SCU alongside their policy proposals. Responsibility fell to the SCU for ensuring the different documents fitted with each other and the overall government agenda. The Research and Information Office (RIO) appeared alongside the SCU in 1999. It was an adaptation of a mechanism Blair had used in opposition. The purpose of the RIO was to facilitate 'rapid rebuttal' of negative news stories via briefings to staff. Blair and his aides promoted a different communications ethos within Whitehall. Staff sought to ensure that civil servants adopted some of the techniques Labour had developed in the lead-up to May 1997, both in No. 10 and across government. A significant portion of Blair's staff had worked for the BBC earlier in their careers, demonstrating the premium placed on media experience.

The prominence Blair and his team attached to public relations proved controversial. Some observers alleged that Blair's aides pursued partisan concerns and disseminated misleading information. Another criticism was that the approach to communications entailed an excessive concentration of authority around the

Prime Minister. Certain commentators held that the prioritisation of presentation distorted the policy-formation process and led to incoherent announcements. A further area of controversy was the alleged unattributable advanced briefing of selected journalists as a means of news management. This technique might involve bypassing Parliament, which by convention was where policy statements were normally meant to be made first. Critics held that some within No. 10 briefed against Blair's own ministers and other allies when they were out of favour. The derogatory term attached to the communications efforts of Blair's team – one often taken up by opposition parties seeking to undermine the credibility of statements – was that of 'spin', practised by 'spin doctors'. Spin was a new way of describing attempts by prime-ministerial staff dating back to the eighteenth century, and aides to other leaders earlier, to present premiers and their governments in the most favourable possible light. Blair's techniques were probably more active, systematic and centralised than before. At the same time the scope of the Prime Minister's expanded communications function should not be exaggerated. Cabinet members would not necessarily do what aides at No. 10 wanted them to. Departmental press secretaries in turn represented their ministers, not Blair. The Downing Street media operation had grown in size, but could not be described as vast. There were limits on how far No. 10 staff and their methods could influence the media. Blair's use of 'spin' itself became a subject of public criticism, and the increased use of partisan aides undermined the credibility of official communications.

The role of outsiders

A prominent feature of Blair's use of aides as Prime Minister was his heavy reliance on staff recruited by his patronage from beyond Whitehall and a reduction in the relative importance of permanent civil servants. This approach helped Blair to work in the way he wanted, but at a cost. Alongside the substantial body of existing staff he brought with him from opposition to government, Blair continued to enlist further outsiders throughout his premiership. The terms on which Blair engaged such aides varied. Some – like Philip Gould – had purely informal positions. Continuing a function he performed in opposition Gould briefed Blair and others in government on opinion research and its strategic implications. Other aides possessed job titles but were unpaid such as Lord (John) Birt. A former Director General of the BBC, Birt joined Blair in an untitled role in 2000. Initially he advised primarily on crime. The following year Birt became Strategy Adviser to the Prime Minister. He continued in this unsalaried position until the end of 2005. Other aides to Blair held ministerial offices. Mandelson became a Minister without Portfolio, based in the Cabinet Office, at the outset of the Blair premiership. He remained, as he had been before May 1997, a close counsellor to Blair. During his spells as Secretary of State for Trade and Industry (1998) and Northern Ireland (1999–2001) he was less available to provide continuous support, because of the demands of these roles.

Some staff worked as impartial officials but were originally temporary recruits from outside Whitehall. Michael Barber and Geoff Mulgan were both special advisers to the Labour government from 1997 before being appointed with the status of permanent civil servants. Mulgan was a member of the Policy Unit from 1997 to 2000 when he became head of the Performance and Innovation Unit. Barber was a special adviser at the Department for Education and Employment from 1997 to 2001 before becoming the first head of the Prime Minister's Delivery Unit. Staff in the Political Office, such as Blair's first Political Secretary Sally Morgan, were not publicly funded, but the majority of Blair's core staff who came from beyond the career civil service were special advisers paid from taxpayers' money. Powell, Campbell, Hunter, Miliband and many others worked on these terms. The number of special advisers across government as a whole expanded at the same time, particularly at the Treasury under Brown.

These outsiders were important for Blair. They were present in significant numbers at key regular meetings. Blair produced notes over the weekend about his priorities for the coming week, which formed the basis for a weekly meeting on Monday at 9 a.m. Most of those in attendance were staff from beyond Whitehall, along with the Principal Private Secretary. Campbell or Powell chaired the Wednesday diary meeting. A special adviser (Kate Garvey in the first term) kept the diary itself. Partisan appointments attended Cabinet. Campbell and Powell, again, came to these meetings, as did Peter Hyman, a special adviser and political strategist, and others. Some precedents existed for this practice. Bernard Donoughue, head of Wilson's and James Callaghan's policy units records that he frequently came to Cabinet meetings. But aides from outside Whitehall attending in such numbers as a matter of course was a major change. These meetings were by tradition the most important in government, and once permanent civil serv- ants were the only officials present. The temporary appointments had extended their role further.

Blair vested substantial authority in his special advisers. He appointed them to significant roles, including what were in practice the two most senior posts at No. 10 – Powell as Chief of Staff and Campbell as Chief Press Secretary (from 2001 to 2003 Director of Communications and Strategy). An Order in Council – a type of legislation issued under the Royal Prerogative not requiring parlia- mentary approval – of 1997 had the effect of exempting them both from the regulation applying to other special advisers restricting them only to providing advice to ministers. Consequently they were able to give instructions to permanent civil servants, inside No. 10 and across Whitehall as a whole. They could authorise expenditure from the budget of the Prime Minister's Office and take part in disciplinary procedures and appraisals for permanent officials. The Order allowed for up to three aides of this kind to be employed. Only Campbell and Powell took up this authority. Strictly how necessary the Order was is debatable, since it had become usual for the Policy Unit, which was headed by a special adviser, to include within it some career officials.

In the early stages of the Blair premiership the encounter between his established team and regular officials generated tension. Powell was suspicious that the Cabinet Secretary, Robin Butler, was trying to throw Blair off balance when he first came to office by overwhelming him with immediate decisions. The more punctilious approach of the permanent civil service did not sit easily with the flexibility and speed of the Blair opposition team. A particularly sensitive issue arose because Policy Unit staff already knew ministers and dealt with them regularly during the opposition period. Consequently they were likely to continue this relationship, compromising the traditional role of the Private Office as the primary conduit. Aides within the Policy Unit were uncomfortable with permanent officials adding comments to their submissions to the Prime Minister. Yet the two groups needed each other and managed to develop ways of collaborating. The permanent officials could work the machine and the irregulars provided a party-political dimension.[164] Despite this emerging accommodation some career civil servants felt the introduction of a substantial group of outsiders at the centre of government led to a decline in the overall status of the career civil service, particularly as a provider of policy advice.

---

164   P. Hyman, *1 Out of 10: From Downing Street Vision to Classroom Reality* (London: Vintage, 2005), pp. 72; 74.

Blair and his staff used working practices less formal than those of the permanent officials. For a while Blair worked in the room previously occupied by Marcia Williams, on the St James's side of the Cabinet room. The problem with this arrangement from the point of view of Powell was that he could not monitor who was seeing Blair. Consequently in 1998 Blair moved to the small room on the other side of the Cabinet room, previously occupied by private secretaries including the principal. It became known as the 'den'. Powell and the other most senior private secretaries now sat in the next office along (with the other private secretaries moved up a small flight of stairs nearby). In his new space Blair's practice of working from a sofa with papers spread out in front of him became famous. When in August 2003 Powell gave evidence to the Hutton Inquiry into the death of weapons expert David Kelly he described 'a sort of running meeting' which took place on 7 July 2003. The venue changed, officials and ministers came and went, some of them participating in a parallel discussion. Powell explained that no minute existed of this meeting, nor of any other that the inquiry was likely to be interested in. The ratio of recorded to non-recorded meetings per day was about three to fourteen. Prompted by evidence of this sort commentators and political opponents attacked the informality of practices in No. 10 under Blair, his 'sofa' government, and his neglect of more formal Cabinet and civil service procedures.

Some analysts portrayed outsiders as being involved inappropriately in the work of the Intelligence and Security Agencies (ISAs).[165] A considerable political controversy of the Blair premiership centred on the role of prime-ministerial staff in the production of the document Iraq's Weapons of Mass Destruction, published in September 2002. This paper was a central part of

---

165 See for instance: P. Knightley, 'Spinning the spooks: a Downing Street disaster', *Sunday Times*, 1 June 2003.

the government's case for taking action against the regime of Saddam Hussein. After the invasion of Iraq in March the following year the occupying forces could find no such weapons. Later in the year No. 10, and in particular Campbell, engaged in a ferocious dispute with the BBC over these events. The BBC ran a story on 29 May that year claiming there was an allegation from within government that Downing Street had changed the text of the Iraq document to make it more dramatic, against the wishes of staff within the ISAs. The author of the story, Andrew Gilligan, later wrote a press article on the subject which named Campbell in connection with the claim about the handling of the text. Following the death of David Kelly, a government weapons inspector who believed he was Gilligan's source, Blair established the Hutton Inquiry to determine what had happened. It concluded that ultimate control over the drafting of the paper had remained with John Scarlett, Chairman of the Joint Intelligence Committee (JIC). While No. 10 made suggestions about the text intended to strengthen its impact, Scarlett included only wording that was consistent with the available intelligence. Hutton left open the possibility of subconscious influence on Scarlett and the JIC. While the outcome of Hutton was favourable to Blair and Campbell, the overall chain of events and the attention they received were politically damaging.

The extensive use Blair made of outsiders as aides, the powers he vested in them, the methods they used and the range of activities in which they engaged led to claims about the abuse of the constitution as a whole and the values of the civil service in particular.[166] Critics frequently used the term 'politicisation' but rarely did they define it. Some held that Blair's informal methods, reliance on special advisers and reduction of collective Cabinet

---

166 For an illustration of this school of thought see: P. Oborne, 'You've reached the top now stop the rot', *Evening Standard*, 23 April 2002.

involvement in decisions suggested a failure by career officials to fulfil a duty of upholding proper standards. Permanent civil servants, however, had little choice. Since they were constitutionally subordinate to the elected government of the time, they had an obligation to implement prime-ministerial decisions about procedure, organisation and the roles of staff.

Career officials were still important in supporting Blair. They continued to fill the post of Principal Private Secretary, traditionally the most senior post in No. 10. To some extent the importance of this job decreased following the introduction of Powell as Chief of Staff. But the Principal Private Secretary was still potentially an important player at No. 10, as was demonstrated by Jeremy Heywood, who held the post from 1999 to 2003. Blair expanded the number of regular civil servants attached to the Prime Minister inside No. 10. Some of these impartial aides developed close working and even personal relationships with Blair's partisan assistants, and came to be regarded as part of the supposed inner circle, such as David Manning, the Prime Minister's foreign policy adviser. Like previous prime ministers Blair relied on career officials beyond No. 10 as well – and had no choice but to do so. Cabinet secretaries, with whom Blair had a practice of holding a 10 a.m. Monday meeting after his 9 a.m. strategy meeting, were of particular value because of their ability to make the administrative machine work for him. Blair entrusted to successive holders of this post (who since 1983 were simultaneously head of the home civil service) a central role in implementing his primary policy goal: public service reform. Powell describes how the civil service was effective in blocking an attempt to recruit a Cabinet Secretary from outside Whitehall. The negative publicity associated with the Hutton Inquiry and other political difficulties experienced by Blair's government from 2003 seem to have helped bring about a change in the centre of gravity back towards career civil servants and their methods. Over time some of Blair's most prominent special advisers, such as Campbell, left No. 10, compounding this tendency.

Campbell and Powell were the most senior outsiders at No. 10 during the Blair premiership but outsiders in more explicit policy roles were important too. David Miliband was head of the Policy Unit from 1997. He held the post until 2001, initially in an acting capacity. Miliband was the son of the renowned socialist intellectual, Ralph. David's brother, Ed, was a special adviser to Gordon Brown at the Treasury. Both David and Ed later became Labour MPs, Ed beating David in the Labour leadership contest of 2010. When the Policy Unit merged with the Private Office into the Policy Directorate in 2001 Andrew Adonis became head of policy. Adonis was, like two other policy advisers to Blair, Derek Scott and Roger Liddle, previously a member of the Social Democratic Party, the Labour right-wing breakaway group formed in 1981. The use of such aides fitted with Blair's centrist orientation, and probably helped aggravate those within Labour who disliked the pro-market approach they felt No. 10 was imposing.

Adonis promoted policies which were controversial within the Labour movement, including academy schools. He hoped to provide Blair with a legacy equivalent in importance to the National Health Service for the Labour governments of 1945–51. In 1999 Adonis made a proposal to Blair and the Education Secretary, David Blunkett, for schools outside local authority control. The aide won the backing of the Prime Minister. Over the coming years Adonis took an active role in developing and actively implementing this controversial programme, first from No. 10 and then from 2005 as a schools minister in the House of Lords. His activities in the early phase went far beyond the restrictions John Hunt had hoped to impose on the Policy Unit through the concordat he agreed with Bernard Donoughue in 1974. Though he was expanding the reach of the premiership through his activities Adonis appreciated the limits on what he could do. Any authority he possessed was dependent upon the active backing of the premier, and on building alliances within and outside No. 10. Adonis saw a key part of his role as one of persuasion. The high turnover of career officials in particular jobs and their associated lack of expertise was a source of frustration for him.

Geoff Mulgan became head of policy for Blair in 2003 (though whether he fully supplanted Adonis is not clear). Mulgan, like other Blair allies such as Mandelson, had previous connections with the extreme left of British politics. Subsequently he had become the first director of the think tank Demos. Though it became popularly associated with New Labour, Demos was not a partisan organisation and had an eclectic approach. A think tank with an even closer link to the Labour governments was the Institute for Public Policy Research (IPPR). Numerous recruits to No. 10 and other departments had IPPR associations. A former director of the organisation, Matthew Taylor, was chief adviser on political strategy to Blair from 2003 to 2006. A further think tank with a No. 10 connection was the Social Market Foundation, whose former director, Philip Collins, became chief speech-writer to Blair in 2005. After his third successive election victory in 2005 Blair appointed David Bennett as his chief policy adviser. Bennett had previously been a director at the McKinsey & Co. consultancy. McKinsey had connections with a growing number of former and existing Blair aides, such as Lord Birt and Michael Barber (and with John Major's final senior policy adviser, Norman Blackwell). One commentator noted this trend and registered concern at increasing public expenditure on consultancies, as well as casting doubt on the value of their services.[167] The

---

167 See for instance: N. Cohen, 'Natural born billers', *Observer*, 19 June 2005.

appointment of staff such as Bennett expressed Blair's desire to apply private-sector management approaches to public services in an effort to make them function more effectively, but reports emerged of doubts within government about Bennett's lack of political background and knowledge of policy.

Jonathan Powell (1956–)

Jonathan Powell directly supported Blair for longer than any of his other aides. From 1997 onwards Powell was one of the two most important special advisers at No. 10, though observers did not always fully appreciate his significance. Powell joined Blair almost at the beginning of his Labour leadership, in 1995. He stayed on after others had gone. In one account Powell's great-est ambition was to equal the achievements of his elder brother, Charles, who had been a foreign affairs private secretary at No. 10 and one of Margaret Thatcher's most important aides.[168] Jonathan Powell, who entered the Diplomatic Service himself in 1979, surpassed this goal. Blair valued him for his knowledge of Whitehall procedures, his immense capacity for work and swift grasp of information, and for his personal fit with the philosophy of New Labour. Blair judged his aide, the son of an Air Vice-Marshall, as having a middle-class disposition and an affinity for the business sector.

From a post at the British Embassy in Washington he took up in 1991, Powell had closely observed the campaign of the Democratic presidential candidate, Bill Clinton, who went to his Oxford college. Clinton's overhaul of his party proved to be an important influence on the New Labour project. Powell was a Labour supporter who was greatly disappointed at the outcome of the 1992 British general election. He accompanied Gordon

---

168   J. Rentoul, 'Jonathan Powell', *Independent*, 27 September 2003.

Brown on his visit to the Democrat Convention that year. Both Blair and Brown visited the US in January 1993, and Powell introduced them to Clinton's campaign team. Powell maintained contact with Blair and after becoming Labour leader Blair invited Powell to join him. He was recruited following an interview with Blair and Lord (Derry) Irvine, a key Blair ally who became Lord Chancellor in 1997. Powell took the title Chief of Staff, which had an American ring to it and was used in the White House. His civil service background was valuable within the Blair team where such experience was lacking. Blair describes how Powell found the transition difficult at first but he soon became effective. Even in the early period at No. 10 Powell felt he did not have the full support of Blair and at one point in 1998 Levy told him he was about to be removed. Powell encouraged Blair to pursue a domineering premiership. In opposition he informed a private meeting that Blair would replace the existing feudal approach to government with a more Napoleonic system. He subsequently stressed that the premiership does not possess the power many outsiders believe it to enjoy, and that it must cooperate with other groups within and outside government to achieve its goals. Powell liaised with the No. 10 Principal Private Secretary, Alex Allan, and the Cabinet Secretary, Robin Butler, for more than six months before May 1997 to coordinate the transition of power that seemed inevitable.

Shortly before he became Prime Minister Blair also discussed with Robin Butler his plans for the organisation of No. 10. Butler pressed on Blair that Powell should not become Principal Private Secretary. To appoint him to this role would be to break with the arrangement traceable to the 1920s that this post was not a patronage appointment. Butler emphasised the various problems that could easily arise. It was inappropriate for a partisan recruit to perform certain functions that included overseeing honours and dealing with the opposition and the Palace. Blair agreed that, at least initially, he would settle for a dual role. Allan would stay on, working alongside Powell, with the two dividing duties between them as appropriate. Blair sustained this arrangement, in form at least, for his entire premiership. Powell insists he never had any designs on the Principal Private Secretary job. He believed Butler was haunted by memories of his brother, Charles, and his unorthodox tenure at No. 10. According to Powell Butler later offered him the job but he declined. Though the nature of Powell's position at No. 10 was unusual, it would be a mistake to caricature his relationship with permanent officials as wholly antagonistic.

Powell described his role to the Hutton Inquiry as one of acting as a 'conduit of information' to Blair, to advise the Prime Minister and to coordinate the activities of No. 10. He gave Hutton a description of his varied work for Blair on one day, 8 July 2003, which showed he was continually and closely involved in every part of the premier's professional life. The Prime Minister saw his Chief of Staff at the outset of each day and maintained contact throughout. Powell was able to influence the papers Blair received and which people he saw. Powell played a prominent part in policy on Northern Ireland. He gave advice to Blair and took part in negotiations, including for the historic Good Friday Agreement of 1998, which bound the main Loyalist and Republican groups to the peace process. Blair was moved to write that there would not have been a peace without Powell. Another function of Powell was to convey sensitive messages across government. He counselled Blair on ministerial appointments and government reshuffles, and the timing of elections. The Chief of Staff helped manage sometimes strained relationships between Cabinet members. With his special interest in foreign policy Powell could be a contact point with governments internationally. He was a firm Atlanticist and supporter of British participation in European integration. While Powell was not a speech-writer, he managed to provide Blair with one of his most memorable lines, when the Labour leader announced in 1996 that his three priorities were 'education, education, education'. Powell sought to provide Blair with a second opinion on the advice he received, from the perspective of a person loyal to the Prime Minister.

Powell was well-placed within the physical geography of No. 10 to wield influence. He worked in an office next door to the 'den' to which Blair moved early on in his premiership. Consequently anyone visiting Blair had to pass through the door in Powell's room. Powell never formally took on the post of Principal Private Secretary, but he became in practice the most senior official at No. 10 with ultimate responsibility for all its functions (though the Cabinet Office sometimes sought to deny this development had taken place). Powell was the first temporary appointment in such a position of authority since the 1920s. In his case, unlike that of David Wolfson for Thatcher, the title Chief of Staff seemed accurately to describe some of his functions. In February 2000 Richard Wilson, the Cabinet Secretary, provided the House of Commons Public Administration Select Committee with a No. 10 organogram. All the lines on it led to Powell. He had achieved a rare combination of different sources of influence for an aide: physical proximity, authority within the administrative machine and a shared partisan interest. He saw himself as growing to become more like Blair, as his brother did with Thatcher, and was able to take certain decisions on behalf of Blair as he came to know his mind. But Powell was not a friend of Blair, and saw a certain distance between them as important to retaining a degree of objectivity. In this lack of personal closeness to the Prime Minister, Powell differed from his fellow aide, Campbell.

Alastair Campbell (1957–)

Campbell was, alongside Powell, the most senior special adviser to Blair. A tabloid journalist by background, he made a major contribution to the initial spectacular success of Blair's communications methods, and had a close association with their growing controversy. In a press interview published in 2004, the year after his departure from No. 10, Campbell explained that Blair appointed him because of his commitment to Labour, his capacity for intense and sustained work, and his dynamism and creativity. But, Campbell went on, the same features that brought benefits to the party and to Blair helped contaminate the relationship with the media.[169] In his autobiography Blair described how he saw Campbell as a 'crazy' person who was able to channel this quality into constructive activity. Blair felt that at times Campbell's volatility could be a source of brilliance and that Campbell was capable of being almost his 'alter ego'. At the same time Blair felt it was impossible to control someone like Campbell, who was always on the verge of problematic behaviour into which he eventually tipped. Observers – especially those who were critical – depicted Campbell as synonymous with the Prime Minister's centralised, activist and partisan public-relations techniques and his broader style of government. In their biography of Campbell Peter Oborne and Simon Walters claim the true significance of Campbell was that he personified the effort by Tony Blair to govern without reference to traditional features of the British constitution such as Parliament, Cabinet and the civil service.[170]

During the long period of Conservative government from 1979 to 1997 Campbell found objectionable what he saw as

169 Ian Katz, 'I'm very tribal, I'm Labour, I'm Burnley, I'm Campbell', *Guardian*, 8 March 2004.
170 Oborne and Walters, *Alastair Campbell*, pp. 358–9.

overwhelming media bias against Labour. He became an aide to Blair at the outset of his Labour leadership in 1994. Blair had discussed with Mandelson a few candidates for a role he regarded as crucial. They considered some broadsheet journalists but Blair decided he wanted someone from a tabloid, and that Campbell was the one. Campbell was reluctant to join, but the future Prime Minister, demonstrating how seriously he took staffing matters, showed up at Campbell's holiday home in the south of France in August 1994 to win him over. With hindsight Blair believed the appointment proved of immense benefit to him, but may not have turned out to be as good for Campbell.

When Blair became Prime Minister in 1997 the initial post Campbell held was Chief Press Secretary. A central function was acting as the Prime Minister's official spokesman, talking to the press lobby. Campbell introduced the practice of giving briefings on the record – though they were not supposed to be attributed to him personally. The purpose of this change was to increase the authority of statements and the coherence of the government message. Over time Campbell took part in these events less, with two permanent civil servants assuming the task. He was always more than someone who simply organised contact with the media. Increasingly Blair drew on him as a strategic adviser, particularly when Mandelson became less available. From 2001 to 2003 Campbell's title was Director of Communications and Strategy. His task involved assisting Blair and the government as a whole on developing its overall 'communications strategy' and dealing with 'specific issues' which arose. In this role he ran the communications section at No. 10, which comprised the Press Office, SCU and RIO. Drawing on his closeness to Blair and his authority under the 1997 Order in Council, he was able to intervene in government activity beyond No. 10, including during the outbreak of foot-and-mouth disease in 2001. In the lead-up to the Iraq War he chaired a cross-departmental body called the Iraq Communications Group.

Blair has remarked on the ability of Campbell to command loyalty in his communications team composed of special advisers and permanent officials, and to mesh them into an effective group. Both allies of Campbell and others agreed he was a brilliant political communicator. His reputation became international when he was loaned to the North Atlantic Treaty Organization during the Kosovo conflict of 1999. Campbell was an effective sloganeer and creator of sound bites inserted into Blair's speeches. He invented the phrase 'New Labour, New Britain' used for Blair's first conference as leader in 1994. Campbell's earlier tabloid career was useful. But Campbell had a negative view of much of the press. Equally many journalists resented him for taking on a political role. They criticised him for his abrasiveness and sought to link him with the dissemination of misleading information. Campbell became better known than many Cabinet members. He provided inspiration for various creative writers, and a press article in 2006 suggested the introduction of an award for 'best portrayal of Alastair Campbell in a drama or comedy'.[171]

The public profile Campbell obtained, and his ability within government to speak, sometimes abruptly, to ministers on behalf of Blair, helped create the idea he was a power in his own right. Some regarded Campbell as 'effectively Deputy Prime Minister'.[172] Campbell disputed such claims. In the first Blair term he argued that journalists exaggerated his importance because he was the person in government they saw the most. Campbell insisted any

---

171 J. Ross, 'You couldn't make him up. Oh yes, you can!', *Sunday Times*, 16 April 2006.

172 R. Christopherson, 'Arise Campbell the real deputy prime minister', *Sunday Times*, 10 January 1999.

power he possessed came from Blair and he had no separate
authority, though he acknowledged his exceptional closeness
to the Prime Minister. On policy, though he took part in key
discussions, he did not always achieve the outcomes he wanted.
He seems to have disliked the agenda for more choice in public
services which Blair increasingly came to pursue. Campbell
denied the existence of an inner circle of aides, including himself,
around Blair usurping the decision-making power of Cabinet
ministers. Further limitations on Campbell were that he could
not completely control all the communications activities going
on within the government, nor could he dictate to the media the
stories they would run.

Employing outsiders and political sympathisers in a job similar
to Campbell's had ample precedent. But the nature of Campbell's
role and the way he operated within it received exceptional scrutiny. On a number of occasions attention focused on whether he
had broken rules applying to special advisers. After Campbell
left No. 10, his post ceased to exist. David Hill became Director
of Communications (without the Strategy part of Campbell's
title). Hill was a special adviser without the powers provided for
under the 1997 Order in Council which had applied to Campbell.
This change was in accordance with the recommendations
of an Independent Review of Government Communications,
chaired by Bob Phillis, chief executive of the Guardian Media
Group. Blair established this body in response to apparent
media and public distrust of official communications. A second
alteration which Phillis prompted was the appointment in
the Cabinet Office of a Permanent Secretary, Government
Communications. These changes in the post-Campbell era
represented a shift of authority away from partisan appointments at No. 10 and towards the career civil service and the
Cabinet Office.

Reorganisation and expansion

After winning the June 2001 general election Blair immediately implemented sweeping changes to his support team. In doing so, rather than demonstrating his supremacy, he expressed frustration that he had not yet been able to achieve his goals. Powell remained his Chief of Staff, while Campbell became Director of Communications and Strategy. Campbell and the staff working under him moved to No. 12 Downing Street, while the previous occupant of this address, the Chief Whip, had to move to No. 9 – reflecting the reduced status of MPs compared with the media. Another freshly created role was that of head of Government Relations. Anji Hunter was the first occupant, with responsibility for dealing with different parts of government, certain foreign administrations and the devolved governments. Taken together it is easy to see these functions as threats to the traditional functions of the No. 10 Private Office and even the Foreign Office.

Jeremy Heywood, the Principal Private Secretary, who as such had formal responsibility for the management of staff and budgets at No. 10, became head of a new entity, the Policy Directorate. As an amalgam of the Private Office and the Policy Unit, its establishment was momentous. The former body had properly come into being in the interwar period (though its name emerged only gradually). It had for a time been the clear, pre-eminent force within No. 10, and even after the appearance of challenges, in particular from the Policy Unit, it had remained prominent. Now the Private Office was no more. The Private Office and Policy Unit were already working closely together by 2001. But this change was a further dissolution of the boundary between impartial civil servants and partisan outsiders (though there had been some career officials in the Policy Unit before). This experiment in administrative fusion did not last. In 2006 a request under the Freedom of Information Act from the present authors revealed that the Private Office was a separate entity once more. Powell records that the two functions they performed were too different to be merged.

Early on in his premiership Blair had added two foreign affairs private secretaries. Some staff were concerned that he, Campbell and Powell were focusing excessively on external policy.[173] In June 2001 Blair created a European Adviser's Office, which Stephen Wall ran, and Foreign Policy Adviser's Office, under David Manning. In 2003 Nigel Sheinwald succeeded Manning and Kim Darroch followed Wall in 2004. The holders of the two posts combined their attachment to Blair with being heads in the Cabinet Office respectively of the European Secretariat and Overseas and Defence Secretariat.

This arrangement represented a blurring of the boundaries between No. 10 as a specifically prime-ministerial entity and the Cabinet Office as a collective support body. When introducing it, Blair met with resistance from career civil servants. The establishment of these offices – which came to be known jointly as the Foreign Policy Directorate, numbering as many as seven – represented a further extension of Blair's desire to participate in foreign affairs. Although they drew staff from the Diplomatic Service they presented a challenge to the Foreign Office. Another Blair aide, Lord Levy, who was not from the Foreign Office, posed a further threat. Alongside his fundraising role Levy travelled around the Middle East using the title 'Personal Envoy to the Prime Minister and Adviser on the Middle East', establishing contacts with a view to easing tensions in the region. His activities generated some hostility within the Diplomatic Service.

The precise status of the staff within the Cabinet Office secretariats headed by Blair's foreign and European policy advisers

---

173 L. Price, *The Spin Doctor's Diary*, (London: Hodder & Stoughton, 2005), diary entry for 25 March 1999, p. 88.

was uncertain. Did they serve the premier or the Cabinet as a whole? In 2004 the review of intelligence and weapons of mass destruction conducted by the former Cabinet Secretary Lord (Robin) Butler found that combining posts in this way tilted the responsibilities of those who held them towards the Prime Minister more than the Cabinet.

Blair made more extensive direct use of staff based in the Cabinet Office than any other Prime Minister. He did so both through establishing new bodies and enlisting the services of existing staff within it. These tendencies became more pronounced in the second term, but began in the first. An initial impetus came from a concern prominent in political and administrative circles at the turn of the twentieth/twenty-first century. A theory existed that individual Whitehall ministries were inclined to operate only in their particular 'silos' while social problems often fell across departmental boundaries. To tackle them properly different parts of government needed to become 'joined-up' and work together. This outlook pointed to a need for new teams at the centre to ensure the necessary cooperation took place. Geoff Mulgan, an originator of the 'joined-up government' school and a subsequent Blair aide, took this view.[174]

In 1998 the Performance and Innovation Unit (PIU) appeared in the Cabinet Office. Influences on the formation of PIU included similar experiments in France and the Central Policy Review Staff (CPRS) which Edward Heath had created in 1971. It looked at cross-departmental concerns and considered the long-term. Its brief was wide, covering issues from the international to the local. Mainly No. 10 commissioned its work, though it could take cues from elsewhere in government. PIU reported through

---

174 G. Mulgan, 'Joined-Up Government: Past, Present, and Future' in V. Bogdanor, *Joined-Up Government* (Oxford: Oxford University Press/ British Academy, 2005), pp. 181–2.

the Cabinet Secretary to Blair. Its first director was a career civil servant, Suma Chakrabarti. Like the CPRS it comprised career officials and outsiders. After Labour secured re-election in 2001 Blair formed a partner body to PIU, the Forward Strategy Unit (FSU). It was explicitly labelled the Prime Minister's Forward Strategy Unit and reported directly to Blair. Between them PIU and FSU had a combined staff varying from fifty to 100. Unlike PIU, FSU dealt with individual departments, rather than focusing on joining-up. This emphasis suggested a shift towards a new administrative managerial concept and priority: 'delivery'.

During his first term of office Blair became increasingly frustrated with a lack of progress by his government, and his inability to make departments follow his agenda. He drew the conclusion that he needed more administrative support than existing arrangements could provide. Consequently Blair enlisted the Cabinet Office more extensively and explicitly for prime-ministerial purposes. The reorganisation of the No. 10 staff which followed Blair's second election victory in June 2001 coincided with changes in the Cabinet Office. The main priority in reforming public services was to ensure they met the needs of recipients. Blair promulgated four 'key principles for public service reform'. They involved a 'national framework of standards and account-ability'; 'devolution of power to frontline professionals'; 'better and more flexible rewards and conditions' for those staff; and 'more choice' for 'consumers'.

Blair sought to drive this new programme from the centre. He wanted to form around him the types of structures that would be available at the head office of a multinational corporation. Blair established: the Prime Minister's Delivery Unit, FSU (which was merged with PIU the following year to become the Strategy Unit) and the Office of Public Service Reform (OPSR). They were based in the Cabinet Office but were either partly or wholly prime-ministerial in their remits. When justifying this expansion of his staff Blair claimed as a precedent the Efficiency Unit formed by Thatcher. On 11 July 2002 Tony Wright MP, chair of the House of Commons Public Administration Select Committee (PASC), put it to the respective heads of the Delivery Unit, OPSR and Strategy Unit, Michael Barber, Wendy Thomson and Geoff Mulgan, that they constituted the 'Prime Minister's department' and asked why there was any point in having a Cabinet and ministers under such arrangements. In response Mulgan stressed that, relative to a civil service of around half a million, the centre remained small. The bulk of policy work had to be carried out in the departments. These new units had little formal power or money and worked mainly through influence.

The OPSR was a body of about twenty-five staff. Its function was to support the Prime Minister and the government in advancing public service reform. Focusing on 'competence and capacity', the remit of OPSR covered not only the civil service but all public services, including local government. It seems not to have been a success and by 2006 had quietly expired. The Prime Minister's Delivery Unit and the Strategy Unit both made a greater impact. Blair initially intended the Delivery Unit to ensure the government attained its key objectives in four specific areas: crime, education, health and transport. Subsequently he added asylum to this list. Michael Barber, the first head of the Delivery Unit, was an education expert and special adviser to David Blunkett as Secretary of State for Education and Employment from 1997 to 2001. [175] Barber was formerly a Labour councillor and parliamentary candidate but became a permanent official as the Prime Minister's Chief Adviser on Delivery. As an aide to Blair he shared an office in No. 10 with Wendy Thomson, a former local

---

175 See: M. Barber, *Instruction to Deliver: Fighting to Transform Britain's Public Services* (London: Politico's/Methuen, 2008).

authority chief executive and now head of the OPSR. After Barber
left Whitehall in 2005, his successor as head of the Delivery Unit
was Ian Watmore, a Cabinet Office Permanent Secretary.

In its first year of operation in 2001 the Delivery Unit had
around twenty-five staff, rising to about fifty by 2006, comprising insiders and outsiders. It helped the Prime Minister monitor
the progress selected departments were making towards specific
agreed outcomes. Regular stocktaking meetings took place involving ministers and Whitehall officials and the unit with Blair in the
chair. Barber insisted to PASC in July 2002 that his unit was not
engaged in micro-management and that departments had become
'enthusiastic' about the help it provided. A wider purpose of the
Delivery Unit was to afford No. 10 a greater role in the extensive system of Public Service Agreements that the Treasury had
established under Gordon Brown during the first Labour term of
office. When first formed the idea of the unit had caused concern
within the Treasury, including over whether it would lead to the
appearance of rival targets and possibly cause upward pressure
on spending. The broader issue was a longstanding power struggle between the Treasury and No. 10, but to function properly
the unit had to work with the Treasury. For practical reasons,
by 2002 the Delivery Unit staff had shifted – physically but not
organisationally – to the Treasury.

The Strategy Unit was formed from a combination of the PIU
and FSU in 2002. Mulgan, who first joined Blair's Policy Unit
in 1997, had been head of PIU since 2000 and of FSU since its
inception in 2001. From 2003 to 2004 Mulgan added to his
Strategy Unit role that of head of policy for Blair. This final amalgam represented a desire to achieve more cohesion of functions
within the prime-ministerial team, which had passed through a
period of intense expansion, innovation and churn. Mulgan left
the Blair staff in 2004 amid speculation that he had a strained

relationship with Lord Birt, the Prime Minister's Strategy Adviser.[176] The successor to Mulgan as head of the Strategy Unit was Stephen Aldridge, a career civil servant (as Mulgan had become, after starting out as a special adviser). The Strategy Unit, which reported to Blair through the Cabinet Secretary, was the single largest body ever formally attached to a Prime Minister, varying from roughly fifty to 100. It came to be based in Admiralty Arch, by this time a Cabinet Office building. Again it was a mixed team of staff from within and beyond Whitehall. The Strategy Unit reviewed long-term policy objectives in substantial areas of concern, covering both the domestic and international fields. It took an interest in cross-cutting issues. A task of the unit was to 'promote strategic thinking' within the departments with which it worked. Strategy Unit reports came to Cabinet for approval with plans for their implementation.

As well as creating new support teams within it Blair altered the remit of the Cabinet Office to tilt it towards prime-ministerial as opposed to collective activities. Traditionally the responsibility of the Cabinet Office was to support ministers as a group, and the Prime Minister in his capacity as chair of the Cabinet. But progressively from 2000 changes began to occur. The phrase 'collective decision making' disappeared from its terms of reference in 2000 as did the purpose of servicing Cabinet in 2001. In 2002 its first objective (of four) became 'To support the Prime Minister in leading the government'.[177] By 2004–5 Cabinet Office accounts showed more than 750 full-time equivalent staff

---

176 D. Charter, 'Top Blair adviser to leave No 10', *The Times*, 10 March 2004; M. White and P. Wintour, 'Class of '97 clear their desks', *Guardian*, 12 March 2004.

177 *2000 Spending Review*, HM Treasury; Cabinet Office, *Resource Accounts 2000–2001*, Cm 5443 (London: Stationery Office, 2002); HM Treasury, *2002 Spending Review* (London: HM Treasury, 2002); Cabinet Office, *Departmental Report 2003*, Cm 5926 (London: Stationery Office, 2003).

deployed specifically on this task (of a total of about 2,400 in the Cabinet Office). The tendency later reversed. The number of aides deployed specifically supporting the Prime Minister fell from the 2004–5 highpoint. In 2006 – perhaps reflecting a decline in Blair's political authority and the approach of the new Cabinet Secretary, Gus O'Donnell, who had taken up the post the previous year – 'Supporting the Cabinet' appeared once again as a purpose of the Cabinet Office and the phrase 'Supporting the Prime Minister' no longer had the words 'in leading the government' after it.[178] Before the end of the Blair tenure the support staff to the premier was scaling down, but not before it had come closer than at any point since the mid-nineteenth century to resembling a fully-blown department at the disposal of the Prime Minister.

Members of the Blair camp had contemplated further centralisation. In January 1998 Powell proposed an Office of Management and the Budget, incorporating the public-expenditure divisions of the Treasury with the functions of the Cabinet Office, and aides around Blair considered the idea again in 2005. The idea did not progress because it would clearly have been unacceptable to Brown. Another prospect that surfaced more than once was for the introduction of a formal department of the Prime Minister. Powell recounts that the Cabinet Secretary, Richard Wilson, threatened to resign rather than accept this development in February 1999, and that Wilson later suggested the Cabinet Office and No. 10 merge as a way of pre-empting it. Though Powell himself saw arguments in favour of enhancing the prime-ministerial team, he did not agree with a 'large prime minister's department', which would lose its flexibility and responsiveness to the prime minister.

One motive driving Blair and his No. 10 team in building up the Cabinet Office was their hostility to the Gordon Brown and

---

178   Cabinet Office, *Departmental Report 2006*, Cm 6833 (London: Stationery Office, 2006).

the Treasury. An enhanced Cabinet Office resembling in some ways a Prime Minister's department would be a counterweight to Brown's Treasury. What Brown would do when eventually he became Prime Minister in 2007 was an intriguing question.

Gordon Brown and his aides

The Gordon Brown premiership was relatively short but eventful.[179] During his time at No. 10 he faced serious economic, political and personal difficulties. Brown struggled to establish his authority and direction as successor to Blair. Often his personal standing in the opinion polls and that of his party was low, and much of the media were hostile towards him. The decisions Brown made and the way he operated were subject to criticism. Frequently his Cabinet was divided and his leadership seemed under threat. Connected to these various difficulties were problems involving his aides. His team had internal divisions and provoked public controversy. Brown's dithering and interventionist style that focused on details reduced the chances of his staff performing satisfactorily. But at a crucial moment for the British and world economy he and the aides he gathered around him proved effective.

Like many previous prime ministers, Brown sought to distinguish himself from his immediate predecessor. He had spent many years – since 1994 – being regarded as the man most likely to succeed Blair as Labour leader and Prime Minister. At the same time he felt the need constantly to press to ensure he received what he felt Blair owed him. The Blair governments (1997–2007) suffered from factionalism and resentment between Brown and his camp on the one hand, and Blair and his on the other hand. When he finally came to power in mid-2007, Brown wanted to

---

179   See: A. Seldon and G. Lodge, *Brown at 10* (London: Biteback, 2011).

operate differently from Blair and for the public to perceive the change. One obvious way of achieving this goal was through taking a different approach to aides.

A controversial feature of the Blair tenure was his heavy reliance on a large group of aides, within which special advisers, some of whom had special legal authority, were prominent. A frequent criticism was that this team facilitated an excessive emphasis on presentation over content, and enabled Blair to undermine other ministers and Cabinet as a whole. The new Prime Minister set out to employ fewer special advisers. He revoked the Order in Council which gave up to three aides executive authority over permanent officials. Brown retained the post of Chief of Staff established in 1997 under Blair. Whereas in the Blair period Jonathan Powell, a party-political appointment, had filled this post, Brown chose a career official from the Treasury, Tom Scholar, who was simultaneously Principal Private Secretary. Beyond No. 10 Brown shifted the Delivery Unit, which Blair had set up to help him monitor and enhance departmental performance in selected areas, organisationally into the Treasury (it was already based there physically). One innovation retained from Blair was the practice of external policy advisers to the Prime Minister heading secretariats within the Cabinet Office.

The changes were part of a broader approach Brown took at the outset of his premiership. The new Prime Minister sought to stress his inclusive credentials, making a series of non-partisan and expert appointments to ministerial and government advisory posts. He set out a programme called the 'Governance of Britain' through which he sought to overhaul the constitution as whole. It was ambitious in scope and included within it the idea of possibly introducing a Bill of Rights and a written constitution. Ultimately these latter plans were not realised, but an important change with implications for prime-ministerial staff emerged from the

Governance of Britain agenda. Part one of the Constitutional Reform and Governance Act 2010 gave for the first time a statutory basis to the civil service. It stipulated that the Prime Minister (in the guise of Minister for the Civil Service) had the power to manage the home civil service. This power already existed but including it in an Act of Parliament arguably strengthened it. Other provisions introduced constraints on the way premiers might use this authority in the configuration of their own staff. The Act required the Prime Minister to publish a code for special advisers which had to include a stipulation debarring these partisan aides from exercising management functions. It enshrined the principle that with limited exceptions, including special advisers, civil servants should be appointed on merit through free and open competition. Any future Prime Minister seeking radically and openly to displace career officials within her or his team, or even more modestly to restore the arrangement existing for Blair when his two senior special advisers could give orders to permanent civil servants, would probably need to change primary legislation. Such a process would involve a prolonged period of parliamentary controversy. This consideration would create a strong disincentive towards action, and could make the position of the permanent civil service more secure than it might otherwise be. But special advisers in general had since 2005 been strengthened since they were now permitted to assist rather than simply advise ministers.

Though it had long-term implications for the way in which Whitehall functioned, Brown's attempt at a smaller, more inclusive, less media-driven and less partisan approach to the prime-ministerial staff contained flaws. A first problem involved what Brown left behind in his transition to No. 10. Moving to his new post was a jolt. First of all the job was different. It did not have a specific policy portfolio. At the Treasury the focus was on financial and economic policy, and on key events such as budgets and spending reviews. Though Brown had taken an interest and sought to intervene in many different parts of government, now his role had become much broader. In addition to taking on a changed task, he lost the support of a full department of staff. Its main replacement was a team which was smaller than the Treasury; it had already shrunk in the later Blair years and Brown had chosen to reduce it further. While once prime ministers had normally been in direct control of the Treasury, Brown as premier did not have this support. Indeed the Treasury, and the Chancellor of the Exchequer at its head, Alistair Darling, would sometimes be in conflict with him over the coming years.

Brown not only lost the institutional support of the Treasury, but was unable to deploy as aides individuals who had previously supported him at the Treasury. Ed Balls had been an economic adviser to Brown in opposition and a special adviser to him as Chancellor of the Exchequer. Balls had become Brown's closest aide, but he was now an MP and Brown appointed him to the Cabinet as Secretary of State for Children, Schools and Families. While Brown still obtained intermittent counsel from him, Balls could not operate in the day-to-day support role he once had and perhaps Brown would have liked. Another former Brown special adviser who was now a minister was Ed Miliband. His post as Minister for the Cabinet Office enabled him to support Brown more directly than Balls, but he could not be a close aide in the same way as before.

Not bringing certain aides with him may have been difficult for Brown. Yet at the same time the group he did import proved problematic. Brown sought to make good the divisions produced by the competition between him and Blair over the previous decade. This consideration influenced his Cabinet-making, with key allies of the former premier given prominent ministerial posts across

Whitehall and some of Brown's own supporters disappointed. But there was little continuity of high-level aides at No. 10 between Blair and Brown. Accounts differ as to whether Brown made a concerted effort to recruit a number of existing staff but failed or simply had no interest. Whether enticing more of the Blair team would have solved any problems is a matter of speculation. The outcome of not doing so was that the appearance of a Brown clique brought into No. 10 was difficult to avoid. It included partisan aides such as Spencer Livermore, his strategist who had helped plan the transition; Sue Nye, who had supported him throughout his career in government; and Damian McBride, who had a media-handling role. Established members of the Brown inner circle clashed with others at No. 10. Even within the close team around Brown divisions existed, with suspicions that some members were briefing the press against others.

A further problem with the Brown support staff arose from his personal style as Prime Minister. While he wanted to appear a more consensual leader than Blair, and perhaps intellectually saw value in such an approach, his natural inclinations lay elsewhere. He was not disposed towards collective discussion of major decisions. In this sense he did not differ from Blair. But Blair had delegated large amounts of work to staff, in place of facilitating Cabinet deliberation or ministerial autonomy. Such habits made Blair similar to Disraeli, though the earlier premier passed on responsibility more to a single private secretary, Montagu Corry, than a whole group as Blair did. Brown was prone to obsessive involvement in detail. For this reason he could be likened to Gladstone though he was dissimilar to Gladstone in a key way. While Gladstone was obsessively organised and focused on an efficiently running office, Brown was unsystematic, even chaotic. The overall functioning of his staff reflected this characteristic. Chains of command and delineation of functions were unclear.

He might take advice from anyone within his immediate team, or others from outside. Aides were less able to provide firm central coordination as they did at times under Blair. For this system to work, it required the Prime Minister himself to be decisive. Often he was not. Given his love of minutiae he needed to feel he had all the information at his command before he committed to a course of action. Such an approach may have been more viable in the Treasury, with a clearer focus on specific policy areas and a more predictable calendar of events, but with the wider and more volatile brief of a Prime Minister it became a bigger problem. Another way in which Brown's actions differed from the path he initially tried to take as Prime Minister was in his attitude towards presentation. While he had a genuine and extensive interest in high policy, he coupled it with a fixation on day-to-day media coverage, and often charged staff to influence it.

A particular choice Brown made early on in his premiership brought to the fore a variety of problems involving his aides. After he became Prime Minister in the summer of 2007, poll ratings were favourable. He considered calling a snap general election to capitalise on this advantage. An early proponent of this course of action was Livermore. Following the party conference season that autumn, when the Conservatives regained some of the political initiative through tax-policy announcements, Brown decided against. This vacillation took place in public, since the Brown team had intentionally encouraged speculation in the media that Brown might seek a fresh mandate soon. The reputation of the Prime Minister never fully recovered. Prolonged discussions with various political aides, including opinion-poll experts, had not led to a satisfactory outcome. In the aftermath some Brown aides appeared to recriminate through briefing the media that others within the prime-ministerial circle were to blame.

The period that followed saw upheaval in the prime-ministerial team. Staff came and went, and organisation changed. Two who left relatively early were Livermore and Scholar. At the end of 2007 Blair resolved to recruit two new senior aides to No. 10. The first was Jeremy Heywood, a permanent official from the Cabinet Office. He became the first ever Permanent Secretary to the Prime Minister's Office, acting as the head of the permanent civil service component in the office. The second new recruit was Stephen Carter, who came from outside the civil service from public relations. Carter sought to impose more structured working arrangements on No. 10. He was not a strongly party-political person and his tenure seems to have been difficult. He left in autumn 2008, becoming a minister in the Lords. Shortly before the departure of Carter, Brown set up a new base of operations in No. 12 Downing Street. This building was the traditional home of the whips, though under Blair they made way for the media team from 2001. Brown had returned the whips to this building, but now they had to make way for him again. In this new location Brown was able to seat his key staff at a horseshoe-shaped set of desks. The idea was he would have ongoing access to his key staff, achieving more systematic and coherent working.

While this innovation may have achieved some of what was hoped, it did not prevent the occurrence of difficulties for Brown in his use of aides. In April 2009 Damian McBride left No. 10 in a highly publicised and controversial episode. Emails he had sent discussing how to spread rumours online about Conservative politicians had found their way into the public domain. Then in February 2010 claims appeared about Brown behaving abusively towards staff at No. 10, and that the Cabinet Secretary had played some role in seeking to modify the Prime Minister's behaviour. Amid all the various problems of the prime-ministerial team under Brown, the most senior permanent official Heywood, and

the permanent civil service as a whole, obtained an increasingly
strong position.

The pathologies associated with Brown's staff arose from the
character of the Prime Minister. Brown had spent more than
a decade seeking to secure the succession to Blair, and often
drew his aides into pursuit of this goal. While ultimately he was
successful in attaining this prize, it did not mean he or his team
were properly prepared for how to operate in No. 10. The way he
worked encouraged disruption around him. Ultimately the lead
and the decisions had to come from him. Earlier prime ministers
found having different sources of sometimes contradictory advice
useful – they do not necessarily have to induce paralysis. Too
many of his aides over the years were abrasive and seemed too
willing to carry out hostile anonymous briefings of journalists to
be a coincidence. Even if he chose to distance himself from some
of the more unpalatable business, he must have had a general idea
of what his staff were doing. Often these activities were counterproductive. Yet when he acted more positively – which he was
capable of doing – he enlisted his staff in such endeavours too.

In autumn 2008, following the collapse of Lehman Brothers
bank in the US, the world financial system was in genuine peril.
Brown did much to promote a concerted response at the national
and global levels. Help on this task came from aides, including
Heywood and Jon Cunliffe, the Prime Minister's Adviser on
Europe and Global Issues, a post he combined with responsibility in the Cabinet Office for EU coordination. Another key aide
at this time was Shriti Vadera. She had been an aide to Brown
at the Treasury and was now a member of the House of Lords
and minister in the Business Department. Like a number of other
Brown staff she had a reputation for toughness. In these circumstances the quality was useful, as was Vadera's support for the
Prime Minister. Brown recounts how he could 'always rely on her

to be laser-like in her focus and direct in her answers'.[180] Brown responded to the crisis with structural innovation, establishing a National Economic Council, regarded in autumn 2008 as a 'War Cabinet' for the credit crunch. This body was a Cabinet committee advised by a panel of outside experts, linked to a Regional Economic Council. Brown took the chair, and Heywood and Dan Corry, head of the Policy Unit and Senior Adviser to the Prime Minister on the Economy, had an important input into its work. Through the Council Brown was able to expand back into the economic policy area he had moved away from when becoming premier – though the Treasury sought to limit what it could cover.

Gus O'Donnell (1952–) and Jeremy Heywood (1961–)

While Blair's approach had posed the greatest challenge to the position of the career civil service yet, this institution remained significant. Brown reversed the provision Blair had introduced in 1997 to confer on No. 10 special advisers executive authority. The permanent officials in the Private Office continued to be critical, as did the Cabinet Secretary. Two particularly important prime-ministerial aides in the post-1997 era came from the career civil service and demonstrated a continuation of the pattern of some individuals serving prime ministers in different capacities over the course of their working lives. They were Gus O'Donnell and Jeremy Heywood.[181]

O'Donnell differed from the generalists who had reached the summit of Whitehall in earlier eras, having been an economics lecturer before joining the Treasury in 1979. He had previous experience as a prime-ministerial aide, having served as Press

---

180 G. Brown, *Beyond the Crash: Overcoming the First Crisis of Globalisation* (London: Simon & Schuster, 2010).
181 See: House of Lords Select Committee on the Constitution, 4th Report of Session 2009–10, HL 30, *The Cabinet Office and the Centre of Government* (London: Stationery Office, 2010).

Secretary to Major as Prime Minister from 1990 to 1994. In 2005 O'Donnell moved from the post of Permanent Secretary to the Treasury to become Cabinet Secretary and head of the home civil service. His initials earned him the nickname 'GOD'.

O'Donnell has noted two key changes between his time at No. 10 under Major and his more recent post: an increasing overseas and global role for the Prime Minister, and the rise of electronic communications, creating more work. Early on in his Cabinet Office tenure O'Donnell launched a major administrative programme involving a series of 'Capability Reviews' that assessed the organisation and effectiveness of Whitehall departments. He expanded his role in overseeing the security and intelligence agencies, as compared with his immediate predecessor, Andrew Turnbull, becoming their accounting officer and taking a strategic interest in their activities and coordination. O'Donnell saw one of his functions as being to ensure that, when a Prime Minister wanted to achieve a particular cross-departmental outcome, the Cabinet Office helped to get this message across within government.

While his two predecessors, Richard Wilson (1998–2002) and Turnbull (2002–5), supported only one Prime Minister, Blair, O'Donnell served three as Cabinet Secretary and head of the home civil service: Blair, Brown and Cameron (and in an earlier post was an aide to Major). He understood the importance of different personalities and circumstances to the way the premiership operated. O'Donnell had to handle two changeovers in incumbent at No. 10. The first, from Blair to Brown in 2007, was fraught but the ultimate outcome had been relatively predictable for some years in advance, and did not involve a change in the party (or parties) of government. More novel and complex were the circumstances of May 2010, when the general election returned a House of Commons in which no single party possessed a

majority, something that O'Donnell had foreseen and prepared
for. No clear official statement existed in the public domain of
what steps should be followed in the event of what is commonly
known as a hung Parliament. O'Donnell initiated and oversaw
the publication of the executive's understanding of what should
happen. It included provision for O'Donnell to facilitate and
support cross-party negotiations, which he did, though his
involvement was limited. These rules eventually formed part
of a volume entitled the *Cabinet Manual* which described
the conventions and practices of a wide range of central-
government activity. It was the latest in a series of documents
which codified features of the British constitution, including
the *Ministerial Code* (published as *Questions of Procedure for
Ministers* in 1992, which had previously existed as an internal
paper), the *Civil Service Code,* and the *Code of Conduct for
Special Advisers*. Often they contained content with implications for the activities of prime ministers and their aides. Having
helped facilitate a smooth transition to the Conservative/Liberal
Democrat coalition, O'Donnell helped devise various arrangements to ensure its effective operation. His office in 70 Whitehall
was equidistant between those of Cameron and Nick Clegg, the
Deputy Prime Minister.

When O'Donnell stepped down at the end of 2011, Cameron
decided to split his post into three: a Cabinet Secretary, a head of
the home civil service and a Cabinet Office Permanent Secretary.
The separation of the Cabinet Secretary post from that of the head
of the home civil service was a historic development. They had
been combined fully since 1983. The new arrangement was that
any Whitehall permanent secretary could apply for the headship
and hold it in tandem with their existing role, while the Cabinet
Secretary would be a freestanding post. The latter job seemed to
offer the most guaranteed access to the premier of the three new

creations. Its first holder was Jeremy Heywood, who had already marked himself out as an important prime-ministerial aide.

Heywood has spent a large portion of his career providing direct support to ministers. He understood the importance of adapting to their varied requirements. He was Principal Private Secretary to Norman Lamont in the early 1990s, at which time he worked with David Cameron who was a special adviser to Lamont. Heywood stayed on as principal when Kenneth Clarke succeeded Lamont. Later he became a private secretary to Blair from 1997, and from 1999 to 2003 Principal Private Secretary at No. 10. He helped facilitate Blair's delivery-focused expansion at the centre of government. Heywood subsequently left Whitehall to work in banking. When Brown became Prime Minister, he managed to recruit Heywood as head of domestic policy and strategy in the Cabinet Office. Then in 2008 Heywood returned to No. 10 as Permanent Secretary to the Prime Minister's Office.

At times in the past prime ministers have sought to include aides within No. 10 with a special status or authority. In 1892 Gladstone publicised that Algernon West was his 'Chief of Staff'. Baldwin and Chamberlain used in Horace Wilson a high-ranking civil servant. Tony Blair appointed Powell as his Chief of Staff, and gave him executive authority (as he did Campbell). Though some regarded Norman Brook as in effect performing such a role, no one before or since Heywood officially held the title of Permanent Secretary to the Prime Minister's Office. It carried with it the implication of the Prime Minister's Office as an institution in and of itself rather than an administrative subdivision of the Cabinet Office, though the resources of No. 10 were slighter than those normally associated with a full department.

Why had this role come about and what was its significance? Heywood's assessment was that Brown had initially opted not to have a Chief of Staff with the equivalent authority to Jonathan

Powell, but after about six months into his premiership decided he needed a figure with more authority to fill the gap left by Powell. While Powell had been a special adviser, in turning to Heywood Brown provided the permanent civil service with an opening to reassert the position within No. 10 it had lost in 1997. Heywood saw the model in which a career official was in charge as prefer-able to the Blair system, which he had experienced first-hand, and he seized the opportunity. He became a senior adviser to the Prime Minister, working day-to-day with Brown. Heywood was available when needed. He sat next to the Prime Minister in the open-plan office set up in 12 Downing Street, and had a second closed office for private meetings. Brown refers to Heywood as 'the peerless and all-seeing Permanent Secretary at Downing Street'.[182] A central difference from the period when he had worked for Blair was that now the financial and economic crisis was an overriding concern. Heywood soon decided he could not perform his new role as well as fulfilling the old function of Principal Private Secretary, so he re-established this position. James Bowler was the first holder of the recreated post, given the task of running the Private Office. Under Cameron, in a coalition government, Heywood further strengthened the position of permanent officialdom by promoting the idea of a Policy Unit that did not include special advisers. He thereby significantly reversed a trend that dated back to the first Harold Wilson premiership of 1964–70.

Working effectively with O'Donnell was important. The general division of functions was that Heywood dealt with ongoing policy issues while O'Donnell had a more strategic position. When a particularly important issue arose they might take it to Brown jointly – strength in numbers, perhaps. Some regarded Heywood as less inclined towards personal publicity

---

182 G. Brown, *Beyond the Crash*.

than O'Donnell, and that he saw anonymity as valuable to effective performance of his duties. It was said that when O'Donnell retired, Heywood did not want the more public-facing head of the home civil service part of O'Donnell's job, which led to the split. But the new Cabinet Secretary could not avoid public exposure. Part of the problem was the wide range of possible tasks into which the holder of the post could be drawn, sometimes leading to unexpected controversy. Heywood was criticised for his investigation of a supposed breach of the *Ministerial Code* by the Chief Whip, Andrew Mitchell in September 2012, involving Mitchell's attempt to ride his bicycle through the Downing Street gates, which ended in the resignation of the Chief Whip.

Assessing aides under New Labour

The Blair experiment in the use of aides to the Prime Minister is historically important. First it represented an exponential expansion of the modifications introduced under an earlier Prime Minister, Harold Wilson. Like Wilson, Blair made heavy use of outsiders, incorporating a personal entourage into No. 10. He challenged the position of the permanent civil service and created a multiplicity of new units. A second facet of the Blair tenure was it tested the limits of the second-phase premiership, creating a prime-ministerial support team that appeared close to being a proper department. Third the experience of the Blair premiership reveals the limitations on what can be achieved by prime ministers and their staff. He sought to govern with little reference to the collective. When his methods failed to deliver what he hoped, he used them even more. They brought with them problems such as resentment among ministers and negative publicity. By the end of the Blair premiership the capacity he had created had dissipated slightly.

The Brown premiership provided another example of the

tendency for vacillations in style between one Prime Minister and the next. Brown understood the value of being seen to be different from Blair. The problem was he did not match the dwindling of the centre he instituted with a genuinely inclusive leadership style. Nor did he adopt an efficient approach to his use of staff. Had Brown deployed the Cabinet and ministers more sensitively and adroitly, then his own support resources would not have mattered as much, since secretaries of state and their departments would have taken some of the strain. Had he been willing to delegate to his personal team, or take decisions more readily himself, his government would have functioned better. Though it was not as large as Blair's, Brown's team generated significant internal disagreements and external controversy. In these circumstances Brown came to rely increasingly on the support of the one institution that could compensate for his personal lack of organisation and suitable outsider appointments. The permanent civil service, and in particular Jeremy Heywood, was able to enhance its position in an important historic shift.

CHAPTER SEVEN

CONCLUSION

Prime ministers have always needed aides. The job is too demanding for premiers to carry out alone and they can achieve more with the help of assistants. These staff have been close to some of the great events in British history: the securing of the Hanoverian succession; the fighting and winning of the Napoleonic, First and Second World wars; the acquisition and management of an Empire and the internal consequences of its collapse. Their association with past controversy has been frequent: the political management methods of Robert Walpole; the Stamp Act in the 1760s; the sale of honours under Lloyd George; appeasement in the 1930s; the Suez crisis of 1956; the 'Poll Tax' in the late 1980s; and the invasion of Iraq in 2003. Aides were often not only connected to such episodes, but their activities could also become a subject of contention in their own right. Individual assistants could gain public prominence and teams of prime-ministerial aides might be a source of fascination, as in the Lloyd George, Harold Wilson and Tony Blair eras. In parallel to the drama, controversy and spectacle was a group of staff that has kept an office at the centre of government functioning day-to-day for nearly three centuries.

In the early period beginning in the early eighteenth century the Treasury, which was then the largest office of government, provided the core of the prime-ministerial staff. From around the mid-nineteenth century the private secretaries became the main team, a smaller support group. During the course of the twentieth century prime ministers added various new functions and teams to their immediate band of assistants. The Cabinet Office came to be a valuable source of support, as could senior officials such as the Cabinet Secretary. A recurring – but not absolutely constant – feature of the prime-ministerial team has been the physical location on which it has centred: Downing Street, particularly No. 10, and the area adjacent to it once known as the Cockpit, where Kent's Treasury was built in the 1730s, now subsumed within 70 Whitehall.

It is difficult to make generalisations about the kinds of individuals involved. Some – such as Montagu Corry for Benjamin Disraeli, Marcia Williams for Harold Wilson or Alastair Campbell and Jonathan Powell for Blair, were attached to only one premier. Others – John Roberts in the eighteenth century, George Harrison and Edward Drummond in the nineteenth, Thomas Jones and Norman Brook in the twentieth, and Jeremy Heywood in the twentieth and twenty-first, had a succession of chiefs. Working as an aide can be the high point of a career, and individuals might gain celebrity specifically for doing so, as did John Colville and Alastair Campbell. They might go on to even greater and more celebrated achievements, like Edmund Burke and Philip Kerr. Some had parallel careers, including George Pretyman in the church, Frederick Lindemann as a physicist and Alan Walters as an economist. Aides may be aspiring party politicians, as were many members of Blair's team.

They might bring to a Prime Minister specialised skills, such as expertise in statistics, analysis of public opinion or academic knowledge of a policy area, or possess close connections to a pressure group, a party or the administrative machine. The aides most valued by prime ministers were those who could connect them to key power centres in society: such as Parliament and the Cabinet, the civil service, pressure groups, indeed any group whose support or acquiescence Prime Ministers needed.

Prime-ministerial aides might be partisan, as are special advisers, or more impartial, as are career civil servants. Some of the inequalities familiar in high politics are apparent: there has been a preponderance of Old-Etonians and Oxford graduates. Both Gladstone and Disraeli wanted aides who had higher social standing than themselves to connect them with the aristocrats who still dominated political life. There has not yet been a female Principal Private Secretary or Cabinet Secretary. Women occupied important roles for Lloyd George, Wilson, Major, Blair and Cameron, but as patronage appointments rather than as career officials. Whatever their backgrounds and profiles aides are often ambitious and hard-working, though there were exceptions to the latter, such as Ronald Waterhouse in the 1920s. Some, like Michael Halls, who died in service for Harold Wilson, and William Armstrong, who experienced a nervous breakdown while supporting Heath, pushed themselves too hard. If for some reason assistants displease a Prime Minister it is uncommon for them to be removed from their positions immediately. Examples of such direct dismissals include David Davies by Lloyd George and Damian McBride by Gordon Brown. Generally those whom prime ministers grow tired of simply lose influence, are moved sideways or are gradually induced to depart.

The development of aides is inseparable from the history of the premiership because these very staff helped to establish the office. In the eighteenth century, assistants such as the Secretary to the Treasury contributed to the instigation and operation of a patronage-fuelled system of political management. By this means Walpole and his successors were able to cultivate the twin sources of their power: Parliament and the royal court, which between them underpinned the premiership itself. Key changes in the structural contours of the office of Prime Minister have involved developments in the size and range of activity of the staff attached to it. The patterns of development of this institution are complex. Sometimes it expands, at other times it contracts. The premiership does not grow ever more pervasive, nor ever weaker.

One modification to the office of Prime Minister involving aides stands out in particular. In its first stage, prime ministers generally had the support of the Treasury providing them with a substantial body of staff and a policy portfolio. Severance from regular direct responsibility for the Treasury during the mid-nineteenth century brought the premiership into its second phase, when prime ministers no longer had a department to sustain them. They now focused on the cross-governmental, coordinating role associated with their position as chair of the Cabinet. They had a less immediate involvement in policy design and implementation, which their attachment to the Treasury had given them.

Subsequently prime ministers made attempts to be more interventionist, using aides to help them. Sometimes they took charge of a department, as Gladstone with the Treasury, Salisbury and MacDonald the Foreign Office, and Churchill with his creation of the Minister of Defence portfolio. Wilson also temporarily took overall charge of the Department of Economic Affairs in the 1960s. (Prime ministers have oversight of the intelligence and security agencies as well.) When prime ministers have sought to extend their reach, it has often been into the spheres of financial and economic policy, and foreign affairs. As high profile and core parts of government business, they are particularly attractive as areas of intervention. When expanding their roles through their staff, premiers have used individual aides with policy roles such as Philip Kerr for Lloyd George, Horace Wilson for Stanley Baldwin and Neville Chamberlain, William Armstrong for Edward Heath, or Alan Walters for Thatcher. Another approach was to create new bodies within the remit of the premiership. Churchill set up his Statistical Section in 1940; Wilson introduced a small team of economists in 1964 and in 1974 formed the Policy Unit, which proved the most long-lived of all such experiments. Thatcher established the Efficiency Unit and Blair the Delivery Unit.

These initiatives represented a testing of the boundaries of the second-phase premiership but not a full departure from them. Blair – particularly during his second term from 2001 – went further than his predecessors, coming closer than any before him to establishing a fully-fledged and specific department of the Prime Minister. He did so by forming a variety of new teams that expanded his reach across government and drew the Cabinet Office increasingly within his orbit. It is possible the Blair era will one day acquire the reputation as having instigated a third phase in the history of the premiership, in which it is supported by a department dedicated to the service of the Prime Minister. Later in Blair's term there was a reduction in the extent of his team. His two successors, Gordon Brown and David Cameron, did not operate on the same scale, though some features of the Blair approach, such as heads of Cabinet Office secretariats serving simultaneously as advisers to the Prime Minister, have survived.

Such approaches and structural developments posed a challenge to constitutional arrangements. The attachment to the premier of staff charged with policy roles or performance management of the civil service threatened the position of existing Whitehall departments and offices. Horace Wilson helped Chamberlain take on functions that might otherwise have fallen to the Foreign Office. The Statistical Section enabled Churchill to scrutinise the performance of departments. In the process it introduced a challenge to the degree of autonomy that they previously possessed, and the section met with resistance to its requests for information. The Efficiency Unit and Delivery Unit performed similar functions to the Statistical Section for Thatcher and Blair respectively. In 1974 the formation of the Policy Unit caused concern on the part of the Cabinet Secretary about the position of the Cabinet Office. Enhancements to the office of Prime Minister might undermine the political heads of departments. Ministers in the Lloyd George government complained about the role of Kerr in foreign affairs. During 1974–79 the Policy Unit took a close interest in the activities of Tony Benn. Nigel Lawson resigned as Chancellor of the Exchequer in 1989, complaining about the behaviour of Walters. When using aides to attain a more active part in government prime ministers may not only challenge particular departments or secretaries of state, but weaken adherence to principles of collective government. Premiers including Lloyd George, Chamberlain, Churchill and Blair all attempted, with the support of staff, to reduce the role of Cabinet in certain key decisions – though to do so required to some extent at least the acquiescence of other ministers.

A more interventionist premiership creates problems of accountability. The broad principle of the British constitution is that the Cabinet as a whole determines the major outlines of policy, while individual secretaries of state take specific decisions within their remit and manage their departments. An expansion in the role of the premiership creates doubt about who really is responsible for policy. The legitimacy of aides taking part in such prime-ministerial enhancement is likely to be subject to challenge, as with criticisms of Horace Wilson, William Armstrong and the team around Blair.

The history of prime-ministerial aides is inextricably linked to the development of the civil service. In the early period of the premiership there was no concept of a clear divide between party-political and administrative work. The Secretary to the

Treasury performed functions that would today be associated with a permanent secretary, but sat in Parliament at the same time, and carried out duties now falling to the Chief Whip, alongside other party-political tasks. The interests of aides and particular premiers were often closely bound together. But from the eighteenth century a permanent civil service began to appear. The principle developed that its employees tended to remain in their posts when the party of government or the political head of a department changed. Officials were not attached to particular programmes or ministers, all of whom they served with equal loyalty. Gradually the civil service became a more coherent entity, whose members exercised substantial influence, although they were constitutionally subordinate to ministers. By the late 1920s, this institution had achieved a pre-eminent position within the premiership. It provided most of the key aides, including the private secretaries who were the core of No. 10.

During the Second World War Churchill's use of outsiders such as Lindemann, head of the Statistical Section, temporarily challenged this civil service pre-eminence, but not past the end of the conflict. By the 1960s the civil service was subject to a wave of criticism, calling into question its skills, motives and organisation. From the first Harold Wilson government of 1964 onwards the grip of permanent officials loosened, with the introduction of various temporary appointments made by the patronage of prime ministers. While there was tension and some conflict between outsiders and regulars, at the same time they needed to cooperate or face stalemate and disaster. Gradually the imports, many of whom had the status of special advisers, became more entrenched. In the Blair period there was a notable development when he legally vested in two aides he brought with him to No. 10, Campbell and Powell, executive powers normally available only to career officials. Were the outsiders gaining the upper hand?

Perhaps not. Under Cameron the Policy and Implementation Unit comprised wholly permanent officials. Its predecessor, the Policy Unit, had in the past been the key base for special advisers in No. 10. Career civil servants continued to fill important roles as aides to the Prime Minister, such as the private secretaries and the Cabinet Secretary.

The balance between temporary and regular staff will probably never tip completely in one direction or another. Their respective roles are more firmly prescribed than ever before according to codes issued under the Constitutional Reform and Governance Act 2010 (CRAG). This practice was part of a wider tendency impacting upon the premiership. The office had become subject to more extensive constitutional definition, both in non-statutory documents such as the *Ministerial Code* and *Cabinet Manual*, and in statutes such as CRAG. Early prime ministers had denied the existence of the premiership. Three centuries later the institution – along with the aides attached to it – continued to edge in the direction of a more formal existence. Transparency could both legitimise and constrain the premiership. Reforms such as the Freedom of Information Act 2000 and the introduction of devolved government to parts of the country created further restrictions. Official inquiries and the 'cash for honours' police investigation entailed additional scrutiny of prime ministers and their aides.

These substantive developments occurred for a variety of reasons. Sometimes they were unintended outcomes. Robert Peel ceded day-to-day handling of Treasury business to a separate Chancellor of the Exchequer in 1841 to enable him to exercise more direct control over government. The eventual consequence of this decision was that prime ministers lost their direct link with the Treasury and its staff. The actions of a later centraliser, Lloyd George, had some similarly perverse long-term impacts. Through the Garden Suburb he created an important precedent for a team directly supporting the premier in overseeing departmental business in more detail. Other Lloyd George innovations were not as straightforward in their outcome. The Cabinet Office, which originated in the secretariat he attached to his War Cabinet in 1916, was intended as a vehicle for prime-ministerial objectives. But in time it helped entrench collective government and could create a barrier to dominance from No. 10 (though it might still be deployed for prime-ministerial purposes as well). Lloyd George oversaw reforms which brought about a more unified, cohesive civil service and created the powerful post of head of the civil service, initially combined with the office of Permanent Secretary to the Treasury. Because of these developments prime ministers became increasingly dependent on staff support from an institution less personally attached to them, which was in practice more of a powerbase in its own right. On the other hand, on some occasions, changes in the structure and operation of the premier's staff developed in intended ways. In as far as he set out to provide the premiership with more involvement in policy and introduce outsiders into No. 10 as a counterweight to the permanent civil service, Harold Wilson's innovations achieved the outcomes he and his advisers hoped for on a lasting basis, though with some regression recently.

These changes did not take place in a vacuum. Often powerful outside events and tendencies drove them. War was often a catalyst. The pressure of the French wars of the late eighteenth and early nineteenth centuries prompted reorganisation at the top of the Treasury, at that time the usual base of the Prime Minister. Lloyd George and Churchill came to No. 10 in dire circumstances during the First and Second World Wars. They oversaw changes that they hoped would enable them to drive conduct of the conflict from the centre. In the period since 1945, domestic concerns have provided a forceful impetus for change. The Harold Wilson changes were part of a programme intended to arrest perceived British economic decline. For Blair, administrative reconfiguration was a means of achieving what he and his aides believed was sorely needed public service reform, and to some extent a response to global security concerns.

Whatever the particular constitutional and administrative structures may be at any given point, at the centre of the premiership and its network of staff lies a single political leader: the Prime Minister, holder of the top prize in British politics. The main lesson of this book is that prime ministers shape their systems of aides. The most important factor determining the structure and operations of prime-ministerial aides is the prime ministers themselves, what they want and their mode of working. If aides are to be understood, both collectively and individually, then it is necessary to understand their relationship with the person they work for.

A variety of general observations apply across different historical periods. Premiers may inherit certain arrangements and procedures but they impose their own ways of working on their staff. Radical changes could take place between one Prime Minister and the next – indeed this phenomenon was common. Disraeli took a relaxed approach, delegating substantial responsibility to his most senior aide, Corry. Gladstone, who twice succeeded Disraeli as premier, spread work more evenly among a team whose activities he obsessively oversaw. Blair vested his personal authority in a substantial number of assistants whom he trusted to know what he wanted without needing to ask him. Brown was less willing to leave work to others. The way prime ministers deploy their teams can vary substantially. A premier such as Lloyd George used his staff aggressively in support of his dynamic style of government, which included seeking to short-circuit other ministers, and in his dealings with the media. By contrast during the sterling crisis of 1976 Callaghan engaged his staff in enabling him to work through collective Cabinet procedures.

The role of aides in the Prime Minister's inner circle is determined partly by their own skills and experience, and the particular tasks they carry out. Proximity is also an important consideration, and it takes a number of forms. An individual may be based physically close to where the premier works, as the private secretaries have been in No. 10; or further away, in 70 Whitehall or Admiralty Arch in the Blair era. Aides may be exclusively attached to the Prime Minister, like the Policy Unit; or have a less direct association with the premier, like the Central Policy Review Staff, which formally supported the Cabinet as a whole through its existence (1971–83). They may have a closer or more distant working relationship with a premier; may be more or less in tune with their chief's political outlook; and their personal connection with the Prime Minister may be stronger or weaker. These distinctions can manifest themselves in complex combinations. Blair's Chief of Staff, Jonathan Powell, worked in the room next to him, was close to his outlook, but not actually a friend. Blair's communications aide, Alastair Campbell, was based in an office slightly further away. He was ideologically not as near a match to Blair as Powell, but was a friend of the Prime Minister. Further ways of differentiating aides include considering how far their employment is dependent upon the fortunes of an individual premier or they have security of tenure. This distinction became increasingly relevant with the rise of the permanent civil service. Finally whether or not they hold a formal post merits considera- tion and, if so, what is their place in the official hierarchy, though specific rank is not all-important.

Aides can sometimes be important players within the political system in their own right, trying to further their own agendas and ambitions. For this reason they may enter into conflicts with one another. Premiers may at times encourage such disputes, or at least find them useful, as a way of motivating and maintaining control over their teams. But taken to excess such internal battles undermine the effectiveness of the staff in supporting the Prime Minister. In the second Harold Wilson premiership the warfare between Marcia Williams on the one hand and Bernard Donoughue and Joe Haines on the other hand was debilitating. The inner team around the premier can share the features of a family. It has often included actual relatives of the Prime Minister in it, or those who take on this quality in surrogate form. This characteristic has positive connotations: trust, informality, shared interests. At the same time, as with real families, jealousy, squabbles, feuds and even bitter separations are possible.

The tendency towards courtly intrigue between different people or factions seeking the ear of the premier underlines our crucial point: ultimately prime-ministerial aides derive their power from the premier. If they are in a position of strength it is because a Prime Minister has allowed it. They can impact upon ministers and officials elsewhere in government in their capacity as staff to the premier only because they possess delegated authority. Prime ministers cannot control precisely how their aides operate at all times, and some assistants can possess considerable bargaining power, especially career officials because of their permanent status, attachment to the administrative machine and the need to secure their cooperation. However, it is difficult to give credence to any idea that assistants can acquire genuine dominance over their chief. A central quality required of a politician who manages to reach No. 10 is the ability to manipulate others, not the reverse. At times prime ministers, consciously or instinctively, may allow the perception to develop that aides have become powers in their own right, partly as a means of diverting unpopularity towards the staff and away from themselves. If aides could control a particular Prime Minister it would probably not be worth doing so, since that premier would be equally weak in dealings with senior ministers and consequently unable to impose any ideas the team had imposed on them.

This realisation leads to a second limitation on the power of aides. Any authority they possess within government is derived from premiers who are in turn subject to a variety of constraints. Prime ministers have always depended on the cooperation of other groups and individuals, such as ministers, parliamentarians, the monarch, parties, the church and public opinion.[183] This reliance is the reason external liaison is such an important part of the work of aides. Premiers cannot be certain of the support or compliance required for them to achieve what they want. Circumstances which are by their nature variable will condition the extent to which they can be successful. Premiers cannot vest in their aides an absolute authority which does not exist to begin with. But assistants can participate in substantial exercises of power, by working with others, or, when circumstances favour and premiers wish to do so, direct prime-ministerial interventions of a more unilateral nature.

What does history suggest about appropriate forms of support for prime ministers and how these structures might develop in future? Managing the balance between outside, patronage-based appointments and career civil servants is an important challenge. Aides drawn from the first group have many advantages from the point of view of their attachment to particular prime ministers. They have a greater personal interest in the success of the premier they support. They can be chosen because they have

---

183 A. Blick and G. Jones, 'Contingencies of prime-ministerial power' in P. 't Hart and R. A. W. Rhodes (eds.), *Oxford Handbook of Political Leadership* (Oxford: Oxford University Press, 2013).

the right partisan attachment and outlook. Such staff may possess contacts, experience and skills lacking within the career civil service. But a stigma surrounds these aides. A common criticism is that, while their presence in the prime-ministerial ambit can be of value, it presents challenges to the proper constitutional order. Often these views emanate from retired career officials and sometimes from former special advisers who claim standards have deteriorated since their day.[184]

Consideration of the history of the premiership as a whole suggests a different emphasis. The permanent civil service is a relative newcomer, which overturned longer-established arrangements. Its most obvious period of strength lasted about four decades, from the late 1920s to 1964, with an interruption during the Second World War. In creating special advisers Harold Wilson partially restored what had been standard practice through much of the development of the office of Prime Minister: the use of aides appointed on patronage by a particular incumbent, rather than impartial permanent staff. Some important tasks exist that career officials are not suited to perform. It is dangerous for them to become publicly too attached to particular premiers and policies: Horace Wilson for Chamberlain and then William Armstrong for Heath are extreme examples. One of the tasks of a premier is to connect party politics with administration. Consequently aides who can do the same, without need for concern about loss of impartiality, are useful.

The exclusion of special advisers from the Policy Unit's successor in the Cameron era amounted to a problematic diminution of the partisan, outsider dimension at No. 10. It compromised the body Harold Wilson introduced in 1974, which was until 2010 composed wholly or mainly of special advisers. Cameron appears

---

184 See: House of Lords Select Committee on the Constitution, *The Cabinet Office and the Centre of Government*, pp. 18–21.

to have recognised that he created problems for himself. The extension of the role of the permanent civil service, rather than of patronage appointments, undermined established constitutional practice. The restoration of a Policy Unit staffed largely or entirely by special advisers is desirable. Equally, no Prime Minister should overlook the importance of the career civil service. A premier should seek diverse sources of support, of which career officials should form one pool. They can provide a different perspective to partisan aides, helping to test the viability of policy proposals. They offer a degree of stability and continuity of practice that may prove useful. It is better for certain tasks – such as handling the intelligence and security agencies and the material they produce – to remain primarily or perhaps exclusively within their remit. To do otherwise can create the perception – and even reality – of partisan abuse. Unless a fundamental reorganisation takes place, prime ministers will continue to need good relations with the permanent civil service if they want successfully to develop and implement policy. The Cabinet Secretary has long been a vital assistant as have the private secretaries in No. 10. A problem associated with the increased use of special advisers has been the creation of confusion across Whitehall about who speaks for the Prime Minister. The Private Office grip on such communications has loosened. In future it would seem wise to introduce a tighter control, though whether this function needs to be under the authority of a career official or an outsider is debatable. If it were to be the latter, then formal empowerment similar to that applying from 1997 to 2007 under Order in Council might be required. Such a change would seem to require primary legislation, and would be politically difficult. The array of opponents would include other ministers who feared interference from special advisers, civil servants both serving and retired, MPs on all sides of the House, and many commentators.

What might be the overall form of the staff of the premier in future? A recurring theme during the twentieth and twenty-first centuries was the possibility of establishing a department of the Prime Minister. Such a project would presumably involve an expansion in the number of staff and the range of activities in which they are engaged. This change could have perverse outcomes. Aides can help premiers to achieve more, but the larger the team becomes and the more it does, the more demanding becomes the task of overseeing it. It would morph into something beyond the Prime Minister's power and ability. Such a department would threaten the flexibility that is crucial if prime ministers are to provide effective personal leadership. Premiers could find themselves struggling to impose their influence on a body established to help them increase their individual impact. Perhaps the reason that a department of this kind has never been established is because premiers have sensed what they might lose by doing so. During the history of the premiership the tendency to transfer staff and tasks away from the office has been as important as a trend towards expansion. The Treasury shifted away in the mid-nineteenth century; the Garden Suburb was wound down after the First World War; and the Delivery Unit which Blair had set up in 2001 to be a counterweight to the Treasury later became absorbed within the Treasury.

A 'Prime Minister's department' raises further practical and constitutional issues. There is not room for it in No. 10. It would require premises, perhaps in 70 Whitehall or somewhere else. It would probably generate controversy in Parliament and the media, and encounter hostility within the departments and from the secretaries of state. It would undermine two core tenets of the British system of government. The first is individual ministerial responsibility. With an increased role for the premiership in decisions, policies and activities, it would be unclear whom

Parliament should hold to account in a particular area: the Prime Minister or the secretary of state.

One way of creating clarity would be to move towards a system under which executive responsibilities and budgets currently vested in various ministers by convention and statute fell to the premiership. But this model would probably require the Prime Minister to be elected directly, separately from the House of Commons – a radical transformation to presidential government. Few are willing to accept this democratic logic. A further possible implication of a department of the Prime Minister would be a diminishing of collective government. It would challenge or supplant the Cabinet Office. It would cut off prime ministers from the system by which they manage government. Whether it would provide an effective replacement remains to be seen. A group of staff without their own power bases in Parliament and party, employed by the premier, would not provide a substitute for the strength of a body of autonomous ministers bound together by their commitment, with the Prime Minister in the chair, to collective deliberation and decision.

LIST OF INTERVIEWS WITH PRIME-MINISTERIAL AIDES

Name	Date of service	Date of interview
Pinsent	1914	20/3/75
Eastwood	1918–34	5/5/75
Harris	1918–61	10/75 (day not known)
Davies	1919–55	16/4/75
Stenhouse	1919–60	16/4/75
Shakespeare	1921–22	4/6/75
Sylvester	1921–23	18/10/75
Vincent	1928–36	18/3 & 30/9/75
Rootham	1933–39	20/6/75
Dunnett	1934–36	16/6/75
Minto	1935–68	15/5/75
Humphreys	1936–38	19/3/75
Colville	1939, 1940s, '50s	9/7/75
Rucker	1939–40	17/3/75
Syers	1937–40	pre-9/75
Bensusan-Butt	1940–42, 46	18/6/80
Bevir	1940–56	19/8/75
Kinna	1940–45	13/8/75
MacDougall	1940–45, 1951–53	1/2/87
Martin	1940–45	17/6/75

Peck	1941–46	19/8/75
Addiss	1945–46	9/11/75
Beards	1945–48	19/12/75
Burke	1945–46	letters: 25/10 & 21/12/76
Jay	1945–46	23/10/75
Gorrell-Barnes	1946–48	10/9/75
Graham	1946–49	16/10/75
Helsby	1947–50	23/7/75
Pumphrey	1947–50	letter: 28/10/75
Osmond	1948–51	17/10/75
Cass	1949–52	10/10/75
Rickett	1950–51	15/8/75
Pitblado	1951–56	1/10/75
Montague-Browne	1952–55	6/11/75
Bishop	1955–59	23/10/75
Cairncross	1955–58	13/11/75
Millard	1955–57	19/11/75
Stephens	1955–61	11/11/75
Zulueta	1955–63	8/11/75
Ramsden	1957	19/11/75
Phelps	1958–61	21/11/75
Hewitt	1961–74	19/11/75
Woodfield	1961–65	25/11/75
Armstrong, W.	1962–74	16/1/80
Reid	1963–66	17/3/76
Balogh	1964–68	17/3, 23/3, 11/5/76
Mitchell	1964–66	4/12/75
Wright	1964–66	7/6/76
Cheminant	1965–68	23/3/76
Andrews	1966–70	29/4/76

Dawe	1966–70	8/3/76
Palliser	1966–69	10/6/76
Gregson	1968–72	24/3/76
Simcock	1969–72	25/3/76
Armstrong	1970–75	11/12/75
Isserlis	1970	5/12/75
Donoughue	1974–79	various
Jaeger	1974–76	1/11/80

CATEGORIES OF WORK

We have identified five core categories of work by Prime Ministers' aides throughout the whole period from Walpole to Cameron:

Providing advice to the Prime Minister on policy and political decisions

Prime ministers have always worked closely with their Cabinet colleagues in this area, on whom they depend to remain in office. In the early period during the eighteenth century the Secretary to the Treasury played an important role, supplemented by other chosen individuals. Later on, private secretaries supplied counsel of various kinds alongside their other duties, though their capacity to do so was limited, and they could often be reticent about directly promoting specific courses of action. From the twentieth century policy specialists appeared, such as the staff of the Policy Unit, who could both scrutinise ideas coming from elsewhere and develop proposals of their own.

Dispensing patronage

The office of Prime Minister has, in part, depended for its authority on the ability to distribute favours of various sorts, such as jobs, honours and – at the outset – money. Over the years, staff have been involved in such functions as deciding who should be chosen and handling the practicalities of patronage. A key part of this general group of activities has also been making ministerial appointments.

Handling the administrative machine

Staff such as the Secretary to the Treasury and later the Cabinet Secretary were important to ensure the bureaucracy worked in the interests of the premier. Tasks in this area included procedural activities such as arranging meetings and recording their decisions, and ensuring policies were set in motion. The late twentieth century saw many prime-ministerial bodies with an interest in civil service performance, such as the Efficiency Unit for Margaret Thatcher and the Delivery Unit for Blair.

Liaising with important groups and individuals, such as other ministers, parliamentarians, the public and the monarch to obtain their views and win their support or acquiescence

Monarchs were major political players in the eighteenth century. Prime ministers had no choice but to pay close attention to them. Their significance has declined substantially, though ongoing communications between No. 10 and the Palace still take place. Managing Parliament has always been a crucial task. Even today ensuring support from the Prime Minister's own MPs is a high priority as shown by David Cameron's appointment of John Hayes and Jo Johnson to roles designed to allay discontent among backbench Conservative MPs. In the early years this duty could be part of the role of the Secretary to the Treasury. The office of the Chief Whip, one of the successor posts to the Secretary to the Treasury, is now central to this function. Parliamentary private secretaries have also operated in the area of parliamentary relations. Private secretaries have played an important role in conducting communications within and beyond government. Handling ministers and Cabinet as a whole has always been vital. Eventually the Cabinet Office became central in such work. Dealing with business interests became an increasingly important task over time. Edmund Burke helped obtain for Lord Rockingham the input of the commercial classes into legislation. Assessing public opinion between elections and seeking to influence elections have been concerns from the outset. As the franchise expanded from the nineteenth century onwards, mass parties, inside and outside Parliament, became increasingly important. Francis Bonham for Robert Peel was an early link with the emergent Conservative Party. From 1964 onwards the Political Secretary was the senior staff member responsible for this task. Dealing with trade unions was also an important task for aides, especially under Labour prime ministers.

Presenting prime ministers and their governments to the public

From Walpole onwards prime ministers deployed aides on public relations duties. Lord Salisbury obtained such informal assistance from Alfred Austin. Not until the 1920s and 1930s did a specialised function of handling the press develop in No. 10. A full Press Office appeared during the post-Second World War, followed under Tony Blair by a Strategic Communications Unit and Research and Information Unit. The role of Press Secretary or Chief Press Secretary has always been difficult to perform, because it is so exposed to journalists, with prime ministers sometimes employing civil servants and at other times people from the media, and all usually facing fierce criticism, meant to damage the Prime Minister.

These broad categories differentiate the work of aides, but do not necessarily indicate clear distinctions between the assistants themselves. Our studies of individual aides show a tendency for them to operate in multiple areas. An aide such as the Cabinet Secretary is likely both to advise on policy and to endeavour to ensure the Whitehall machine implements it. Those responsible for liaising with important groups – such as political secretaries, who handle relations with parliamentary parties – may well make recommendations on government programmes and appointments. Press secretaries are likely to become involved in policy discussions, since prime ministers are interested in how to present decisions and the possible media and public reaction to them.

SELECTED READING

General

A. Blick, *People Who Live in the Dark: The History of the Special Adviser in British Politics* (London: Politico's, 2004)

A. Blick and G. Jones, *Premiership: The Development, Nature and Power of the Office of the British Prime Minister* (Exeter: Imprint Academic, 2010)

P. Hennessy, *Prime Minister: The Office and its Holders since 1945* (London: Penguin, 2001)

P. Hennessy, *Whitehall* (London: Pimlico, 2001)

G. Jones, 'The Prime Minister's secretaries: politicians or administrators?' in J. Griffith (ed.) *From Policy to Administration: Essays in Honour of William A. Robson* (London: Allen & Unwin, 1976)

G. Jones and J. Burnham 'Innovators at 10 Downing Street', in K. Theakston (ed.), *Bureaucrats and Leadership* (London: Palgrave Macmillan, 1999)

D. Kavanagh and A. Seldon, *The Powers Behind the Prime Minister: The Hidden Influence of Number Ten* (London: HarperCollins, 2000)

J. M. Lee, G. W. Jones and J. Burnham, *At the Centre of Whitehall: Advising the Prime Minister and Cabinet* (Basingstoke: Macmillan, 1998)

C. A. Petrie, *The Powers Behind The Prime Ministers* (London: MacGibbon & Kee, 1958)

C. Seymour-Ure, *Prime Ministers and the Media: Issues of Power and Control* (Oxford: Blackwell, 2003)

K. Theakston, *Leadership in Whitehall* (Basingstoke: Macmillan, 1999)

Early years

S. Ayling, *Edmund Burke: His Life and Opinions* (London: Murray, 1988)

D. M. Clark, 'The Office of Secretary to the Treasury in the Eighteenth Century', *The American Historical Review*, vol. 42, no. 1 (October, 1936), pp. 22–45

H. T. Dickinson, *Walpole and the Whig Supremacy* (London: English Universities Press, 1973)

N. Gash, 'F. R. Bonham: Conservative "Political Secretary", 1832–47', *The English Historical Review*, vol. 63, no. 249 (October, 1948), pp. 502–522

B. W. Hill, *Sir Robert Walpole: 'Sole and Prime Minister'* (London: Hamish Hamilton, 1989)

T. Horne, 'Politics in a Corrupt Society: William Arnall's Defense of Robert Walpole', *Journal of the History of Ideas*, vol. 41, no. 4 (October – December, 1980), pp. 601–614

B. Kemp, *Sir Robert Walpole* (London: Weidenfeld and Nicolson, 1976)

G. Keppel, J. Roberts and J. E. Tyler, 'John Roberts, MP and the First Rockingham Administration', *The English Historical Review*, vol. 67, no. 265 (1952), pp. 547–560

F. P. Lock, *Edmund Burke: Volume I, 1730 –1784* (Oxford: Clarendon Press, 1998)

R. Pares, *King George III and the Politicians: The Ford Lectures Delivered in the University of Oxford 1951–2* (Oxford: Clarendon Press, 1953)

H. Parris, *Constitutional Bureaucracy: The Development of British Central Administration since the Eighteenth Century* (London: Allen Unwin, 1969)

J. H. Plumb, *Sir Robert Walpole: The Making of a Statesman* (vol. 1) (London: Cresset, 1957).

J. H. Plumb, *Sir Robert Walpole: The King's Minister* (vol. 2) (London: Allen Lane, 1972)

H. Roseveare, *The Treasury: The Evolution of a British Institution* (London: Allen Lane, 1969)

J. C. Sainty, 'The Evolution of the Parliamentary and Financial Secretaryships of the Treasury', *The English Historical Review*, vol. 91, no. 360 (July, 1976), pp. 566–584

N. Sykes, *Edmund Gibson: Bishop of London, 1669–1748* (Oxford: Oxford University Press, 1926)

D. O. Thomas, *The Honest Mind: The Thought and Work of Richard Price* (Oxford: Clarendon Press, 1977)

T. S. Urstad, *Sir Robert Walpole's Poets: The Use of Literature as Pro-Government Propaganda, 1721–1742* (Newark: University of Delaware Press, 1999).

M. Wright, *Treasury Control of the Civil Service: 1854–1874* (Oxford: Oxford University Press, 1969)

1868–1914

E. Alexander, *Chief Whip: The Political Life and Times of Aretas Akers-Douglas, 1ˢᵗ Viscount Chilston* (London: Routledge & Kegan Paul, 1961)

A. Austin, *The Autobiography of Alfred Austin: Poet Laureate, 1835–1910* (London: Macmillan & Co., 1911)

D. W. R. Bahlman (ed.), *The Diary of Sir Edward Walter Hamilton: 1880–1885* (vol. 2) (Oxford: Clarendon Press, 1972)

D. Brooks (ed.), *The Destruction of Lord Rosebery: From the Diary of Sir Edward Hamilton, 1894–1895* (London: Historians' Press, 1986)

E. Campion (ed.), *Lord Acton and the First Vatican Council: A Journal* (Sydney: Catholic Theological Faculty, 1975)

O. Chadwick, *Acton and Gladstone* (London: Athlone Press, 1976)

Viscount Chilston, 'Lord Salisbury as Party Leader (1881–1902)', *Parliamentary Affairs*, 13 (1960), pp. 304–17

N. B. Crowell, *Alfred Austin: Victorian* (Albuquerque: University of New Mexico Press, 1953)

A. Godley Kilbracken, *Reminiscences of Lord Kilbracken* (London: Macmillan & Co., 1931)

R. Hill, *Lord Acton* (New Haven: Yale University Press, 2000)

H. D. Hutchinson (ed.), *Private Diaries of the Rt Hon Sir Algernon West, G C B* (London: John Murray, 1922)

R. A. Jones, *Arthur Ponsonby: The Politics of Life* (Bromley: Helm, 1989)

F. W. Leith-Ross, *Money Talks: Fifty Years of International Finance* (London: Hutchinson, 1968)

G. G. Leveson-Gower, *Years of Content: 1858–1886* (London: John Murray, 1940)

J. Sandars, *The Sandars Centuries: A Brief History of the Sandars Family with Sketches of Some Notable Figures from the Family Past* (London: J. Sanders, 1971)

A. West, *Recollections: 1832–1886* (vol 1 and 2) (London: Smith, Elder & Co., 1899)

1914–1945

G. Bennett, *Churchill's Man of Mystery: Desmond Morton and the World of Intelligence* (London: Routledge, 2009)

R. Cockett, *Twilight of Truth: Chamberlain, Appeasement, and the Manipulation of the Press* (London: Weidenfeld and Nicolson, 1989)

J. Colville, *The Churchillians* (London: Weidenfeld and Nicolson, 1981)

J. Davies, *The Prime Minister's Secretariat: 1916–1920* (Newport: R. H. Johns, 1951)

E. L. Ellis, *T. J.: A Life of Dr Thomas Jones, CH* (Cardiff: University of Wales Press, 1992)

F. W. Furnaux Smith, 2nd Earl of Birkenhead, *The Prof in Two Worlds: The Official Life of Professor F. A. Lindemann, Viscount Cherwell* (London: Collins, 1961)

R. F. Harrod, *The Prof: A Personal Memoir of Lord Cherwell* (London: Macmillan, 1959)

R. R. James, *Memoirs of a Conservative: J. C. C. Davidson's Memoirs and Papers, 1910–37* (London: Weidenfeld and Nicolson, 1969)

T. Jones, K. Middlemas (ed.), *Whitehall Diary*, vol. 1, *1916–1925* (Oxford: Oxford University Press, 1969)

J. F. Naylor, *A Man and an Institution: Sir Maurice Hankey, the Cabinet Secretariat and the Custody of Cabinet Secrecy* (Cambridge: Cambridge University Press, 1984)

G. Peden, 'Sir Horace Wilson and Appeasement', *The Historical Journal*, vol. 53, no. 4 (December, 2010), pp. 984–1014

C. P. Snow, *Science and Government* (Oxford: Oxford University Press, 1961)

A. J. P. Taylor (ed.), *My Darling Pussy: The Letters of Lloyd George and Frances Stevenson, 1913–41* (London: Weidenfeld and Nicolson, 1975)

J. A. Turner, 'The formation of Lloyd George's "Garden Suburb": "Fabian-like Milnernite Penetration"?', *The Historical Journal*, vol. 20, no. 1 (1977), pp. 165–184

J. Turner (ed.), *The Larger Idea: Lord Lothian and the Problem of National Sovereignty* (London: Historians' Press, 1988)

J. Turner, *Lloyd George's Secretariat* (Cambridge: Cambridge University Press, 1980)

R. W. Thompson, *Churchill and Morton: The Quest for Insight in the Correspondence of Major Sir Desmond Morton and the Author* (London: Hodder and Stoughton, 1976)

N. Waterhouse, *Private and Official* (London: Jonathan Cape, 1942)

J. Wheeler-Bennett (ed.), *Action This Day: Working with Churchill* (London: Macmillan, 1968)

T. Wilson, *Churchill and the Prof* (London: Cassell, 1997)

1945–1997

W. Clark, *From Three Worlds: Memoirs* (London: Sidgwick & Jackson, 1986)

B. Donoughue, *The Heat of the Kitchen: An Autobiography* (London: Politico's, 2003)

B. Donoughue, *Downing Street Diary: With Harold Wilson in No. 10* (London: Jonathan Cape, 2005)

B. Donoughue, *Downing Street Diary Volume Two: With James Wilson in No. 10* (London: Jonathan Cape, 2008)

Lord Egremont, *Wyndham and Children First* (London: Macmillan, 1968)

J. Haines, *Glimmers of Twilight: Harold Wilson in Decline* (London: Politico's, 2004)

J. Haines, *The Politics of Power* (London: Jonathan Cape, 1977)

B. Ingham, *Kill The Messenger … Again* (London: Politico's, 2003)

B. Ingham, *The Wages of Spin: A Clear Case of Communication Gone Wrong* (London: John Murray, 2003)

D. Jay, *Change and Fortune: A Political Record* (London: Hutchinson, 1980)

D. MacDougall, *Don and Mandarin: Memoirs of an Economist* (London: John Murray, 1987)

F. E. Williams, *Nothing so Strange: An Autobiography* (London: Cassell, 1970)

M. Williams, *Inside Number 10* (London: Weidenfeld and Nicolson, 1972)

Since 1997

A. Adonis, *Education, Education, Education: Reforming England's Schools* (London: Biteback, 2012)

M. Barber, *Instruction to Deliver: Fighting to Transform Britain's Public Services* (London: Methuen, 2008)

F. Beckett and D. Hencke, *The Blairs and Their Court* (London: Aurum, 2004)

G. Brown, *Beyond the Crash: Overcoming the First Crisis of Globalisation* (London: Simon & Schuster, 2010)

A. Campbell, *The Blair Years: Extracts from the Alastair Campbell Diaries* (London: Arrow, 2008)

House of Lords Select Committee on the Constitution, *The Cabinet Office and the Centre of Government* (London: Stationery Office, 2010), fourth report of session 2009–10, HL 30

P. Hyman, *1 Out of 10: From Downing Street Vision to Classroom Reality* (London: Vintage, 2005)

J. Powell, *The New Machiavelli: How to Wield Power in the Modern World* (London: Vintage, 2011)

L. Price, *The Spin Doctor's Diary: Inside Number 10 with New Labour* (London: Hodder & Stoughton, 2005)

D. Scott, *Off Whitehall: A View from Downing Street by Tony Blair's Adviser* (London: I. B. Tauris, 2004)

INDEX